EURODÉLICES

FISH & SEAFOOD

Eurodélices

Fish & Seafood

DINE WITH EUROPE'S MASTER CHEFS

KÖNEMANN

Acknowledgements

We would like to thank the following people, restaurants and companies for their valuable contributions to this book:

Ancienne Manufacture Royale, Aixe-sur-Vienne; Baccarat, Paris; Chomette Favor, Grigny; Christofle, Paris; Cristalleries de Saint-Louis, Paris; Grand Marnier, Paris; Groupe Cidelcem, Marne-la-Valée; Haviland, Limoges; Jean-Louis Coquet, Paris; Maître cuisiniers de France, Paris; Les maisons de Cartier, Paris; Philippe Deshoulières, Paris; Porcelaines Bernadaud, Paris; Porcelaine La Farge, Paris; Puiforcat Orfèfre, Paris; Robert Haviland et C. Parlon, Limoges; Société Caviar Petrossian, Paris; Villeroy & Boch, Garges-les-Gonesse; Wedgwood-Dexam International, Coye-la-Forêt.

A special thank you to: Lucien Barcon, Georges Laffon, Clément Lausecker, Michel Pasquet, Jean Pibourdin, Pierre Roche, Jacques Sylvestre, and Pierre Fonteyne.

Skill ratings of the recipes:

✢   easy

✢✢   medium

✢✢✢   difficult

Photos: Studio Lucien Loeb, Maren Detering
Copyright © Fabien Bellhasen and Daniel Rouche
Original title: Eurodélices – Poissons, Crustacés, Coquillages

Copyright © 1998 for the English-language edition:
Könemann Verlagsgesellschaft mbH,
Bonner Str. 126, 50968 Cologne

Translation and typesetting of the English-language editon:
Translate-A-Book, a division of Transedition Limited, Oxford, England
Coordinator for the English-language edition: Tammi Reichel
Series project manager: Bettina Kaufmann
Assistant: Stephan Küffner
Production manager: Detlev Schaper
Assistant: Nicola Leurs
Reproduction: Reproservice Werner Pees, Essen
Printing and binding: Neue Stalling, Oldenburg

Printed in Germany

ISBN 3-8290-1129-6

10 9 8 7 6 5 4 3

Contents

Foreword

The Eurodélices series brings a selection of European haute cuisine right into your kitchen. Almost 100 professional chefs, many of them recipients of multiple awards and distinctions, associated with renowned restaurants in 17 countries throughout Europe, joined forces to create this unique series. Here they divulge their best and their favorite recipes for unsurpassed hot and cold appetizers, fish and meat entrees, desserts, and pastry specialties.

The series as a whole, consisting of six volumes with over 1,900 pages, is not only an essential collection for gourmet cooks, but also a fascinating document of European culture that goes far beyond short-lived culinary trends. In a fascinating way, Eurodélices explores the common roots of the different "arts of cooking" that have developed in various geographic locations, as well as their abundant variety.

For eating is much more than the fulfillment of a basic bodily need; cooking is often elevated to the level of an art, especially in association with parties and celebrations of all kinds, in private life and in the public sphere. Young couples plan their futures over a special dinner at an elegant restaurant, partners gather at table to launch new business ventures, heads of state are wined and dined. Every conceivable celebration involves food, from weddings to funerals, from intimacies shared over coffee and cake to Sunday dinners to Passover and Thanksgiving feasts.

We often have our first contact with the cultures of other lands, whether nearby or across an ocean, through their food. Precisely because the various contributing chefs are rooted in their distinct traditions, some flavors and combinations will be new to North American readers, and occasionally ingredients are called for that may be unfamiliar or even difficult to locate. The texts accompanying each recipe help elucidate and, wherever possible, suggest substitutes for ingredients that are not readily available in North America. A glossary is also included to explain terms that may not be obvious, listing some ingredients.

Because precision is often crucial to the success of recipes of this caliber, a few words regarding measurements and conversions are in order. In Europe, it is customary to use metric units of liquid volume or weight, that is, milliliters or grams. Every household has a kitchen scale and solid ingredients are weighed, rather than measured by volume. Converting milliliters to fluid cups and grams to ounces is straightforward, if not always neat. More problematic are ingredients given in grams that North Americans measure by volume, in tablespoons and cups. Throughout the Eurodélices series, the original metric measurement follows the North American equivalent. The conversions are painstakingly accurate up to 100 ml and 100 g (which necessitates some awkward-looking amounts). Thereafter, they are more neatly, and thus less accurately, rounded off. As with all recipes, measurements are approximate for many ingredients, and a wide variety of factors ranging from temperature and humidity to accuracy of kitchen implements to the way food is sold will affect the amount actually used. If the reader wants to recreate the recipes as given, however, the use of a kitchen scale is strongly recommended.

The unique collection of around 750 recipes contained in Eurodélices aims to excite its readers' curiosity. Classic dishes, which have been enjoyed for generations and thus form the foundations of modern cookery, are liberally presented. But there are also new and surprising pleasures, familiar foods prepared in novel ways, as well as culinary delights composed of ingredients from far away places that we experience for the first time. Allow yourself to be inspired by the European master chefs to try and, perhaps, try again.

Clam

Preparation time: 2 hours
Cooking time: 5 minutes
Difficulty: ★

Serves 4

28 clams, such as littlenecks
2 oz/50 g shiitake mushrooms
4 baby zucchini

2 lychees
⅓ cup/50 g corn kernels, fresh or frozen
2 leaves gelatin, or 4 tsp powdered gelatin
6½ tbsp/100 ml chicken stock
a little olive oil

For the lemon thyme butter:

3½ tbsp/50g butter
1 sprig of lemon thyme

Catalonia may well be several thousand miles from China, but this hasn't stopped Fernando Adría from drawing inspiration from oriental cuisine in the preparation of fresh clams. He also makes clever use of the specialties of his native region, by combining the clams with chicken stock, thus offering a fresh approach with familiar ingredients.

Although clams are plentiful throughout the Mediterranean, Adría maintains that the best clams in Europe come from Galicia in northwestern Spain, with its Atlantic coastline. His preference is not for the largest sort, but for the pale-shelled variety weighing between 1–1¾ oz/30–50 g each, which he cooks quickly over high heat. As soon as the clams open they are shucked, cooled and glazed with a mixture of their own juices and the gelatin—the gelatin being crucial to the success of this *chaud-froid*.

The influence of Chinese cooking can be seen chiefly in the finely sliced vegetables, with the stark contrast between the tender baby zucchini and crunchy corn dominating. Shiitake mushrooms should be used if possible, but may be replaced by other wild varieties such as cèpes, horns of plenty or chanterelles.

This recipe may be made with other shellfish, our chef recommending, for example, mussels. These abound on the rocks of the Spanish Costa Brava, and he uses them from time to time with great success.

1. Plunge the clams into a pot of water over high heat for 2 minutes until they open. Immediately remove them from their shells with a knife, taking care not to damage them. Reduce the cooking water to ¾ cup/175 ml. Soften the gelatine in a little cold water and add to the cooking water. Refrigerate until syrupy.

2. When completely cool, place the clams on a rack and glaze with the jellied liquid. Next, prepare the lemon thyme butter sauce: Infuse the thyme in 6½ tbsp/100 ml of boiling water. Boil this liquid down to 2 tbsp and pass through a strainer. Over low heat, whisk in the butter.

chop suey

3. Peel the lychees and reserve. Cut the zucchini into thin rounds and slice the mushrooms finely, then sauté in a little olive oil over low heat until both are tender. Add the lychees and the corn with the chicken stock and cook for 1 minute.

4. Arrange the vegetables in the center of the dish, pouring the lemon thyme butter sauce all around. Top with the clams just before serving.

Sea cucumber with

Preparation time: 1 hour
Cooking time: 5 minutes
Difficulty: ★★★

Serves 4

1 lb 5 oz/600 g fresh sea cucumbers
1 lamb's brain, cooked
20 thin strips of bacon

3½ oz/100 g chanterelles
1 head Belgian endive
1 tbsp tomato peeled, roughly chopped
4 tsp/20 g butter
6½ tbsp/100 ml rich meat stock
a little olive oil
salt and freshly ground pepper
a few chervil leaves

What are we to make of the sea cucumber? More delicate than the squid and not as plump as the razor clam, to which it nevertheless bears a slight resemblance, the sea cucumber is not a vegetable, still less and mollusk, but rather an echinoderm like the sea urchin and starfish. This peculiar creature abounds in most marine environments, but, outside of Asia, it is only in Spain (and more specifically in Catalonia, where it goes by the name of *espardenya*), that it is elevated to main-course status.

To give the uninitiated an idea of what the sea cucumber is like, its flesh resembles that of the octopus and its iodine tang is inevitably reminiscent of its natural habitat. It tastes best pan-fried or deep fried, and is less well suited to poaching. Nor does it combine well with just any accompaniment. Those with no previous experience of preparing echinoderms should keep faithfully to the cooking times and accompaniments given by Fernando Adría.

Generally speaking, the sea cucumber is still slightly crunchy when cooked. For this reason, one always looks for a contrasting texture, such as lamb's brains—prized for their tenderness, and which must be absolutely fresh—as an accompaniment. The interplay of velvety and crisp, sweet and salty, to which the bacon and Belgian endive contribute, is guaranteed to delight those who love gutsy flavors and originality in their cooking.

Since sea cucumber is not widely available, it may be necessary to replace it with a julienne of squid.

1. First clean the sea cucumbers: Using a sharp knife, remove the fibers on the rubbery portion, taking care not to rip the flesh.

2. Next, gather the sea cucumbers into little parcels and wrap a strip of bacon around the center of each. Separate the head of Belgian endive into leaves. Slice the lamb's brain and wash the mushrooms.

lamb's brains and chanterelles

3. Pour a little oil into a nonstick pan. Sauté the endive leaves and brains, followed by the sea cucumber, until golden brown.

4. Sauté the chanterelles in olive oil until golden brown. Add the butter, which helps to achieve an attractive color. Next, pour in the meat stock and reduce. Arrange the endive leaves in the center of each plate. Top with the sea cucumber parcels and scatter the mushrooms and the roughly chopped tomato all around. Garnish with chervil leaves.

Tuna cutlets

Preparation time: 10 minutes
Cooking time: 10 minutes
Difficulty: ★

Serves 4

8 thin slices fresh tuna
2 onions

2 small tomatoes
1 green bell pepper
1 red bell pepper
a little oil
few drops sherry vinegar
basil or chives
salt and freshly ground pepper

People have fished for tuna since time immemorial. This larger relative of the mackerel with its handsome silver jacket has numerous virtues, chief among which is its meaty, firm and very tasty flesh, which is free from awkward bones. The myriad traditional ways of preparing this fish is a reflection of the esteem in which it is held in many countries. The bluefin tuna (*Thunnus thunnus*) is the favorite of the Basque fishermen in France and Spain.

This recipe requires a certain amount of dexterity, as the tuna cutlets used for this little onion-and-basil-topped sandwich must be sliced paper thin. The fish is seared in a very hot pan for just a few seconds on each side; any longer would produce disastrous results. This treatment ensures that the flesh of the fish retains its original structure and its vitamins.

Ideally, the tuna should be garnished with Spanish (or Bermuda) onions; their slightly sweet taste goes well with the tomatoes and basil. Use whole leaves of fresh basil if possible. Basil flowers may also be used for this dish; their slightly sweet flavor harmonizes well with the onions.

1. Lightly sauté the onions in a little oil. Add 1 finely cut-up tomato and the basil.

2. In a small bowl, make a vinaigrette by whisking together the sherry vinegar, oil and salt. Add 1 washed, seeded and finely diced tomato, and the blanched and finely diced green and red bell peppers.

with vinaigrette

3. Just before serving, flash-fry the tuna cutlets on both sides in a hot pan.

4. Arrange 1 tuna cutlet in the center of each plate and spoon over the onion, tomato and basil mixture. Top with a second cutlet. Spoon the vinaigrette all around, and garnish with deep-fried basil leaves or finely snipped chives.

Cuttlefish

Preparation time: 30 minutes
Cooking time: 15 minutes
Difficulty: ★★★

Serves 4

3¼ lb/1½ kg small cuttlefish (or squid) with
their ink
1 onion
1 green bell pepper
1½ cups/300 g peeled, roughly chopped
tomatoes
a little oil
flat-leaf parsley
salt and freshly ground pepper

For the sauce:
cuttlefish or squid ink
¾ cup/200 ml fish stock
6½ tbsp/100 ml white wine
2 onions
salt and freshly ground pepper
a little oil

The Basques have always had a soft spot for the *chipiron* or small cuttlefish. No bar would consider its selection of *pinxos* (the Basque term for *tapas*) complete without a plate of these small cephalopods in their own ink (*en su tinta*). From 10 a.m. onwards, before their pre-lunch aperitif, San Sebastián bar-goers can enjoy the first freshly caught cuttlefish or squid, prepared simply, expertly and deliciously in the traditional manner.

As a child, Hilario Arbelaitz would often go fishing with his father. Today, in memory of these past adventures, he recommends that you seek out little *chipirones*, which he far prefers to the larger type fished along the North American coasts. The varieties found close to the coast, rather than further out to sea, are more tender, and thus

superbly suited to our purposes.

Whichever sort you choose, it is the body sac of the cuttlefish that is used for this recipe. The ink sac is reserved to color the sauce; if necessary, however, the ink available in little plastic envelopes from fishmongers may be used with equal success.

Most people quickly become firm devotees of Basque cooking, particularly of the varied seafood *tapas*— anchovies, mussels, squid, cuttlefish and octopus. If you enjoy this cuttlefish tartlet, you'll almost certainly be tempted to penetrate the mysteries of Basque cuisine yet further. A world of delicious tastes awaits you!

1. Clean the cuttlefish, reserving the ink for the sauce. Using a metal cutter, stamp out 28 coin-sized pieces from some of the cuttlefish and refrigerate.

2. Cut the remaining cuttlefish into ⅜ in/1 cm dice. Soften the finely chopped onion and green bell pepper in some oil; add the diced cuttlefish and sauté briefly, taking care not to overcook. Set aside. In a separate pan, cook the chopped tomato.

tartlets

3. For the sauce, slice the two onions into thin rings and gently sauté in a little oil until golden. Add the white wine, ink, and fish stock and reduce slightly. Purée the sauce, then put through a fine strainer and adjust the seasoning.

4. Sauté the cuttlefish discs in a little oil; season with salt and pepper. Pour some sauce onto the center of each plate. Place a metal ring on top and spoon in the cuttlefish and onion mixture. Top with the cuttlefish rounds. Spoon the cooked tomato into the center and garnish with parsley.

Hake with clams

Preparation time: 45 minutes
Cooking time: 10 minutes
Difficulty: ★★

Serves 4

4½ lb/225 g hake fillets, or substitute cod
1¼ lb/600 g clams, such as littlenecks
4 cloves garlic
1 bunch of flat-leaf parsley

6½ tbsp/100 ml extra-virgin olive oil
a little flour
2 tbsp water

Hake should be line-caught if possible. It requires careful handling as the flesh tends to fall apart easily. Its taste, however, is particularly fine and delicate, comparable to sea bass or turbot.

Choose a medium-sized hake weighing a generous 2 lb/1 kg, which will yield fine, shiny white fillets. This North Atlantic fish is very popular in France, Spain and Portugal, and is used to good effect in many regional dishes. It is eaten mainly in the summertime, when its flesh is tastiest. Store it in the refrigerator for two days before cooking to ensure the best texture.

Hake should be cooked only briefly. The hake is quite a versatile fish. Even the head has its devotees; it is halved and fried in garlic once the jaws are removed.

As an elegant foil for the hake, our chef recommends clams or similar shellfish. Cooking the clams in olive oil in a lidded pot ensures that they remain tender and open easily.

Firmin Arrambide recommends substituting cod for the hake and cockles or mussels for the clams if either or both ingredients are unavailable.

1. Peel the garlic and slice thinly. Heat the olive oil in a large pot or flameproof casserole, earthenware if possible, and sauté the garlic until just turning golden brown.

2. Season the fish with salt and pepper and add to the pot. Cook in a 350 °F/180 °C oven for 5 minutes, or until done. Wash the clams carefully in three changes of water and steam in a covered pot with olive oil over high heat until they open. Remove the clams from the pot; strain the juices into a bowl.

and a parsley *jus*

3. Take the fish fillets from the oven; remove the fish from the pan and keep warm. Add the chopped parsley and the clam juices to the pan.

4. Gently simmer the oil and the clam juices in a saucepan. Whisk in a pinch of flour and add 2 tbsp water and the chopped parsley. Bring to a boil. Place a piece of hake on each plate, arrange the clams around the fish and pour over the parsley sauce.

Red mullet and cuttlefish

Preparation time:	1 hour
Cooking time:	1 hour
Difficulty:	✳ ✳

Serves 4

6 small red mullet (about 3½ oz/100g each)
12 small cuttlefish (or squid)
2 onions
1 tomato

1 green bell pepper
2 cloves garlic
6½ tbsp/100 ml olive oil
salt and freshly ground pepper

The term *chipiron* is used in both the southwest of France and the Basque Country to refer to the cuttlefish, which is known in the south of France variously as *casseron*, *sépiole*, or *supion*. If it is difficult to obtain, substitute squid. Preparing cuttlefish in its own ink is an authentic Basque culinary tradition.

Our chef recommends preparing the two main ingredients of this recipe—the red mullet and the cuttlefish—separately, so that the flavor of the cuttlefish is not lost. It should be quickly pan-fried for two minutes on each side, so it does not become tough or lose its flavor.

Choose small red mullet, like those caught in the Bay of Biscay by the small fishing boats of Saint-Jean de Luz and Hendaye near the Franco-Spanish border. These fish weigh 3½–7 oz/100–200 g each and are known for their fine flesh. As they have no gall, they are often prepared whole, including the liver. Red mullet and cuttlefish are a good partnership, being similar in size. The mullet cook very quickly.

The ink sauce is prepared like an onion coulis with green bell pepper and tomato. The ink provides color and flavor without being overpowering. It is located in the ink sac and should be strained before being added to the sauce. Squid ink may also be purchased in plastic envelopes.

If red mullet is not available and you have to use a larger fish, such as sea bass or sole, cut the fillets across into several pieces, so that they do not roll up when fried.

1. Clean and fillet the mullet. Prepare 6½ tbsp/100 ml stock from the bones and heads. Gut and clean the cuttlefish, reserving the ink sacs. Refrigerate.

2. Peel the onions and slice into thin rings. Peel and seed the tomato. Halve, core and seed the bell pepper and cut into thin strips. Peel and chop the garlic. Over low heat, heat some olive oil in a pan and gently sauté the onions, garlic and green bell pepper. Cover and simmer briefly. Add the tomato and the fish stock, then simmer, uncovered, until the mixture is soft.

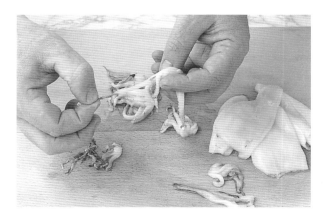

with a black ink sauce

3. Purée the sauce in a blender to thicken. Add the ink and adjust the seasoning. Put the sauce through a fine strainer lined with cheesecloth.

4. Heat a frying pan until very hot. Salt and pepper the mullet and cuttlefish and sauté in olive oil for two minutes on each side, until golden brown. Spoon a little black sauce onto each plate and top with the mullet and cuttlefish.

Pike with

Preparation time: 10 minutes
Cooking time: 15 minutes
Difficulty: ★★

Serves 4

4½ lb/2 kg pike
32 crayfish
3½ tbsp/50 ml olive oil

For the sauce:
2 shallots
4 tsp/20 ml cognac
3½ tbsp/50 ml dry white wine
1 cup/250 ml cream
2 sprigs of fresh tarragon
salt and coarsely ground pepper

The pike, a skillful predator, lives in the lower reaches and backwaters of rivers and in large ponds, but also frequently penetrates high up into the trout zone. It is also raised in small ponds. Before the French Revolution, pike from the breeding ponds of the Louvre Palace graced the table of King Louis XIV.

The firm, white flesh of the pike is extremely fine, but it contains a great many bones, some of which are well hidden and can only be removed with the aid of tweezers. Our chef recommends specimens weighing 4¼ lb–6½ lb/2–3 kg, which he thinks contain fewer bones.

After being immersed in water for about one minute, the fish may be filleted with ease. In this recipe, steaming ensures that the fillets stay nice and tender as well as

cooking through completely. As pike generally has a reputation for being pleasant but bland, the fish is served here with a rather spicy sauce.

Before the crayfish are cooked, the intestine should be removed by pulling out the center fin of the tail.

We recommend that you strain the sauce through a piece of cheesecloth after it is made, then through a fine strainer after it has settled. Whip it gently just before serving, to achieve an even lighter and more appetizing consistency.

The recipe may be prepared with other fine-fleshed freshwater fish instead of pike—or the fish may be left out entirely and replaced by additional crayfish.

1. Fillet the pike and cut it into 4 portions. Season with salt. Wrap each piece in plastic wrap and steam at 160 °F/70 °C.

2. Devein the crayfish and cook in smoking hot olive oil until they turn red.

crayfish

3. Flambé the crayfish with the cognac, then place in a hot oven for 3 minutes. Remove the meat from 16 of the crayfish tails. Reserve 4 whole crayfish for garnish. Break up the shells and remaining crayfish with a pestle or in a food processor. Return to the pan.

4. Add the lightly browned diced shallots and the coarsely ground pepper. Sweat for 2 minutes, then pour in the white wine and reduce by half. Add the cream and tarragon. Cook down to a creamy consistency and season to taste. Strain the sauce. Mask the pike fillets with this sauce, and garnish each portion with 4 crayfish tails and a whole crayfish, and a little blanched tarragon.

Eel with green

Preparation time: 20 minutes
Cooking time: 10 minutes
Difficulty: ✷✷

Serves 4

generous 2 lb/1 kg small eels
14 oz/400 g mushrooms
1 stalk of green garlic
1 head of garlic

2 cups/500 ml Bourgueil or other light-bodied
red wine
1 cup/250 ml milk
6½ tbsp/100 ml red-wine vinegar
3½ tbsp/50 g butter
2 tbsp duck fat
1 sprig of lovage
4 sprigs of parsley
2 sage leaves
pinch of sugar
salt and freshly ground pepper

Despite its somewhat unattractive appearance, the slippery-skinned eel is very delicate-tasting. The eels that go to European markets are born in the North Atlantic in the Sargasso Sea, and over the course of several years swim with the Gulf Stream toward Europe. The females travel up river, and the males remain near the confluence—unless, that is, they are caught and wind up on our plates. If they fail to elude this fate, it is not for want of putting up a fight. You will witness their agility if you buy them live from your fishmonger: time and again they will wriggle out of your grasp, and even once cut up they may not stop moving. The only way to deal with them is to stun them with the well-aimed blow of a stick.

Eel is very rich in vitamin A, and quite fatty. For this reason, tasty mushrooms, such as cultivated mushrooms and oyster mushrooms, are especially suitable as an accompaniment; cèpes or shiitakes, by contrast, would be too rich, and chanterelles too delicate-tasting.

Bourgueil is a high-quality wine from the Loire valley in France, from a region with countless gourmet associations since the time of Rabelais. It enhances the strong aroma and flavor of the sauce, imparting to it a subtle hint of raspberries. Once reduced, this red wine will be rich in tannin. Stirring in a spoonful of sugar helps to mitigate its acidity. In any case, it is important not to whip the sauce, since this could spoil its color.

This is a typical March dish—the month of eels and mushrooms. It can, however, also be prepared in any other month of the year.

1. Buy live eels if available. Skin and fillet the eels and cut into pieces about 3 in/7 cm long.

2. Blanch the unpeeled garlic cloves in milk. Repeat the process twice more, using fish milk each time. Rinse the garlic cloves, place in an ovenproof dish with a pinch of sugar and a little browned butter, and bake until golden brown and tender. Cut the green garlic into thin slices. Clean, trim and slice the mushrooms.

garlic and vinegar

3. Fry the eel in duck fat, then season with salt and pepper. Sauté the mushrooms in butter. Add the parsley, the snipped lovage, and the caramelized garlic and keep warm.

4. Deglaze the eel pan with vinegar and reduce until the liquid has almost disappeared. Add the red wine and sage, and reduce again. Add the butter. Serve on shallow plates. Spoon some sauce over the eel and the mushroom-garlic mixture, and garnish with sage, lovage and parsley.

Swordfish ragout

Preparation time: 15 minutes
Cooking time: 15 minutes
Difficulty: ★

Serves 4

14 oz/400 g swordfish
2 medium eggplants
2 sweet, ripe tomatoes
2 cloves garlic

½ cup extra virgin olive oil
1 sprig of rosemary
2 sprigs of parsley
salt, coarse sea salt, freshly ground pepper
a little white wine

The swordfish, whose scientific name is *Xiphias gladius,* gets its common name from its characteristically long, spearlike upper jaw. This powerful fish, which is 13–16 feet/4–5 meters long, is caught in the Atlantic and the Mediterranean. Fortunately, it is seldom sold live, but almost always cut up into steaks.

The delicate taste of this fish is reminiscent of veal. When shopping, look for shiny, pink flesh. It is important to cook swordfish gently, because its delicate, delicious flavor is quickly spoiled by heavy-handed treatment. Cooks like to enhance its taste by sprinkling it with *fleur de sel* (see page 172), as this salt also improves the texture and

prevents the flesh from falling apart easily. If this is unavailable, use coarse sea salt.

The eggplant accompaniment is especially recommended in summer. Choose fresh, glossy, unbruised fruit with dark purple skin, firm flesh and few seeds. Steer clear of overly large specimens, which may be mealy in texture and lose flavor when cooked.

This ragout can be prepared easily and quickly, substituting other firm-fleshed fish such as monkfish, if wished. Whatever fish you use, be sure to serve it nice and hot.

1. Slice the eggplant into rounds a scant ¼ in/½ cm thick and place on a large colander or baking rack. Salt, and let drain for 2 hours. Pat dry thoroughly and broil for 5 minutes on each side. Keep warm.. Cut the fish into cubes.

2. Heat the olive oil, 1 finely chopped garlic clove and the rosemary in a pan. When the oil is hot, add the fish cubes, and season with sea salt and coarsely ground pepper. Let brown for 5 minutes.

with broiled eggplant

3. Next, add the peeled, seeded and finely diced tomatoes and cook for 5 minutes.

4. Deglaze with white wine and season with the remaining garlic and the chopped parsley, mixing well to combine. Place 3 eggplant slices on each plate, spoon over the seasoned swordfish cubes and drizzle with olive oil.

Sea bass couscous

Preparation time: 1 hour
Cooking time: 15 minutes
Difficulty: ★★

Serves 4

3⅓ lb/1½ kg sea bass
¾ cup/120 g couscous
1 green bell pepper
1 red bell pepper
1 carrot

1 onion
2 shallots
10 black olives
3 cups/750 ml fish stock
1 cup/250 ml extra virgin olive oil
1 cup/250 ml heavy cream
6 cups/1½ l white wine
salt and freshly ground pepper

Couscous is a typical dish of the North African countries of Morocco, Algeria and Tunisia and has been known in France since the conquest of Algeria by Charles X in 1827. Durum semolina and stock are its main ingredients, around which an infinite variety of recipes have sprung up, some of which include fish.

For this recipe, our chef recommends a line-caught sea bass. The delicate, tender flesh of this fish harmonizes superbly with the semolina, which naturally must be of the best quality. The quality in turn hinges on whether the grains were "rolled" properly and retain the proper degree of firmness after the cooking process.

Neither should the crucial role of the vegetables and seasonings be overlooked. In North Africa there are special strongly perfumed spices such as dried rosebuds, or the mixture *ras-el-hanout*, literally "grocer's head," made from at least a dozen spices, including ground black pepper, cloves and cinnamon. Their addition to the couscous will delight connoisseurs. The sauce is made with extra virgin olive oil. It will stay beautifully creamy in texture if the oil is blended in at the last minute.

1. Cook the couscous. Cut little balls from the carrot with the aid of a small melon-baller. Cut ¾ of the olives into small rings.

2. Scale and fillet the sea bass and cut into 4 portions. Make a fish stock using the bones. Fry the fish in olive oil and set aside.

with olive oil

3. Cut the bell peppers, onion and shallots into very small dice. Combine in a bowl with the cooked couscous, reserving a little of the vegetable mixture for a garnish. Spoon some couscous into a round baking ring on each plate, smooth the surface, remove the ring and top with a piece of fish. Garnish with the diced vegetables.

4. Prepare a white-wine sauce with the fish stock. Using an electric hand blender, blend a few pitted black olives and the olive oil into the sauce. Spoon a little sauce onto each plate, and garnish with the olive rings filled with carrot balls.

Russian salmon

Preparation time: 1 hour 30 minutes
Cooking time: 1 hour 30 minutes
Difficulty: ✷✷✷

Serves 12

8 lb 12 oz/4 kg salmon
7 oz/200 g salmon flesh (can be from trimmings), puréed
7 oz/200 g shallots
generous 1 lb/500 g onions
1¼ lb/600 g button mushrooms
3½ oz/100 g wild mushrooms (such as morels or chanterelles)
1¼ cups/300 ml white wine
1⅔ cups/400 ml fish stock
5 oz/150 g shellfish *salpicon* (see glossary)
5 oz/150 g scallop *salpicon* (in season only)
1½ cups/150 g wild rice (cooked weight)

5 oz/150 g basmati rice (cooked weight)
1 oz/30 g *fines herbes*, parsley
8 eggs, hard-boiled
6 cups/1½ l crème fraîche

For the sauce:
¾ cup/200 ml Noilly Prat (French dry vermouth)
¾ cup/200 ml white wine
the salmon braising liquid
6½ tbsp/100 ml jellied meat stock or glace de viande
7 oz/200 g shallots
2¼ lb/1 kg butter
1 tsp/10 g freshly ground pepper

Crêpe batter (see basic recipes)
Brioche dough (see basic recipes)

Marie Antoine Carême achieved fame as a court chef in the late 18th and early 19th century. This koulibiac, which he created to mark his culinary debut at the court of the Russian czar, is a testament to the cosmopolitan nature of his cooking. Originally, it was prepared with ingredients including sturgeon marrow (the valuable vesiga) or poultry. The foremost aim of the koulibiac is to retain the flavor of its individual ingredients. Recipes for more modest variants of this dish also exist, containing cabbage and other vegetables.

Preparation should be approached methodically. The brioche dough should be made the day before. The koulibiac is baked in an oven heated initially to 400 °F/200 °C, then lowered to 350 °F/180 °C. We also recommend that you prepare the garnish a day in advance, saving the assembly for the following day. Only then will you deal with the famous Scottish salmon, now raised in Scotland's crystal clear lochs.

The koulibiac should be brought piping hot straight from the oven to the table. You could also keep it overnight, however, and serve it cold the following day; a little lobster aspic and a cucumber salad with chives would make tasty accompaniments.

1. Line a braising dish with sliced shallots, chopped button mushrooms and parsley sprigs. Pour in the white wine and fish stock. Place the boned, skinned salmon fillets in the dish and season. Cover with aluminum foil and braise in a 350 °F/180 °C oven. Prepare a crêpe batter, adding the finely chopped herbs, and prepare six 7–in/18–cm crêpes.

2. Blanch the sliced button mushrooms and onions; cool and drain. Using the salmon flesh, prepare a rather firm stuffing. Add the other filling ingredients (parsley, onions, wild mushrooms and rice), using the rice to bind the mixture. Correct the seasoning. Slice the hard-boiled eggs into rounds. Prepare the brioche dough.

koulibiac

3. Roll out the brioche dough and transfer to a greased baking sheet; cover with the crêpes. Spread ⅓ of the filling into a rectangle the size of the salmon in the center. Place a fillet on top and cover with another third of the filling. Top with the egg slices. Place the second fillet on top and cover with the remaining filling. Fold over the brioche and seal. Bake at 400 °F/200 °C for 30 minutes; reduce the heat to 350 °F/180 °C and continue baking for another 20–30 minutes.

4. Combine the Noilly Prat, braising liquid, jellied meat stock and the finely chopped shallots in a saucepan and boil down to a syrupy consistency. Remove from the heat and whisk in the cubed butter. Correct the seasoning. Pass the sauce through a fine strainer and add the shellfish salpicon and scallop salpicon, if using.

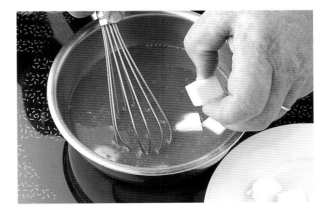

Queen of England's

Preparation time: 1 hour 30 minutes
Cooking time: 25 minutes
Difficulty: ★★★

Serves 4

4 Dover sole (about 10½ oz/300g each)
a few button mushrooms for the braising liquid
10½ oz/300 g button mushrooms
1¾ oz/50 g cèpes, morels, or chanterelles
2 shallots

generous 1 lb/500 g puff pastry
¾ cup/200 ml white wine
2 cups/500 ml fish stock
2 cups/500 ml heavy cream
parsley
salt and freshly ground pepper

The revocation of the Edict of Nantes in 1685 led to French cooks settling in England at the end of the 17th century, as they followed great Protestant families into exile. Since then, under the decisive influence of Marie-Antoine Carême, who cooked for the Prince Regent among others, there have been hundreds of French chefs in London who have endeavored to bring French gastronomy to the British. This dish, created at London's Connaught Hotel in 1977 to celebrate the 25th anniversary of the accession of Queen Elizabeth II to the throne, is one of the restaurant's most famous, and symbolically bears the image of Saint Paul's Cathedral worked into the puff pastry.

Here we have a combination of great French classics such as *sauce bonne femme* and a mushroom *duxelles*: a superb way to combine the classic and the original. The watchword here, though, is advance preparation. Our chef therefore recommends that you begin the puff pastry and filling the day before. It is also worth mentioning that small sole weighing about 10½ oz/300 g each can usually be trusted to have tender, tasty flesh.

According to taste, the *duxelles* filling may contain morels, cèpes or chanterelles, fresh if possible, although soaked dried mushrooms may be used.

The individual ingredients are layered when cold, then wrapped in puff pastry; the fish parcels must rest again before the final cooking stage. Don't forget to make a small "chimney" in the puff pastry, through which a little sauce can be poured just before serving.

1. Skin the soles, remove their heads and braise the fish with the white wine, shallots, fish stock, parsley and a few extra sliced mushrooms. Remove the fish from the braising stock and trim; fillet the fish and keep cool. Add the trimmings from the soles to the braising stock.

2. Reduce to a syrupy consistency. Add the heavy cream and reduce. Put through a fine sieve. Add the chopped parsley and chervil. Chop the cultivated and wild mushrooms. Sweat the chopped shallots in the butter. Add the mushrooms and cook until all liquid has completely evaporated.

Jubilee sole

3. Place some mushroom stuffing on half of the sole fillets. Reassemble the fish by covering with the top fillets.

4. Wrap in puff pastry and place a small puff-pastry emblem on top. Set aside to rest. Bake at 500 °F/250 °C for 15–20 minutes. Pour a little sauce onto the fish through a little hole made in the pastry. Serve the remaining sauce in a sauceboat.

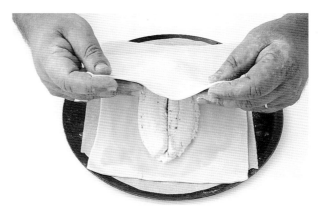

Light pike

Preparation time: 1 hour
Cooking time: 30 minutes
Difficulty: **

Serves 4

16 crayfish
7 oz/200 g mushrooms
3 cups/750 ml *sauce américaine* (see p. 57)
1 bunch of chives

For the filling:
4½ oz/125 g pike flesh
4½ oz/125 g pike-perch flesh or substitute scallops
2 egg whites
1 egg
½ cup/125 g butter, softened
¾ cup/200 ml heavy cream
salt and freshly ground white pepper

Quenelles or dumplings were once the specialty of the traditional cafés of Lyon, where families on their Sunday outings would sit down together for a meal. Christian Bouvarel has fond memories of these special occasions of his childhood and of the ice-cold lemonade that inevitably accompanied the delicious food. In those days he would also set off with his friends to catch crayfish in the nearby rivers, which his mother would then serve with the delicious dumplings.

Although a typical Lyonnais specialty, quenelles are derived—etymologically, at least—from the German *Knödel* or dumpling. Quenelles are usually made from fish, for example, carp or pike, which must be very fresh. Christian Bouvarel is of the opinion that the flavor of the pike should be toned down for this dish by adding pike-perch or scallops to the dumpling mixture.

Lastly, it should be mentioned that traditional quenelles contain a flour-based panada, which Christian Bouvarel prefers to leave out to ensure a lighter texture. Molding the dumplings with the aid of a spoon is admittedly a slightly tricky task. Don't give up, though—it gets easier after the first few botched attempts, and remember that Lyon wasn't built in a day either!

1. Fillet and bone the fish. Refrigerate until needed.

2. To make the quenelle mixture, process the fish flesh, salt and pepper in a food processor. Add the whole egg and egg whites, followed by the well-chilled heavy cream; do not over-process. Lastly, add the softened butter. Press through a sieve, then transfer the mixture to a bowl over ice cubes for 1 hour.

quenelles

3. To form and cook the dumplings, bring some salted water to a boil. Mold the dumplings (3 per person) using 2 tablespoons and poach for 10 minutes without boiling, turning them once. Drain on a kitchen towel.

4. Meanwhile, trim, peel and slice the mushrooms and sauté them in butter. Devein the crayfish, cook in simmering water and remove the tails from their shells. Arrange 3 quenelles and 4 crayfish on each plate and serve hot, with sauce américaine (see p. 57).

Soused whitefish

Preparation time: *1 hour*
Cooking time: *10 minutes*
Difficulty: ✲

Serves 4

4 whitefish
4 white onions
1 red bell pepper
2 carrots
1 rib celery

5½ oz/150 g zucchini
2 tbsp sugar
¼ cup/½ glass white vinegar
4 tsp/20 ml extra virgin olive oil
1 bay leaf
tarragon leaves
salt and freshly ground pepper

Unlike many other recipes for marinated fish hors d'oeuvre, in which the fish is fried, the fish fillets here are steamed, thus retaining their delicate taste and featherlight consistency. This preparation method is particularly suited to whitefish, which are native to the Alpine waters of Lake Geneva and Lake Maggiore, as well as to the Great Lakes of the United States. The flesh of whitefish is too delicate to stand up to long transport times or careless handling. It may, however, be kept for several days in the marinade which Carlo Brovelli recommends here.

The fish rolls themselves are not difficult to make. If you find the whitefish bland, you can pep up the flavor with a dash of white vinegar (balsamic vinegar is too subtle) or a few fresh herbs sprinkled over the dish just before serving.

The fillets must be handled with great care, as they are extremely fragile: one hand rolls the fillets up with the spatula, while the other hand, fingers moistened, carefully holds the skin and flesh together.

This fish can be served with crunchy *al dente* cooked vegetables as a warm appetizer, or you can eat it cold on a still summer evening.

If whitefish is unavailable, which is increasingly the case in Europe at least, choose fish whose fillets are long and thin enough for the rolls, such as sole.

1. Wash the whitefish fillets and remove any remaining bones. Roll them up and fasten with a toothpick. Steam, or bake in a 300 °F/150 °C oven, until just done.

2. Wash the vegetables and cut them up finely. Cook until al dente in simmering water to which a dash of sugar and vinegar have been added.

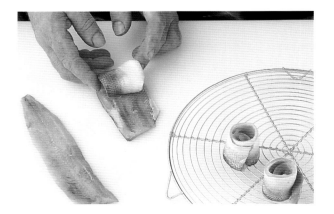

fillet rolls

3. Heat the olive oil in a pan for 10 minutes. Add the lukewarm vegetables, the bay leaf and the whitefish rolls. Marinate for 12 hours.

4. Place 2 fish rolls in the center of each plate. Scatter the vegetables around and sprinkle with the olive oil.

Fillet of sole with

Preparation time: 45 minutes
Cooking time: 15 minutes
Difficulty: ★★★

Serves 4

3 Dover soles, filleted (yields 12 fillets)
1 lobster (1¼ lb/600 g)
1 oz/25 g truffle paste
1½ cups/360 ml thickened lobster stock
(1 oz/25 g cornstarch per 4 cups/1 l)

⅓ cup/80 ml heavy cream
4 tsp/20 ml Madeira
celery leaves for garnishing
salt and freshly ground pepper

A good protein-provider like all other fish, Dover sole has always held a particular attraction for gourmets, who constantly invent superb recipes for it, some with the odd flash of genius. The fillets of this oval flatfish are easy to work with, and its firm white flesh is unusually delicate. Year-round availability is ensured by the great number of areas in which it is fished.

Choose soles weighing a generous pound/500 g each for this recipe. The skin of the fish, which must be shiny and tough, will peel away with a strong tug. To help you roll up the fillets attractively, we recommend that you use plastic or aluminum cylinders, which are also useful for other recipes. The lovely word *salpicon* supposedly derives from the Spanish *picar*, "to chop," preceded by a prefix referring to salt. In any case, here it means a variety of finely diced ingredients made into a ragout or stew, used among other things to fill puff pastry cushions.

The lobster stock takes time to prepare (3–4 hours), in other words considerably longer than the few minutes required to cook the lobster. Ideally, a sufficient quantity of stock should be prepared the day before, so as to have it on hand for other purposes.

1. Gently press the sole fillets flat. Lightly grease 12 cylinders measuring 1–1¼ in/3 cm in diameter and roll the fillets around them with the skin side inwards. Place the fillets in a pot with a steaming rack and steam for 3 minutes over boiling water.

2. Bring the lobster stock to a boil and stir in the cornstarch, which has been mixed in a little cold water. Boil for several minutes. Meanwhile, heat the oil to 300 °F /150 °C. Select a few of the best celery leaves and deep-fry. Drain on paper towels.

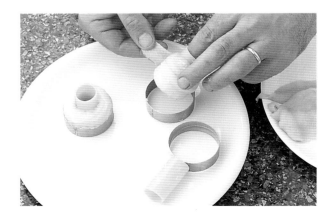

lobster *salpicon*

3. Cook the lobster for 7–8 minutes in boiling water. Shell the lobster, finely dice the tail meat and reserve the claw meat for garnish. Boil down the truffle paste with the Madeira and cream until you have a thickened sauce. Fold in the diced lobster meat. Adjust the seasoning and keep warm.

4. Place the sole fillets on a warmed serving plate and stuff with the lobster mixture, using a demi-tasse spoon. Pass the thickened stock through a fine strainer and pour onto the plates. Arrange the fillets in a triangle and garnish with the tips of the shelled lobster claws.

Breaded turbot

Preparation time: 1 hour
Cooking time: 20 minutes
Difficulty: ✵✵

Serves 4

 a small turbot, weighing 4½ lb/2 kg
16 crayfish
7 oz/200 g broccoli florets
1¾ oz/50 g tomatoes, cut up small
½ celery root

2¾ oz/80 g fresh bread crumbs
3 egg yolks
½ cup/120 g clarified butter
4 tsp/20 ml white wine
2 tbsp/30 g Dijon mustard
salt and freshly ground pepper

Steaming food is now exceptionally popular, particularly with fish. There are numerous reasons for using this technique with turbot. This flatfish, native to the Atlantic Ocean and the English Channel, and known by the Romans as the "king of the seas," has very delicate, fine-tasting flesh requiring gentle cooking. In the North Sea, this fish is found chiefly in the Dutch province of Zeeland, from where it is exported to the United States, where it fetches extremely high prices.

Fresh turbot will have a tough, shiny skin, still covered in slime—proof that it has not been washed. The belly side should be nice and white. Its unusual trapezoidal shape distinguishes it from brill and John Dory, which can successfully replace it in this recipe.

Handle the cooked turbot very carefully, as its delicate, flaky flesh falls apart easily and could make plating difficult. For the breadcrumb coating, it is best to use stale, even-textured white bread, with the crusts removed. It is essential that the turbot fillets rest briefly after baking in the oven, before going under the broiler.

The *sabayon* sauce requires a bit of practice, but preparing it over a water bath or double boiler makes things somewhat less tricky. The egg yolks must thicken without scrambling. The celery root julienne must be fried only very briefly in hot oil—otherwise it will turn black.

1. Skin and fillet the turbot, and cut into 4 portions. Brush the fillets with oil, season and steam for 3–4 minutes over boiling water. Remove from the heat and pat dry. Place on a plate that has been greased with butter. Cover the top with an even layer of bread crumbs.

2. Moisten the bread-crumbed fish with hot clarified butter. Cook for 3–4 minutes in a 375 °F/190 °C oven. Let rest for 2 minutes, then place under the broiler until evenly browned.

fillet

3. Cut the celery root into julienne and deep-fry in oil heated to 300 °F/150 °C. Drain on a hot baking sheet covered with paper towels. Blanch the broccoli florets for 3–4 minutes. Cook the crayfish in a court bouillon for 3–4 minutes. Shell the crayfish tails. Keep warm.

4. Pour the wine and the 3 egg yolks into a saucepan and whisk vigorously. Whip up like a sabayon at the edge of the burner. Fold in the remaining hot clarified butter, the chopped tomatoes (cooked down to a thick purée) and the mustard. Adjust the seasoning. Plate the fish and its accompaniments.

Sea bass cooked

Preparation time: 45 minutes
Cooking time: 25 minutes
Difficulty: ✳

Serves 4

3¼lb/1½ kg sea bass
14 oz/400 g celery root
1¼ cups/300 g butter
⅔ cup/150 ml sauce américaine (see p. 57)

4¼ tbsp/70 ml reduced brown veal stock
1 tsp poppy seeds
1 tsp mustard seeds
2 tsp/10 g Meaux mustard
deep-fried parsley
1 tbsp extra virgin olive oil
salt and freshly ground pepper
coarse salt

It need not always be a highly complicated business to produce a top quality dish. This method of preparing sea bass is simple and delicious and does justice to this fish, which was known in Greek mythology as the "child of the gods" and has retained its reputation to this day.

Sea bass has fine, delicate flesh, silvery-blue skin, and the aroma of iodine. Choose a fine-looking, absolutely fresh fish with clear eyes, weighing 3¼ lb/1½ kg, which will be easy to fillet.

In an effort to leave the sea bass in its natural surroundings, Michel Bruneau recommends an entirely new approach: cooking the fish on a large, thick stone.

This unusual gadget preserves the true taste of the fish, giving it a wonderful appearance and cooking it perfectly. The fillet should be brushed with plenty of oil on its skin side, the only side of the fish that will come in contact with the stone.

A number of gourmets consider sea bass to be a bland fish that must be enlivened with stronger flavors. It is often served with a piquant sauce that enhances without overpowering it. Make sure that you measure the ingredients carefully to produce a creamy sauce garnished with crunchy mustard seeds and poppy seeds. For this dish, we recommend enriching the celery root purée with butter.

1. Cut the sea bass into 8 equal-sized portions and set aside. Peel and coarsely dice the celery root and cook in boiling salted water; drain and blend to a smooth purée with 13 tbsp/200 g butter. Season and set aside to keep warm in a hot water bath.

2. Brush the skin of the sea bass fillets with olive oil and rub with coarse salt.

on a hot stone

3. Place the stone in a 475 °F/250 °C oven for 10 minutes, in order to heat it to about 400 °F/200 °C. Lay the fish fillets on the stone, skin side down, and roast for 5–8 minutes or until done.

4. In a saucepan, combine the sauce américaine with the veal stock, mustard seeds and poppy seeds and reduce by one third. Whisk in the butter and season. Spoon some celery root purée onto each plate, then arrange two fish fillets around it, skin side up. Pour around the sauce and garnish with parsley.

Bourride,

Preparation time: 45 minutes
Cooking time: 25 minutes
Difficulty: ★★★

Serves 4

2 lb 3 oz/1 kg baby turbot
2 lb 3 oz/1 kg John Dory
12 oz/350 g sole
1 lb 5 oz/600 g monkfish fillet
1 lb 5 oz/600 g sea bream
1 baguette (for the croutons)
salt and freshly ground pepper

For the vegetable accompaniment:
4 carrots
4 baby turnips

the white part of 4 young leeks
8 pearl onions
2 tomatoes

1 green and 1 red bell pepper
4 leaves of basil, chives
1 rib celery, chervil, tarragon
6½ tbsp/100 ml white wine
1 cup/250 ml vegetable stock
1 pinch of saffron strands
1 tbsp extra virgin olive oil

For the sauce:
1 small boiled potato
3 tbsp olive oil
juice of ½ lemon
4 cloves of garlic
1 tbsp tomato paste
1 egg yolk
salt, cayenne pepper and freshly ground black pepper

The port of Sète in the south of France has its own version of this fish soup, which Michel Bruneau discovered during a stay in the town. He was so impressed that he renamed his restaurant, until then known as *Au bon accueil* ("The warm welcome") after the dish.

This dish, here cooked "à la Bruneau", honors the traditions of the south of France while incorporating raw materials from Normandy: leeks and carrots, local fish and potatoes for the garlic sauce. The assortment of fish on which *bourride* is based contains one "fine" fish (turbot, brill or John Dory), one flat fish (Dover sole, dab or lemon sole), one fatty fish (sea bream, tuna or mackerel), and, depending on the market, the most recently delivered fish,

say monkfish. Since no one fish should dominate in terms of taste, it may be necessary to reduce the amount of one or the other fish on account of its stronger flavor.

While the saffron should be used sparingly, you may be more lavish with chervil and tarragon. The most difficult part of this recipe is the cooking times for the vegetables and fish, which must be prepared at the last moment in the order given.

Rub the croutons, made from a fresh baguette, with garlic. The shoot in the center of the clove should be removed to make the garlic more digestible. When fried in hot oil, the croutons will not absorb so much fat.

1. Heat the oil in a large saucepan and gently sweat the vegetables, which have all been cut into ¼ in/½ cm chunks. Pour in the white wine and the vegetable stock. Cook, covered, for 10 minutes. Add the saffron, whole basil leaves and chives. Season with salt and pepper and simmer for a further five minutes.

2. Prepare the sauce: Pound the garlic cloves and the boiled potato in a mortar, then add the egg yolk, salt and pepper. Add the olive oil in a thin stream, stirring constantly. Finally, add the tomato paste and the juice of ½ lemon. Transfer to a saucepan.

my way

3. Cut each fish into 4 equal-sized pieces, and season both sides with salt and pepper. Cook the fish on top of the boiling vegetables in the following sequence: monkfish, 5 minutes; sole, turbot and John Dory, 4 minutes; sea bream, 3 minutes. Cook, covered, without turning the fish.

4. Over a low heat, add 3 tbsp of the cooking liquid to the garlic mixture, which should not boil again under any circumstances. Serve the fish and vegetables in very shallow bowls, accompanied by croutons that have been rubbed with garlic, then fried in olive oil. Pass the sauce separately in a sauceboat.

Sole in the

Preparation time: 1 hour
Cooking time: 20 minutes
Difficulty: ★★

Serves 4

4 small Dover sole, no more than
10½ oz/300 g each
4 new carrots
20 baby leeks

4 sprigs of thyme
1 tsp/5 g grated ginger
1 tbsp peanut oil
3½ fl oz/100 ml hard cider
6½ tbsp/100 g butter
6½ tbsp/100 ml *crème fraîche*
chervil for garnishing
salt and freshly ground pepper

Solea Jovis—Jupiter's sandal—is what the gourmets of ancient Rome called their favorite fish, the Dover sole, which reached the apex of its popularity at the court of Louis XIV at Versailles. Nowadays, this fish is still highly prized for its firm, supple flesh. Dover sole is caught mainly in the North Sea, and in Senegal and Morocco, and so is available on the European market year-round. It is also exported to the United States.

Smaller sole, with plump, fine-tasting fillets are preferable for this recipe. Other small, fleshy flatfish, may also be prepared according to this recipe. Our chef recommends that you use carrots with a delicate, sweetish flavor, which harmonize perfectly with ginger. The ginger should be smooth and firm; peel before grating. Because of its strong flavor, only a little is needed to enhance the other ingredients.

The leeks must be cooked only until *al dente* , that is crisp yet tender, so they remain an appealing accompaniment. Leeks that are overcooked look gray and sludgy.

1. Fillet the sole. Cook the leeks and carrots with the grated ginger. Purée 3 of the carrots and cut 1 into rounds.

2. Stuff the sole fillets with leek and carrot slices. Decorate with leeks, carrots and thyme.

French style

3. Heat the butter and oil in a skillet and fry the sole fillets for 2 minutes on each side. Drain and keep warm.

4. Whisk the crème fraîche and butter into the carrot purée. Adjust the seasoning. Place each sole fillet on a warmed plate and pour some sauce around it. Garnish with chervil leaves.

Crown of scallops

Preparation time: 30 minutes
Cooking time: 15 minutes
Difficulty: ★★

Serves 4

12 sea scallops
2 black truffles
generous 2 lb/1 kg fennel
2 shallots
1 leek

1 carrot
1 onion
1 tomato
1 lemon
2 tsp shrimp-sauce extract
6½ tbsp/100 ml olive oil
6½ tbsp/100 g butter
4 tbsp snipped chives
sprigs of chervil
salt and freshly ground pepper

In this recipe land and water, with their respective raw materials, enter into a marvelous partnership in which the scallops are set off to particular advantage by black truffles. Choose medium-sized extremely fresh scallops with very little coral (the orange roe sac), either dry-packed or, if possible, in their shells. Scallops that do not react when a knife is inserted into the shell are not fresh and should be discarded.

The black truffles lend visual contrast to the dish, and they contribute the most subtle of flavors. Alain Burnel believes that they originated in Valréas, the several-hundred-year-old papal enclave near Avignon in Provence, where these valuable fungi are still found at unbeatable prices. The truffles should be cut into very thin slices, like the scallops.

Keeping to the same black and white color scheme, slices of firm-fleshed fish can be used in place of the scallops, but to considerably less impressive effect. In any case, the important thing is to combine subtle-tasting ingredients. The exception to this is the shrimp-sauce extract, which is used to enhance the flavor of the star ingredient, the scallops.

The fennel, which may also be replaced by baby fennel when in season, gives the dish a refreshing hint of aniseed.

1. Finely slice the leek, shallots, chervil, carrots and onions. Simmer in salted water to make a little court bouillon; dice the tomatoes and add to the bouillon. Strain.

2. Halve the fennel; cut into slices lengthwise, then cut on the diagonal into chunks. Simmer for 8 minutes in the court bouillon. Drain and refrigerate, reserving the court bouillon.

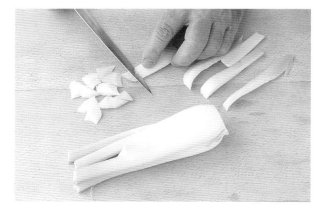

and fresh truffles

3. Slice the scallops into thin rounds, then do the same with the truffles. Add olive oil, salt, pepper and lemon juice. Macerate until the scallops turn opaque.

4. Sauté the fennel with the shallots in butter and add the chives. Mound the fennel in the center of the plate, and surround it with 2 circles of alternating scallops and truffles. Reduce the fennel stock; add the shrimp extract and whisk in the oil to form a sauce. Before serving, place a sprig of chervil on top of the fennel.

A little Provençal

Preparation time: 2 hours
Cooking time: 50 minutes
Difficulty: ★★★

Serves 4

3¼ lb/1½ kg assorted fish: (red) scorpion fish,
John Dory, red mullet, gurnard, conger eel,
wrasse
2¼ lb/1 kg rock fish
2 tomatoes
1 fennel bulb

3 small potatoes
2 onions
6 cloves garlic
1 leek
1 baguette
saffron threads
2 egg yolks
6½ tbsp/100 ml olive oil
freshly grated Parmesan cheese
sprigs of parsley
cayenne pepper
salt and freshly grated pepper

Every family in the south of France has its own recipe for bouillabaisse, with a few common denominators: scorpion fish, red scorpion fish, gurnard, conger eel and red mullet. Few of these ever show up in American markets, but you can make a delicious fish soup using local fishes.

Alain Burnel recommends a handful of small rock fish as a basic ingredient, to give the soup body and flavor. The problem, however, is getting them, unless you live near a Mediterranean fishing port. The soup base must be reduced before the larger fish are cooked in it, so it is best to prepare it the day before and to deal with the fish shortly before serving: the plumpest ones such as the conger eel

and scorpion fish first, and the more delicate ones like the red mullet last.

To merit its nickname of "golden soup," bouillabaisse must be enriched with saffron, a delight to both the eyes and palate. Harvest conditions have not changed since the time of the Crusades: 150,000 crocus flowers must be hand-picked to yield just one kilo (2.2 lbs) of the threads, which explains why it is the world's most expensive spice. You may take it for granted that cheap saffron has been adulterated, usually with annato or safflower—very effective food colorings that lack the subtle flavor of the real thing.

1. Scale, gut and clean all the fish. Cut the larger ones into pieces, leaving the small ones whole. Slice the baguette on the diagonal. Rub these croutons with garlic and put to one side.

2. Heat the oil in a saucepan until very hot, then start the soup off with the small fish, a bouquet of herbs, the onions and the white part of a leek, finely sliced, the 2 tomatoes, peeled, seeded and finely chopped, the garlic, saffron and fennel. Cook for 30 minutes and put through a food mill.

bouillabaisse

3. Cook the 3 potatoes in this soup. Remove, peel, and pound in a mortar with the egg yolks; gradually add the olive oil. Reserve this rouille.

4. Cook the remaining fish in the soup for 10 minutes, starting with the largest, then adding the other fish in descending order of size. Season to taste with salt and cayenne pepper. Serve in a covered soup tureen, garnished with chopped parsley. Pass the grated Parmesan, rouille and garlic croutons separately.

Cod in dark beer

Preparation time: 45 minutes
Cooking time: 15 minutes
Difficulty: ✶

Serves 4

1¼ lb/600 g cod
generous 1 lb/500 g hop shoots
1 lemon
2 egg yolks

2½ oz/75 g fresh white bread crumbs
1 cup/250 g butter
½ cup/120 ml Belgian *Koninck* beer (or other dark beer)
1 cup/250 ml fish stock
1 tsp fresh brewer's yeast (not active dry yeast)
salt and freshly ground pepper

While somewhat humbler than the "noble" fish such as European turbot or Dover sole, fish of the cod family (including haddock, pollack and whiting) nevertheless are very popular fish. Fresh cod is readily available, and lends itself well to an enormous variety of dishes.

Jan Buytaert prepares cod in the Flemish style, with the dark Belgian *Koninck* beer he so loves, and which he holds up as an example of the versatility of beer in cooking. This heady dark brew would have gone down well at the 16th century Flemish *kermis*, or fair, with its tipsy, red-cheeked villagers, as portrayed in the paintings of the Brueghels. If

you cannot get hold of *Koninck* with its many subtle nuances, the recipe may be made with any other dark beer.

The second crucial factor for the sauce is the butter. Use fresh, premium unsalted butter with plenty of flavor.

No less typically Belgian than the beer are the hop shoots. Popular since the 19th century for their high sugar content, they are traditionally compared to asparagus; many people actually prefer them. In any case, this unusual vegetable, whose harvest time is dubbed the "fifth season" by its Belgian fans, certainly repays closer acquaintance.

1. Cut the cod into 4 portions of about 5 oz/150 g each. Reserve the bones and trimmings and make into a stock. Place the cod on a baking sheet that you have buttered and sprinkled with salt and pepper, and cook in a preheated 375 °F/190 °C oven for 5–8 minutes, or until half-done.

2. Carefully clean the hop shoots and cook in the fish stock, which has been seasoned with the juice of half a lemon. Remove the shoots and keep warm.

with hop shoots

3. Add the beer to the hop-cooking liquid and reduce by half. Add the yeast and whisk in some butter. Pass through a fine strainer and correct the seasoning. Mix the bread crumbs with a little butter, forming into thin "cakes." In a double boiler, whisk the 2 egg yolks together with 2 tbsp water until foamy. Remove from the heat, then whisk in the remaining clarified butter to make a sabayon. Season.

4. Mound some hop shoots in the center of 4 buttered plates. Top with a piece of cod and a breadcrumb "cake." Bake briefly in the oven, until the fish is cooked through and the bread crumbs are golden brown. Pour some of the beer sauce around the fish, and spoon a bit of the sabayon on top before serving.

Turbot cheeks

Preparation time: 45 minutes
Cooking time: 30 minutes
Difficulty: ✭✭

Serves 4

generous 1 lb/500 g turbot cheeks (or substitute cod cheeks)
8 large langoustines (or substitute crayfish)
2¼ lb/1 kg mussels
juice of ½ lemon

1 egg yolk
1 bunch of flat-leaf parsley
1 bunch of chervil
6½ tbsp/100 g butter
3½ tbsp/50 ml dry white wine
½ cup/120 ml heavy cream
6½ tbsp/100 ml light cream
250 ml/1 cup white veal stock
salt and freshly ground pepper

Chervil was once dubbed "the parsley of the rich." In traditional medicine it is known as a liver stimulant and depurative (blood cleanser). Many legends are connected with this herb, for example that of the princess disfigured by illness who recovered her former beauty by applying chervil face masks.

The Umbelliferae family to which chervil belongs contains a number of poisonous species such as hemlock, administered in ancient Greece to those condemned to death, and infamous as the means by which the great Socrates died. Chervil, however, is absolutely harmless. Its subtle but distinctive taste is reminiscent of anise and parsley combined. Together with chives, tarragon and parsley, chervil is one of the four *fines herbes* of French cooking.

Gourmets consider turbot to be one of the very best eating fishes, but true turbot is rarely imported to the United States. Its origins are also important: as far as the Belgians are concerned, the finest turbot comes from Zeeland in the Netherlands. Turbot cheeks are highly prized, and consequently seldom available.

For the accompaniment, you will need the finest mussels available. Treat them with the respect they deserve by cooking them with a good white wine, perhaps a chardonnay.

1. Scrub the mussels thoroughly under cold running water and pull off their beards. Cook them in a pan with the wine, half of the veal stock, half of the butter, and some salt and pepper. Remove them from their shells and keep warm in a little of the cooking liquid. Strain the remaining cooking liquid through some cheesecloth and reserve.

2. Season the turbot cheeks and cook in the remaining veal stock just until the flesh turns opaque. Combine the reserved mussel-cooking liquid, the turbot-cooking liquid and the heavy cream in a saucepan and reduce by half.

with chervil

3. Strip the parsley and chervil leaves from their stalks, then wash and chop finely. Finish the reduction in step 2 by binding with the light cream mixed with the egg yolk, then adding the juice of ½ lemon and the chopped herbs.

4. Shell the langoustines, season, and pan-fry in the remaining butter. Arrange the turbot cheeks into rosettes on warmed plates, mounding the langoustines and mussels in the center. Pour the remaining sauce all around.

Dover sole with caviar

Preparation time: 30 minutes
Cooking time: 10 minutes
Difficulty: ☆

Serves 4

4 small Dover sole (about 5 oz/150 g each)
2¹/₂ oz/75 g osetra caviar
generous 1 lb/500g small heads of Belgian endive
1 egg yolk

½ cup/125 g butter
1 cup/250 ml white veal stock
5 oz/150 ml heavy cream
5 oz/150 ml light cream
Salt and freshly ground pepper

A flatfish known for its fine flavor and delicate flesh, the Dover sole dwells on the sandy sea floor, taking on the color of its surroundings so completely that it can barely be distinguished from them. This camouflaging is a strategic ploy, since the sole is a ruthless predator that consumes anything that comes within striking distance. How much more pleasant it is, therefore, for us to admire this attractive fish cooked and on a plate—especially the small sole recommended for this dish by Jan Buytaert, whose size makes them the ideal size for individual portions. If you must substitute another flatfish, choose a firm-fleshed variety.

Belgian endive is the blanched shoot of the chicory plant, forced in the dark. It was discovered more or less by accident in French-speaking Belgium in the 19th century.

High in fiber and potassium, this vegetable can form a valuable component of the modern diet and is very popular in its native Belgium. Choose small specimens with light, slightly yellowish leaves. Once cut into strips, the endive need only be cooked briefly in a stock that has enough body to allow it to be extended with cream.

In order to glaze the sole properly just before serving, you will require a source of intense heat, such as a preheated broiler. If the procedure is not carried out quickly enough, the sauce could collapse, spoiling the appetizing appearance of the dish.

Use osetra caviar to garnish the reassembled sole fillet; its good-sized golden grains are the prettiest, and its fruity flavor sets the other ingredients off to the best advantage.

1. Carefully rinse and drain the Belgian endive and slice into fine strips. Transfer to a buttered saucepan and pour over the veal stock. Cook, covered, over moderate heat for 4 minutes. Drain, and strain the cooking stock.

2. Clean and skin the sole. Butter a baking sheet and place the fish on top. Season with salt and freshly ground pepper and dot with a little butter. Bake for 7 minutes at 430 °F/225 °C, then fillet the fish, yielding 4 small fillets per fish.

and Belgian endive

3. Reassemble each sole on a plate, filling with the Belgian endive. Combine the vegetable cooking juices with the heavy cream and reduce. Finish off the sauce by adding half of the light cream mixed with the egg yolk, then adding the other half, whipped.

4. Mask the sole fillets with this sauce and glaze under the broiler. Spoon a dollop of caviar on the Belgian endive between the two top fillets and serve.

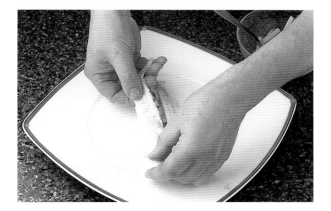

Stuffed velvet swimming

Preparation time: 1 hour 15 minutes
Cooking time: 35 minutes
Difficulty: ★★

Serves 4

20 large velvet swimming crabs

For the stuffing:
9 oz/250 g crab meat (from a large edible crab)
½ ripe mango

½ cup/125 ml béchamel sauce
1 tbsp fresh basil
1 tsp reduced *sauce américaine* (see p. 57)
1¾ oz/50 g Parmesan, freshly grated

For the sauce:
¾ cup/200 ml highly seasoned *sauce américaine* (carrots, onions, white wine, lobster stock)
1 tbsp/15 g butter
1 tbsp finely chopped chives
1 tbsp finely diced, peeled tomato

Among the 5,000 or so known species of true crabs, the velvet swimming crab is a fine example of the subclass of swimming crabs. It is distinguished by a flattened fifth pair of legs located just above its abdomen, which serve as flippers when it moves around. Unlike most of the other members of its class, therefore, this crustacean is relatively nimble and swims chiefly in very deep water, which is extremely useful for escaping from its enemies.

From a culinary viewpoint, however, it is very good value, has quite fine, delicate meat and can be made into excellent bisques, mousses or stuffings. Jacques Cagna has a novel way with it, filling the shell with a stuffing made from the meat of the large crab, while using the flesh of the swimming crabs as a main ingredient in the *sauce américaine*.

The disciples of Prosper Montagné still persist in calling the highly seasoned *sauce américaine sauce armoricaine* ("Armorican sauce"), despite the fact that none of the ingredients are even remotely reminiscent of Brittany. Here, Jacques Cagna offers us a new taste experience by also adding some finely diced mango, whose mellowness counterbalances the piquancy of the other ingredients. Our chef recommends a mango ripe enough not to be fibrous, but still firm.

1. Make the stuffing: Prepare a béchamel sauce out of butter, flour and milk. Peel the mango and cut into tiny dice. Chop the basil leaves. Mix together all the stuffing ingredients.

2. Cook the swimming crabs quickly in a court bouillon. Extract the flesh from their shells and reserve for the sauce américaine. Wash the reserved shells, fill with the stuffing and cover with grated Parmesan.

crabs with dried tomatoes

3. To prepare the sauce américaine, sauté the reserved crab meat in a little olive oil. Add the diced carrot and onion and brown slightly. Deglaze with white wine, then reduce. Add the lobster stock and cook for 10 minutes.

4. To finish the sauce, pass through a fine strainer, reduce by half, whisk in the butter and add the chopped chives and the peeled, finely diced tomato. Season and keep warm. For each serving, spoon sauce over the bottom of a shallow bowl, place 5 swimming crabs on top and brown briefly under a very hot broiler.

Crépinette of skate

Preparation time:	1 hour
Cooking time:	30 minutes
Difficulty:	★★

Serves 4

One 4½ lb/2 kg skate
4 oz/115 g pork caul
2 oz/60 g pancetta
1 head Savoy cabbage
2 tsp/10 g black olive paste

For the juniper butter:
¼ cup/65 g softened butter
rounded ½ tsp/3g juniper berries

1 small shallot
½ oz/15 g unsmoked bacon
¾ tsp mustard
½ sprig of thyme

For the vinaigrette:
¼ cup/4 tbsp olive oil
2 lemons
salt

For the black olive paste:
3½ oz/100g black olives
5 basil leaves
1 tbsp olive oil
salt and freshly ground pepper

Reaching lengths of up to 4 ft/1.2 m, *Raja clavata*, the European thornback ray or skate, propels itself forward in a graceful wavelike motion in its North Atlantic and Mediterranean habitat. The skate is the most widespread and frequently eaten European member of the family *Rajidae*, the true rays, but it is not easy to catch, because of its size and self-defense system, which enables it to administer electric shocks at short distances. Jacques Cagna recommends it for its delicacy and low fat content.

Since very large skates can be insipid and mealy, use the wing of a medium-sized specimen. It is difficult to handle without braking, but the fillets come away easily from the central cartilage.

The juniper butter draws its inspiration from certain German and Nordic recipes, and is pleasantly reminiscent of game preparations. In this recipe, Jacques Cagna gives it the specific task of enhancing the texture and taste of the skate, which one could hardly conceive of eating without some additional flavoring.

For the Provençal-style olive paste, we recommend that you use the small black olives from Nice.

1. To prepare the juniper butter, finely process the juniper berries followed by the ½ oz/15 g bacon. Add the chopped, sweated shallot, mustard, thyme, and then the softened butter. Season and pass through a sieve. Reserve.

2. Clean, skin and fillet the skate. Cut the pancetta into thin slices. Make a vinaigrette by whisking together the olive oil, lemon juice and salt. Cut the cabbage into thin strips and pan-fry in butter.

with juniper butter

3. To make the black olive paste, pit the olives and purée with the basil. As soon as they form a compote-like consistency, add the olive oil and season. Push through a sieve.

4. Spread out the pancetta on the work surface. Place a skate fillet on top. Spread with some olive paste. Top with a second skate fillet and wrap in the caul. Brown for 3–4 minutes on each side, then transfer to a 350 °F/180 °C oven for 10 minutes. Place on a bed of Savoy cabbage and pour a little vinaigrette all around.

Grilled sea bass with

Preparation time: 1 hour
Cooking time: 30 minutes
Difficulty: ★★

Serves 4

2 small sea bass (about 2 lbs/1 kg each),
filleted, or 4 4–6 oz/125–175 g fillets
24 baby carrots
24 baby turnips
12 baby zucchini
12 cherry tomatoes
8 star anise
1 tbsp butter

For the court bouillon:
⅔ cup/150 ml olive oil
1 tbsp white wine vinegar
1 tbsp cider vinegar
2 tsp lemon juice
½ tbsp/15 g honey
1 pinch/2 g saffron threads
1 tbsp/5 g coriander seeds
¼ cup, loosely packed /5 g flat-leaf parsley
½ tbsp/5 g black peppercorns
1 bay leaf
salt and freshly ground pepper
sprigs of fresh dill to garnish

The fish known in France as *bar* or *loup de mer* ("seawolf") goes by the name of "sea bass" in English-speaking countries. In the territorial waters of the United Kingdom this fish occurs in its largest numbers off the Scottish coast, not all that far from the Turnberry Hotel, over whose kitchens Stewart Cameron presides. Our chef is thus certain of obtaining the freshest specimens for his grill, just a few yards away from where they are landed.

In Scotland, sea bass are a lovely blue-gray color and can weigh between 8¾ lb–11 lb/4–5 kg. Stewart Cameron, however, prefers medium-sized specimens of about 5 lb/2.5 kg. The flesh of the sea bass is especially delicate-tasting, but quite different fish such as mackerel or cod

may be substituted in this recipe, in which case the approach preparation of the vegetables rather than of the fish is of prime importance.

The beauty and elegance of this dish are enhanced by the use of small vegetables, which also absorb the subtle flavors of the court bouillon better and more quickly. It is important to stick rigorously to the quantities given for the court bouillon ingredients, so that the seasonings do not overwhelm the individual flavors of the vegetables. An excess of vinegar would also spoil the delightful taste of this dish. This recipe offers a chance for the turnip to shine. This humble root vegetable, long neglected, has experienced a much-deserved increase in popularity over the last few years.

1. Place all of the ingredients for the court bouillon in a saucepan and simmer very gently over a low heat for 3–4 minutes.

2. Wash and trim all the vegetables, peeling the turnips and carrots. Cook each separately in the court bouillon until al dente, then place in a shallow bowl.

poached baby vegetables

3. Trim the fish fillets and remove any remaining bones; score the skin decoratively. Brush with a little butter. Pan-fry the fish in some butter for 5 minutes; the skin should be crisp. Reheat the vegetables in the court bouillon.

4. Whisk the butter into the hot court bouillon, then strain the mixture. Place a sea bass fillet in the center of each plate, surround with the vegetables, pour over the sauce and garnish with the star anise and the sprigs of dill.

Fillets of brill and mackerel

Preparation time: 45 minutes
Cooking time: 30 minutes
Difficulty: ✶✶

Serves 4

1 brill (generous lb/500g) (sea bass or cod may be substituted)
2 mackerels
24 hardshell or littleneck clams
1 cup/250 ml fish stock

For the mustard sauce:
6½ tbsp/100g coarse-grain mustard such as Scottish Arran mustard (if available) or French Meaux mustard
2 shallots
1 lime
4 tsp Scotch whisky
6½ tbsp/100 ml fish stock
¾ cup/200 ml heavy cream
5 tsp/25 g butter
½ bunch of chives
salt and freshly ground pepper

sprigs of fresh dill to garnish

To a large proportion of its guests, the Turnberry Hotel and its environs mean golf, and Tom Watson winning the 1977 British Open. Just a stone's throw away across the Firth of Clyde, however, lies a better-kept secret: the lovely Isle of Arran, where the only Scottish mustard is made, a coarse-grained condiment comparable to French Meaux mustard.

Add to this the mackerel, which abound in these waters throughout the summer and which are, more often than not, served broiled; the brill, which are no less plentiful; and the traditional hardshell clams, and you have a combination whose origins reach far back into Scottish folklore. Hardshell clams are easily recognized by their thick, mottled shells with their concentric grooves. Since their shells are often full of sand from burrowing into the sea bed, they should be rinsed thoroughly before cooking.

If hardshell or littleneck clams are unavailable, other varieties may be substituted successfully.

The iodine tang of the clams, accentuated by the mustard, is intended to enhance the more delicate taste of the mackerel and brill. The two different sorts of fish are held together with a toothpick, which like a magic wand turns them into a single fish with the advantages of both. Be prepared for one or more of your guests—never having heard of omega-3 fatty acids—to turn up their noses at mackerel, finding it too fatty. If this should happen, keep them happy by substituting herring.

In any case, we recommend that you wrap the fish fillets in plastic wrap to prevent them from falling apart during the poaching process.

1. Cut the brill into fillets weighing about 4 oz/120 g each and bone them. Do the same with the mackerel, whose fillets should weigh about 2 oz/60g each.

2. Wash the clams and rinse well to remove any sand. Cook in the fish stock over high heat for 2–3 minutes, or until they open. Poach half of the brill and mackerel fillets in the fish stock for several minutes.

with a mustard sauce

3. For the mustard sauce, melt the butter in a saucepan and gently sauté the finely chopped shallots with 10g of chopped chives and the juice of ½ lime. Add the whisky and fish stock. Reduce by half and stir in the heavy cream. Strain. Reduce again and add the mustard. Correct seasoning.

4. Using the remaining fish fillets, wrap a brill fillet around a mackerel fillet and fasten together with a toothpick; steam till the fish flesh is firm and opaque. Spoon some mustard sauce onto each plate and place the fish in the center. Arrange the clams and steamed fish all around. Garnish with sprigs of fresh dill.

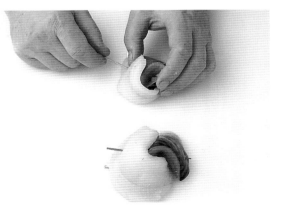

Dover sole fillets with

Preparation time: 30 minutes
Cooking time: 10 minutes
Difficulty: ✶

Serves 4

4 sole
7 oz/200 g spinach
3½ oz/100 g truffles
salt

For the rosemary oil:
1 sprig of rosemary
6½ tbsp/100 ml extra virgin olive oil
1 tbsp Dijon mustard
juice of 1 lemon
salt and freshly ground pepper

Rosemary, you will surely agree, is both a delightful-tasting and delightful-sounding herb (*rosmarino* in Italian). It plays a key role in many Italian recipes: in marinades, salads, terrines, ratatouilles and braised vegetables. Caution is advised, however, since rosemary has a very strong flavor that could overpower the other ingredients if not used with discretion.

That would be a particular pity here for the julienne of black truffles that grow chiefly in Umbria and the Marches. Once, and only once, our chef tried replacing them with stronger-flavored white truffles. An open conflict ensued, with both the rosemary and white truffles vying to gain the upper hand, rather than blending harmoniously.

The starring role in this recipe naturally goes to the Dover sole. In order to preserve their freshness they should be filleted at the last minute. These fillets are also lovely garnished with pomegranate seeds, whose translucent ruby color and tart flavor are a delight to both eye and palate.

A crispy note is furnished by the deep-fried spinach, whose light texture provides a superb foil for the delicate fish. A comparable effect could be achieved with Swiss chard. Our chef leaves it to the imagination of the individual cook to adapt this simple and tasty recipe encapsulating the charm of traditional Emilia-Romagna.

1. To prepare the rosemary oil, finely chop the rosemary and combine well in a bowl with the mustard, lemon juice, salt and oil.

2. Carefully pull off the skin from both sides of the sole, then fillet the fish. Steam the fillets.

rosemary on crispy spinach

3. Rinse and dry the spinach leaves. Deep-fry in hot oil, drain on paper towels and season.

4. Arrange the fried spinach in the center of 4 heated plates. Place the sole fillets on top. Pour over the rosemary oil and sprinkle with the julienned truffle.

Parmesan-crusted sea bass

Preparation time: 45 minutes
Cooking time: 8–10 minutes
Difficulty: *

Serves 4

4 thick sea bass fillets (6 oz/180 g each)
2 long eggplants
2 medium-sized zucchini
2 green bell peppers
2 red bell peppers

4 tomatoes
1 white onion
4 cloves garlic
3 sprigs of basil
2 sprigs of flat-leaf parsley
1 sprig of thyme
1¾ oz/50 g freshly grated Parmesan
2 tbsp/30 g butter
1¼ cup/300 ml extra virgin olive oil
salt and freshly ground pepper

This recipe contains no fish-stock-based sauce: the sea bass fillets are pan-fried, the dish is moistened with vegetable *jus* made by straining a ratatouille.

The success of the recipe lies not only in the consistency of this *jus*, which should be thick and flavorful, but also in how well it harmonizes with the vegetable strips, which are sautéed separately. Using extra virgin olive oil in the preparation of both naturally promotes this harmony.

If you do not buy sea bass fillets, choose a whole fish weighing 4¼–6½ lb/2–3 kg in order to obtain the required thickness of fillet. The sea bass is found in the Atlantic and the Mediterranean, and is referred to as *bar* or *loup* in France. Pan-fried quickly in butter, the Parmesan-coated fillets take on an appetizing crunchiness.

Farmers in the countryside around Nice offer a great variety of top-quality vegetables. In this recipe, a number of these are used to make a slow-cooked, melting ratatouille. More vegetables are sliced into thin strips and lightly sautéed, contributing both their unadulterated Provençal flavors and the touch of crispness which goes well with the crunchy sea bass.

If sea bass is unavailable, or you want a change, Francis Chauveau recommends sea bream as a highly satisfacory alternative.

1. Cut 1 eggplant and 1 zucchini lengthwise into 16 strips each, and 1 red and 1 green bell pepper into 8 strips each. Peel and seed 2 tomatoes, then cut into 16 equal strips. Broil 1 green and 1 red bell pepper until they char and blister; rub off their skins under cold water, then core and seed them.

2. Finely slice the remaining vegetables and stew in a pan in some olive oil. Add 2 chopped cloves of garlic and the basil, parsley and thyme. Bring to a simmer, season, and cook, covered, over low heat for about 1 hour. Place in a fine-mesh strainer and press to produce an oily jus.

with vegetable ribbons

3. Heat some olive oil in a skillet and gently sauté the vegetable strips. Thinly slice 2 cloves of garlic and deep-fry; also deep-fry 4 basil leaves.

4. Dredge the tops of the sea-bass fillets in grated Parmesan and pan-fry on both sides in a little olive oil. When the fillets are nearly cooked through, add the butter and fry until the topping is golden brown and crunchy. Place a fish fillet in the center of each plate, inserting a deep-fried basil leaf in the topping to garnish. Arrange the vegetable ribbons all around, alternating the colors. Place the garlic "petals" on the vegetables at intervals and pour the jus all around.

Spiny lobster

Preparation time: 15 minutes
Cooking time: 10 minutes
Difficulty: ★

Serves 4

4 spiny lobsters (generous 1 lb/500 g each)
8 black and 8 green olives
½ lemon
3½ tbsp/50 g butter
4 tsp chicken stock
¼ cup/4 tbsp *sauce américaine* (see p. 57)
2 tbsp olive oil
additional olives for garnish

For the vegetable garnish:
7 oz/200 g fennel
1 tbsp olive oil
a few dill sprigs
salt and freshly ground pepper

For the court bouillon:
1 carrot
1 onion
a little vinegar
thyme, bay leaf, flat-leaf parsley
salt and black peppercorns

Jacques Chibois' favorite kind of lobster remains the Mediterranean pink spiny (or rock) lobster, rarer than its ubiquitous red cousin, the common spiny lobster. Like all other crustaceans, the spiny lobster moves about with difficulty on the rocks, making it easy to catch. If you are not lucky enough to catch your own, choose a live one from a lobster tank weighing 1–1¼ lb/500–600 g, preferably a female, as its eggs can be used in the sauce. The flesh of the rock lobster is more delicate than that of the American lobster and must be cooked gently or it will become tough. Seasonings should also be used with discretion, so as not to mask its flavor.

In the Provençal manner, Jacques Chibois teams up green

and black olives with this Mediterranean crustacean; the combined flavors will instantly transport you to the south of France. Do not forget to blanch the black olives five times, to rid them of their bitter taste.

Fennel makes a pleasant accompaniment for the lobster. The white bulbs, which should be quite firm, are rich in vitamin C and are known for their digestive properties. Once upon a time, this highly edible plant was used to frighten away witches and evil spirits.

If you are unable to find any spiny lobster to your taste, you may also make this recipe with American lobster, langoustines, or large shrimp.

1. Cut the fennel into tiny dice and the olives into thin julienne (blanch 5 times). Cook the fennel in boiling salted water until tender—it should not be at all fibrous. Refresh and drain the fennel. When ready to serve, heat in a pan with a little olive oil, salt and pepper.

2. Cook the lobsters in the court bouillon for 5 minutes. Shell them, reserving the legs and heads with their antennae; halve the heads lengthwise. Cut the lobster tails into rounds.

with olives

3. Heat the lobster meat together with the chicken stock and the sauce américaine; season with salt and pepper to taste. Finish the sauce by whisking in the butter, olive oil and the julienned olives.

4. Pit the additional olives and thread them onto the reserved lobster legs. Arrange the fennel in the center of a shallow bowl and top with the lobster meat, placing the legs and head at the edge. Mask with the sauce and garnish with the dill sprigs.

Mediterranean fish

Preparation time: 30 minutes
Cooking time: 10 minutes
Difficulty: ★

Serves 4

2¼ lb/1 kg deep-sea Mediterranean fish (or substitute fish such as hake)
3½ oz/100 g potatoes
1 tsp/3 g chopped green garlic
¼ cup plus 2 tsp/70 ml olive oil
8 tsp/40 g butter

⅔ cup/150 ml boiling water
8 saffron threads
¼ tsp/1½ g rosemary
a few sprigs of chervil
salt and freshly ground pepper

For the vegetable accompaniment:
14 oz/400 g eggplant
1 clove garlic
1 tbsp olive oil
2¾ oz/80 g coarse salt

In the past, fishermen in the Mediterranean would use the *palangre*, a line equipped with sinkers and hooks that was lowered to the sea bed to catch deep-sea fish such as conger eel, dogfish, sea bream or red pandora. Nowadays, the same word is used by extension to refer to the fish caught in this way.

Since the *palangre* is becoming increasingly rare in the Mediterranean, however, we are obliged to fall back on other fish such as hake or whiting, which must be absolutely fresh. These fish can spoil very quickly.

This fragility should be borne in mind when you are cooking the fillets. Your main concern, however, will be to ensure that the skin is crisp, offering a delightful contrast to the soft flesh.

The potato sauce should be thoroughly blended to ensure that it is free from lumps. It is also important to add just the right amount of garlic, rosemary and saffron, so that the balance of flavors is not spoiled by excessive seasoning.

Eggplants, those summer vegetables *par excellence*, should be salted and drained before cooking. The process robs them of none of their nutritional value, but rids them of excess moisture (they consist of approximately 92 percent water).

Other vegetables popular in the Mediterranean, such as zucchini or tomatoes, may be substituted for the eggplant; finely chopped, sautéed with garlic and well seasoned, they too make for a winning combination of flavors.

1. Peel the eggplants and cut into small even-sized cubes. Salt and place in a strainer to drain for 20 minutes, then cook until tender in boiling salted water. Refresh, drain and press gently to expel excess water. Heat a little olive oil in a pan and fry the eggplant with one minced clove of garlic. Adjust seasoning.

2. Gut and fillet the fish and cut into 4 portions. Cook the potatoes in boiling water until tender.

with rosemary

3. Transfer the cooked potatoes to the blender. Add the olive oil, the butter, boiling water, garlic and saffron threads. Blend until you have a smooth, lump-free emulsion. Cook gently for 2–3 minutes with the rosemary, then adjust the seasoning.

4. Salt and pepper the fish; place in a hot pan and brown over low heat in a little butter. Cover the pan for 5–8 minutes. Place the sautéed eggplant in the center of the plate and top with the cooked fish. Pour over the sauce, scatter a few sprigs of chervil around the fish and garnish with a sprig of rosemary.

Broiled sea bass with

Preparation time: 40 minutes
Cooking time: 20 minutes
Difficulty: ☆

Serves 4

One 3¼ lb/1½ kg sea bass
4 heads Belgian endive
juice of 1 lemon
2 shallots

1 tsp/15 g sugar
⅔ cup/150 ml red wine vinegar
6½ tbsp/100 ml port wine
10 tbsp/150 g butter
salt and freshly ground pepper

The sea bass inhabits the temperate waters of the Atlantic and Mediterranean, and is highly prized for its delicate flesh. You can tell a fresh fish by the fact that it is firm, stiff and shiny. When pressed lightly with a thumb, the flesh should spring back, leaving no indentation—another reliable indicator of freshness.

Oddly enough, gastronomic opinion is sharply divided on the sea bass, some attributing an inimitable flavor to the fish, others dismissing it as bland. In any case, it is best to choose a line-caught wild sea bass if you can find one. Our chef recommends scoring the skin of the fillets; this provides for an even more attractive final result, as well as

allowing the heat to penetrate more effectively without drying out the flesh.

The sauce is a delicate juxtaposition of red wine vinegar with port wine. Both ingredients must be of the highest quality. The vinegar should be prepared from a good red wine that has been fermented slowly. Although a product of Oporto in Portugal, the main market for port is France, where tawny port, a mixture of several vintages is preferred. This dish offers a good opportunity to try an old tawny, in spite of its expense.

This simple but exquisite dish is best served piping hot.

1. Scale and fillet the sea bass. Remove any stray bones carefully with tweezers.

2. Cut the Belgian endive into strips and place in a bowl. Season with salt, pepper, lemon juice and sugar, and mix well. Melt 3½ tbsp/50 g butter in a saucepan. Add the endive and cook over very high heat.

a port and vinegar sauce

3. Place the vinegar and the finely chopped shallots in a saucepan and reduce to a syrupy consistency. Season and add the port. Reduce once more and whisk in the remaining butter. Pass the sauce through a fine strainer and keep warm.

4. Cut the fish into 4 portions. Score the skin diagonally, season the fillets and place in an ovenproof nonstick pan. Brush with butter. Cook under a very hot broiler or in a very hot oven. Place a spoonful of Belgian endive onto each of 4 heated plates. Top with a fish fillet and pour some sauce all round.

Cod with

Preparation time: 30 minutes
Cooking time: 30 minutes
Difficulty: ☆

Serves 4

1 small cod, about 2 lb 10 oz/1.2 kg, or 4 cod
fillets, 6 oz/175 g each
2 medium-sized tomatoes
1 red bell pepper
3½ tbsp/50 ml lemon juice

⅔ cup/150 ml extra virgin olive oil
5 tsp/25 g butter
chives
tarragon
basil
scant 2½ oz/70 g coarse salt
salt and freshly ground pepper

The Atlantic cod or *Gadus morhua* enjoys great popularity all over the western world, in both its fresh and dried forms. The Portuguese claim a thousand different ways of cooking salt cod alone, and recipes for the fresh fish also abound. On the other side of the Atlantic, in Newfoundland, cod fishing is considered a great maritime adventure, inspiring literature such as the 20th-century French novelist Roger Vercel's *Jean Villemeur*.

In order to preserve this fish, caught in cold, distant waters, European sailors used to salt it themselves on the fishing boats. It then formed the bulk of their diet during the sea crossing. Now that cod-fishing boats are veritable floating refrigerated factories, salting is no longer necessary, but the tradition is still carried on.

Choose a fleshy fish, preferably with yellow skin; use only the "loin" part of the fillets, reserving the belly for later use, in a *brandade*, for example. Serge Courville recommends marinating the fish fillets in coarse salt for 24 hours in order to firm them up nicely. They should be brushed with butter before cooking to impart an attractive color.

The *sauce vierge* or "virgin sauce" takes its name from the extra virgin olive oil, appreciated nowadays for its health-giving properties as well as its incomparable taste. Produced chiefly in the northern Mediterranean countries of Greece, Italy, Spain and France, it has the lowest acidity of any oil (1%).

1. Fillet and skin the cod. Carefully separate the "loin" fillets from the belly flesh, and remove all remaining bones.

2. Wash the fillets, pat dry and cut into individual-sized portions. Place in a bowl, sprinkle with coarse salt and refrigerate for 24 hours.

sauce vièrge

3. Peel and seed the tomatoes and cut into small dice. Wrap the red bell pepper in aluminum foil and bake in a hot oven, then peel and finely dice the bell pepper. Place the tomatoes, red bell pepper, chopped herbs, olive oil and lemon juice in a small saucepan; season and keep warm over low heat.

4. Pat the fish dry, then brush with butter and place in a heated nonstick pan. Cook the fillets until nicely colored on one side, then turn them over and cook until golden brown on top and opaque in the center. Ladle some sauce onto each plate and place the fish on top.

Breaded turbot

Preparation time: 45 minutes
Cooking time: 20 minutes
Difficulty: ★★

Serves 4

One 3¼ lb/1½ kg European turbot
chervil to garnish

For the julienne of vegetables:
1¾ oz/50 g carrot
1¾ oz/50 g leek
1¾ oz/50 g celery root
3½ tbsp/50 g butter

For the fish stock:
bones and trimmings from the turbot
2 oz/60 g shallots
1 cup/250 ml champagne
1 cup/250 ml cream
5 tbsp/75 g butter
1 bouquet garni
salt and freshly ground pepper

For the crumb coating:
1 oz/25 g Comté cheese
5 tbsp/75 g butter
1 oz/25 g fresh white bread crumbs

The story of the "roving eye" is guaranteed to appeal to connoisseurs of natural oddities. At birth, turbot and other flatfish have an eye on each side of their heads, but at a certain stage one eye migrates to the other side. Up until this point, the baby turbot spends much of its time swimming about, but afterwards it is content to settle down on the sea bottom, where it gradually takes on the color of its surroundings.

This nutritional powerhouse of a fish with its rough, scale-free skin is prized for its exceptionally delicate flesh which nevertheless holds its shape well during cooking. Gourmets agree that April is the best month for this fish, whose freshness can be gauged by its extremely shiny skin and immaculate white belly. Be sure not to confuse true turbot, generally imported from the Netherlands, with the lesser fish often sold under that name in U. S. markets.

Be forewarned that the crumb topping cooks extremely quickly, whether in the oven or under the broiler. Here we should stress the importance of the Comté, a French mountain cheese whose characteristic mildness is crucial to the success of this dish. Comté browns very quickly, and you are therefore advised to watch it like a hawk when it is cooking.

Hailing from the Champagne region in northeast France, our chef naturally recommends that you make the sauce with champagne, although another dry white wine would also fit the bill. It must be admitted, however, that champagne is unbeatable for lending zing to a sauce, and will do nothing but flatter the turbot in this recipe.

1. Scale and gut the turbot; carefully fillet the fish, then cut into portions.

2. Using a vegetable mandoline or a knife, cut the carrots, celery root and leek into very fine julienne. Blanch the vegetables, stew in 3½ tbsp/50 g butter and season.

in champagne

3. Make a fish stock from the turbot bones and trimmings, 2 oz/60 g finely sliced shallots, the champagne and the bouquet garni. Cook for 20 minutes, then strain through a fine-mesh strainer. Reduce and add the cream, followed by 5 tbsp/75 g butter. Season and keep warm.

4. For the crumb coating, press the Comté and the bread crumbs through a coarse sieve or box grater and mix with 5 tbsp/75 g softened butter. Spread the seasoned turbot fillets with the coating. Transfer to a baking sheet and bake for 5 minutes in a 425 °F/220 °C oven. Spoon some of the vegetable accompaniment into the center of each plate, top with a piece of fish and pour the sauce around. Garnish with chervil.

Sautéed langoustines

Preparation time: 30 minutes
Cooking time: 45 minutes
Difficulty: ★★

Serves 4

4½ lb/2 kg langoustines (about 28) or jumbo shrimp
10 oz/300 g chanterelles
10 tbsp/150 g butter, softened
1⅔ cup/400 ml dry white wine
6½ tbsp/100 ml oil
1 pinch saffron threads
salt

The chanterelle, with its little funnel-shaped cap, is familiar to all lovers of wild mushrooms. These fragile mushrooms should never be washed, but only brushed gently. After rinsing them rapidly under the faucet, they should be drained very quickly on paper towels and cooked immediately.

Medium-sized langoustines weighing between 2¾–3½ oz/80–100 g each are ideal for this dish. Our chef makes use of the superb langoustines caught in the Bay of Biscay, particularly during the summer.

To ensure that your langoustine tails are tender on the inside and nice and crisp on the outside, they must be peeled raw and then flash-fried in very hot butter. Naturally, this preparation method is also suitable for large shrimp, should you wish to use these instead of langoustines.

Saffron, obtained from the stigmas of a crocus, has been used in the kitchen since at least the Middle Ages, when spices played a large role in the European kitchen. It imparts a rich yellow color and a subtle flavor to the dishes in which it is used.

1. Peel the langoustines or shrimp and refrigerate the tails. Brown the heads and shells for 3–4 minutes in smoking-hot oil.

2. Add the white wine, season with salt, and simmer, partly covered, for about 30 minutes. Strain through a very fine strainer, add the saffron and reserve.

with chanterelles

3. Carefully clean the chanterelles and sauté quickly in butter. Enrich the white wine sauce by adding the softened butter bit by bit.

4. Just before serving, season the reserved langoustine tails or shrimp and sauté them in a mixture of oil and butter. Spoon some chanterelles into the center of each plate, arrange the langoustines around them in a semicircle and pour over the saffron sauce.

Grilled wild salmon

Preparation time: 30 minutes
Cooking time: 10 minutes
Difficulty: ✶✶

Serves 4

One 2¼ lb/1 kg wild salmon, or 4 salmon steaks
9 tbsp/140 g butter
¾ cup/200 ml oil
salt and freshly ground pepper

For the béarnaise sauce:
4 egg yolks
2 shallots
3½ tbsp/50 ml vinegar
2 tbsp water
10 tbsp/150 g butter, clarified
1 bunch each of tarragon and flat-leaf parsley
⅓ oz/10 g coarsely ground black pepper

For the garnish:
2 medium zucchini
2 medium carrots
8 small potatoes

Few fish enjoy such a high reputation as the salmon. This sea fish that swims upstream to spawn, leaping over all barriers with brio, never fails to stir the hearts of nature-lovers or the taste buds of gourmets, who have delighted in its tasty pink flesh for centuries. Rich in vitamin A, salmon is one of the most coveted species of fish—especially wild salmon, leaner than its farmed cousins.

Unfortunately, wild Atlantic salmon is increasingly rare in European waters, and the Adour river in the southwest of France, where our chef used to find beautiful fish, is no exception. Poaching and water pollution must share the blame, as no law of nature could prevent the salmon, driven by instinct, from swimming upstream to spawn. Moreover, it is not universally known that once they have

spawned, Atlantic salmon swimming back downstream to the sea have lost most of their body mass, and only a sojourn in sea water can rejuvenate them.

Salmon cut into steaks stays tender when cooked, and the cooking process can be more easily monitored than when the fish is whole. The steaks are done when the flesh near the bone is pink. This dish should be served piping hot; do not reheat.

Béarnaise sauce, scented with tarragon, is the ideal accompaniment for grilled fish and enhances the salmon without masking its true flavor. It is important to prepare the béarnaise just before serving, ideally in a double-boiler, so that the temperature can be regulated.

1. Clean the fish. If using a freshly caugt fish, gut it and remove the fins, working from tail to head. Carefully wash the salmon under clear running water and drain on paper towels. Cut into steaks of equal thickness.

2. Peel the carrots and potatoes and cut these and the zucchini into olive shapes. Heat some oil in another pan and toss the vegetables until crisp-tender. For the sauce, combine the chopped shallots, chopped tarragon, coarsely ground pepper and vinegar in a heavy braising pan and reduce until almost all of the liquid has evaporated.

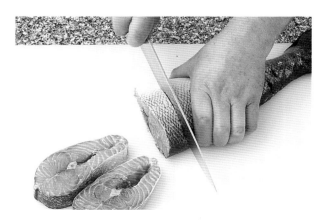

with béarnaise sauce

3. Add the egg yolks and water to the reduction and whisk in a double boiler until the mixture falls from the whisk in a thick ribbon. Now add the clarified butter in a thin, steady stream, whisking vigorously all the while. Pass the sauce through a strainer lined with cheesecloth. Salt to taste and add the tarragon and the finely chopped parsley. Set the béarnaise sauce aside in a warm place.

4. Marinate the salmon steaks for several minutes in the olive oil and 8 tsp/40 g clarified butter, turning 2 or 3 times. Meanwhile, steam the vegetables until the potatoes are cooked and the carrots and zucchini are crisp-tender; keep warm. In a stovetop grill pan, grill the salmon over moderately high heat for 1 minute on each side, until medium-rare, or to taste. Arrange the vegetables in a flower shape next to the salmon and serve the béarnaise sauce separately.

Dover sole

Preparation time: 30 minutes
Cooking time: 10 minutes
Difficulty: ★★

Serves 4

Four 9 oz/250 g Dover soles
2¼ lb/1 kg fresh cèpes or porcini mushrooms
2 shallots
1 onion
1 medium carrot
1 bunch of parsley
1¾ oz/50 g all-purpose flour

13 tbsp/200 g butter
2 cups/500 ml oil
2 glasses sweet Jurançon or other medium-sweet white wine
2 cups/500 ml water
salt

It is said that Henri of Navarre, later to become Henri IV of France, was fed Jurançon wine while in infancy. The product of a fertile soil and of a mixture of different types of vines, Jurançon is a spicy, full-bodied wine that acquires hints of Madeira as it ages. The distinctive taste of Dover sole is ideally enhanced by the flavor of this wine.

Highly esteemed since ancient times, Dover sole is caught in the Atlantic and the English Channel, but also in more distant waters, thus ensuring a year-round supply. Unfortunately, it rarely appears in American fish markets. It should be cooked on its central bone, which imparts quite a noticeable aroma and flavor to the flesh as well as preventing it from drying out. A fresh sole should be stiff, with bulging eyes and skin tightly attached to the fillets; it will not require more than a few minutes' cooking.

Use a damp cloth to sponge away the earth clinging to the stalks of the mushrooms. Preparation is in two stages: first, the mushrooms are sautéed in oil and drained; then, just before serving, they are reheated in a little butter.

The (Dover) sole (*solea solea*) may be replaced here by the more modest lemon sole. Somewhat similar to the sole in appearance, its flesh is not so fine; it too requires only brief cooking.

1. Clean the sole: trim off the fins, cut off the heads and tails, then pull off the skin with a single sharp tug.

2. Prepare the sauce: gently sauté the heads and fins of the sole in oil and butter until lightly colored. Add the thinly sliced onion and carrot. Moisten with the Jurançon and about 2 cups/500 ml of water. Add a pinch of salt. Simmer gently for about 1 hour. Strain through a fine strainer, pressing to extract all of the juices. Just before serving, reduce to a slightly syrupy consistency and whisk in 3½ tbsp/50 g butter.

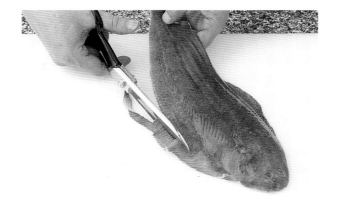

with cèpes

3. Clean the mushrooms with a damp cloth (do not wash). Peel the stalks, then cut the cèpes into ⅜ in/1 cm slices. Heat some oil in a skillet and sauté the cèpes until golden. Drain on paper towels. Just before serving, reheat in butter with the shallots and parsley.

4. Sauté the sole in oil and butter until golden brown. Fillet and place on buttered plates. Arrange the piping hot cèpes on top of the fish and serve, passing the sauce separately.

Sea bass with crispy

Preparation time: 30 minutes
Cooking time: 10 minutes
Difficulty: ★★

Serves 4

One 4½ lb/2 kg sea bass, or
4 7–8 oz/200–250 g sea bass fillets
2 ripe, red tomatoes
3½ oz/100 g fresh chanterelles
4 cloves garlic
½ shallot

4 sprigs of fresh thyme
1 bay leaf
generous 5 oz/150g fresh basil
3½ tbsp/50 g clarified butter
¾ cup/180 g butter
3½ tbsp/50 ml olive oil
3½ tbsp/50 ml fish stock
4 sprigs of fresh thyme
1 pinch *fleur de sel*
salt and freshly ground pepper

According to some sources, basil came originally from India, where a decoction of the leaves was used both as a remedy and condiment. Basil is very popular in Itlay and France, particularly Provence, and is the basis of the famous pesto and pistou, the garlic enriched sauces that originated there.

Nowadays, fresh basil is available everywhere. Naturally, it lasts longer if bought as a potted plant. Basil is the ideal accompaniment for tomatoes, and it harmonizes beautifully with garlic, thyme and bay leaf, all of which add their fragrance and flavor of Provence to this dish.

The sea bass, native to the coasts of France, is known as *loup de mer* ("sea wolf") in the Mediterranean and *loubine* around La Rochelle in the Bay of Biscay. This fish can reach lengths of up to 40 in/1 m. In addition to its impressive size, this member of the *Serranidae* family boasts lean, vitamin-rich flesh. Sea bass should always be absolutely fresh: stiff, with clear, bulging eyes and shiny scales.

Richard Coutanceau prepares the flavored oil a week in advance. To make it, place a clove of garlic in a little olive oil, add ¾ cup/200 ml peanut oil, some thyme and a bay leaf, and set aside to steep.

1. Skin and halve the tomatoes; squeeze gently to remove the seeds and excess liquid. Place in a baking dish, pour over some oil flavored with garlic, thyme, and bay leaf and bake for 40 minutes at 190 °F/90 °C. Clean the sea bass and cut into 4 fillets.

2. Blanch a generous 5 oz/150 g basil. Refresh quickly in cold running water, dry thoroughly and transfer to a blender. With the motor running, add 3½ tbsp/50 ml olive oil. Season with salt and pepper. Bring 3½ tbsp/50 ml fish stock to a boil and whisk in 10 tbsp/150 g butter.

skin in a basil sauce

3. Add enough fish stock to the basil paste to achieve a pouring consistency. Sauté 3½ oz/100g chanterelles in a little oil, adding ½ finely sliced shallot toward the end of cooking.

4. Score the skin of the fish in a lattice pattern. Add 2 tbsp/30 g clarified butter and the remaining thyme to a nonstick pan. Cook the fish fillets, skin side down, for 7 minutes without turning. Place ½ tomato on each of 4 heated plates and top with a crispy sea bass fillet. Sprinkle with the fleur de sel and thin shreds of basil. Pour the sauce around the fish.

Mussels in white wine with

Preparation time: 35 minutes
Cooking time: 15 minutes
Difficulty: ✻

Serves 4

4½ lb/2 kg (farmed) mussels
2 cups/500 ml white wine
1 shallot
1 bouquet garni (thyme, bay leaf, parsley)

juice of ½ lemon
⅓ cup/80 g butter
⅔ cup/150 ml heavy cream
1¾ oz/50 g all-purpose flour
1 tsp curry powder

In the past, lovers of fine food were often deprived of these delicious mollusks, as people were discouraged from eating mussels. Indeed, until some time in the 19th century it was believed that mussels should be eaten only in moderation, because they were supposedly hard to digest. Today, thanks to advances in farming methods, the shellfish on our plates are fresh, healthy and easy to digest.

Mussels are eaten when two years old. In France they are farmed mainly opposite the Ile de Ré, in the Baie de l'Aiguillon, where the mussel farmers carefully monitor the growth of the *moules de bouchot*. These small, highly esteemed mussels are cultivated on stakes driven into the shallow coastal beds. These aristocrats among shellfish are traditionally prepared as a *mouclade*: cooked in white wine and served with a thick butter and cream sauce.

Mussels should be eaten the day they are purchased. First of all, any open or damaged mussels are discarded, and the remaining ones are carefully scrubbed and debearded. Overcooking toughens them, which ruins them beyond redemption.

To season this dish from the Charente region of France with curry powder may seem odd. One need only think back, however, to the proud past of La Rochelle, a port of call for Dutch merchants on their return journey from the Far East, bearing Indian spices back to Europe.

1. Sweat the finely sliced shallot in a little butter. Add the thyme, bay leaf, parsley and white wine. Bring to a boil and add the mussels, cooking for 2–3 minutes or until they open. Drain the mussels, reserving their liquor and cooking liquid.

2. Make a roux from the butter and flour and whisk in the reserved liquid. In another saucepan, combine and heat together the curry powder, cream, and juice of ½ lemon.

a butter-and-cream sauce

3. Whisk the curry-cream mixture into the roux-and-mussel-liquor mixture. Stir over low heat for several minutes and strain.

4. Remove the top shell from each mussel and arrange the mussels on the half shell decoratively in shallow bowls. Pour over the mouclade sauce. Serve hot.

Scallop cakes

Preparation time: 30 minutes
Cooking time: 15 minutes
Difficulty: ✷✷

Serves 4

20 sea scallops
6 heads of Belgian endive
4 shallots

juice of ½ lemon
1 pinch of saffron threads
1 pinch of sugar
4½ tbsp/100 g sesame seeds
3½ tbsp/50 g butter
⅔ cup/150 ml cream
3 cups/750 ml dry white wine
3½ tbsp/50 ml oil
salt, freshly ground pepper, dry pink peppercorns

With a little imagination you can conjure up a delicious dish from almost any ingredient—even from scallops accidentally squashed on the way home from fishing. This mishap served Jean Crotet as the inspiration for a recipe in which chopped scallop meat is transformed into appetizing patties.

Whole, top-quality scallops may of course also be used. Buy dry-packed or, better, live scallops. If you can find these, first remove the coral (the reddish-orange roe sac) from the white meat, since the liquid it contains could increase the likelihood of the patties falling apart.

The farm-style preparation of the Belgian endive, which is sliced into thin strips, gives this seafood dish a rustic touch. Take care not to cook the leaves for too long.

The use of sesame, with its Arabian Nights associations, gives this dish a subtle Asian note. This blends successfully with the flavor of the scallops, particularly when enhanced by a little vermouth, which gives body to the white wine in the sauce.

If by misfortune you do not enjoy the taste of cooked Belgian endive, you can replace it with roughly shredded cabbage sautéed in butter.

1. Slice the Belgian endive into strips, then place in a pot with the butter, sugar, salt, pepper and juice of ½ lemon. Cook over high heat for 5–6 minutes, stirring frequently to bind the butter.

2. Remove the reddish orange coral (roe sac) from the white scallop meat, then chop the scallops by hand. Season with salt and pepper, then form into patties about 4 in/10 cm across. Smooth the patties and sprinkle with sesame seeds.

with sesame seeds

3. Reduce the white wine and the finely sliced shallots; add the cream and saffron. Season and set aside.

4. Heat the oil in a nonstick pan. Place the scallop cakes in the skillet sesame-seed-side down. Cook for 3–4 minutes over low heat until golden, then turn and briefly cook the other side. Arrange the cooked endive in the center of the plate, top with a scallop patty and pour the sauce all around. Sprinkle with a few crushed pink peppercorns.

Pandora fillet with

Preparation time: 45 minutes
Cooking time: 3–4 minutes
Difficulty: ✳

Serves 4

Two 1¼ lb/600 g pandoras or porgies
2 medium-sized zucchini
5 tomatoes (for the *confit*)
1 lemon
1¾ oz/50 g small Niçoise olives
generous 5 oz/150 g small capers
3½ tbsp/50 g butter

extra-virgin olive oil, preferably French
2 tbsp roast-meat juices or reduced veal stock
balsamic vinegar
16 basil leaves
thyme
flat-leaf parsley
salt and freshly ground pepper

For the chick-pea crêpes:
¼ cup/65 g chick-pea flour
⅞ cup/230 ml water

0The people of Nice are extremely partial to a savory crêpe, served hot off the pan, and called *socca* after the local name for the chick-pea flour from which it is made. Chick peas or garbanzos, once disparaged in the Mediterranean as poor man's food, have undergone a recent social and culinary rehabilitation. They have also become better known as a popular ingredient in North African cooking.

The *socca* is accompanied here by the Mediterranean pandora fish, known in France as the *pageot*. This fish is sometimes confused with its cousin, the sea bream, the delicacy of whose flesh it cannot, however, match, although it yields pink, highly aromatic flesh and relatively fleshy fillets. Certain varieties of the pandora journey from the Mediterranean to the Atlantic, and they are widely available in Franc.e

Preparation of the *socca* is child's play: chick-pea flour and water are made into a batter, which should be set aside in a cool place for 24 hours. The crêpe is first cooked in a pan, where it puffs up, then collapses. It is then transferred to the oven and baked until crisp. If you are preparing the crêpes several hours in advance, place them on a cake rack once cooked. If left on a plate, they would become soggy.

Be careful to measure the capers and olive oil carefully to balance the tart flavor of the lemon.

1. Prepare the chick-pea crêpe batter by mixing together the chick-pea flour and water. Season the batter with salt and set aside in a cool place for 24 hours.

2. Prepare the tomato-and-thyme confit. Assemble the garnish: the lemon, peeled and finely diced, the Nice olives, pitted and thinly shaved, the flat-leaf parsley in sprigs and the capers. Wash, fillet and bone the fish.

chick-pea crêpes

3. Make a beurre noisette by heating the butter until it turns brown and gives off a nutty smell. Add 2 tbsp meat juices or reduced stock and a little balsamic vinegar and oil. Cut uniform shavings from the zucchini peel; sauté in oil without browning, then drain and set aside. Deep-fry the basil leaves and reserve.

4. Make the chick-pea crêpes in a pan, then transfer to a 425 °F/220 °C oven for 2 minutes. Heat the butter in another pan and add the garnish (lemon, capers, olives and parsley). Pan-fry the fish. Place a crêpe on each plate and spoon over some zucchini shavings and confit tomatoes. Top with a fish fillet and the fried basil and pour some sauce over before serving.

Braised

Preparation time: 30 minutes
Cooking time: 1 hour 30 minutes
Difficulty: ✶✶

Serves 4

2 John Dory
28 thin stalks green asparagus
40 morels, fresh or dried and reconstituted
1½ cups/350 g butter
a little olive oil
1 bunch of chives
12 sprigs of chervil
salt and freshly ground pepper

For the white stock:
2 chicken carcasses
2 onions, studded with cloves
1 medium carrot
1 leek
1 bouquet garni

Michel Del Burgo prefers Mediterranean fish: sole, sea bream, sea bass or John Dory. This recipe, in which John Dory fillets are braised on their backbone, has earned him many accolades; he stresses that it achieves perfection only if made with a genuine Mediterranean John Dory, whose fine white flesh puts it head and shoulders above its Atlantic cousins.

Fillet the fish, keeping the heads for a fish soup, and reserve the central bone. After brushing the fillets with oil, simply put the fish back together again and transfer it to the oven. This is easy, as the bone slips right back into place. The fish is done when the fillet sticks to the bone and is an attractive pink color there, which contrasts with its otherwise translucent appearance. This procedure brilliantly preserves the sea flavor of the fish.

Green asparagus is best for this recipe: French connoisseurs will prefer that grown in the Aude area. The choice between all-green asparagus and the blanched sort with touch of violet where it has had some sun depends on its appearance and your own preference. The important thing is for all asparagus stalks to be of the same thickness and of a regular cylindrical shape. The morels may be fresh or dried, as long as they are soft and aromatic. Mousserons may be substituted, but, unlike morels, they do not yield a juice, which imparts a aspecial flavor to the John Dory.

1. Fillet the John Dory. Brush the fillets with oil and salt lightly, then reform the fish around the central bone and set aside. Prepare the white stock: Cover the chicken carcass with cold water, add the remaining ingredients and cook for about 90 minutes, skimming several times. Strain when done. Wash the morels.

2. Wash the asparagus, peeling if necessary. Cook in boiling salted water until crisp-tender, then refresh. Place the John Dory in a buttered baking dish; add the morels and pour over some white stock. Cover with aluminum foil and cook for 5 minutes at 400 °F/200 °C. Remove from the oven, turn the fish over and cook for another 6 minutes.

John Dory

3. Pour the juices from the cooked fish into a saucepan. Reduce and whisk in the butter. Finely chop the chives.

4. Finish the garnish by adding the morels and the asparagus tips to the sauce mixture. Adjust the seasoning. Remove the skin and any remaining bones from the fish. Arrange the morels and asparagus on the plates, top with the fish and pour the sauce all around. Sprinkle with the finely chopped chives and decorate with sprigs of chervil.

Braised turbot with

Preparation time: 45 minutes
Cooking time: 30 minutes
Difficulty: *

Serves 4

One 4½ lb/2 kg turbot
1 bunch of green asparagus
1 bunch of large golden grapes, such as
muscat grapes

2 shallots
2 medium leeks
4 medium carrots
6½ tbsp/100 g butter
1 cup/250 ml *crème fraîche*
2 cups/500 ml muscadet
chervil
salt and freshly ground pepper

Originating in the south and southwest of France, an *estouffade* is a dish that is slowly stewed in a lidded pot, preserving intact the taste of all of the ingredients used in it, whether vegetables, meat or fish. In this recipe, we use European turbot, which can be recognized by its clear eyes and shiny skin.

The turbot lives on sandy sea beds in cold waters and can weigh up to 11–13 lb/5–6 kg. It is primarily caught at night with the *palangre*, a line equipped with sinkers and hooks. Popular since ancient times, there are a wealth of recipes for this splendid fish. However, turbot is very delicate and must be cooked carefully.

The accompaniment of early vegetables mounded in the center of the plate is dominated by the asparagus tips. Select small, firm specimens. The remaining vegetables are chosen according to what is in season and tastes best. The important thing is to cook them together with the turbot in muscadet. The fine bouquet of this wine is the pride of the Nantes countryside.

This dish owes its originality in part to the grapes, which should have a slightly musky taste. Once peeled, they should be slowly steamed, or cooked for a few seconds in the microwave. This unusual garnish lends a freshness to the entire dish and will not fail to delight your guests.

1. Fillet and skin the turbot. Carefully remove all bones from the fish. Cut the fillets into large cubes.

2. Cook the asparagus tips in boiling salted water. Refresh at once. Cut 1 leek into 2 in long/4–6 cm long pieces, then into thin slices. Using a very small melon-baller, cut the carrots into tiny balls, or cut into small dice. Peel the grapes, cut up small and steam for several minutes.

muscadet and early vegetables

3. Peel the shallots, finely dice and sweat them in butter. Blanch the leek and the carrots and add to the shallots. Salt and pepper the turbot chunks and add these to the pot. Briefly sweat the vegetables and fish and pour over the muscadet to cover. Bring to a boil and remove from the heat at once. Cover and leave for 5 minutes.

4. Remove the turbot and keep warm. Reduce some of the vegetable-wine mixture until the liquid has evaporated, then purée in a blender. Add the crème fraîche. Reduce to a velvety consistency and correct the seasoning. Whisk the butter into the sauce. Arrange the remaining vegetables and grapes in the center of the plate. Surround with the chunks of turbot and pour some sauce all around.

Sweet-and-sour John Dory

Preparation time: 20 minutes
Cooking time: 15 minutes
Difficulty: ✶✶

Serves 4

One 4½ lb/2 kg John Dory
generous 1 lb/500 g oyster mushrooms
1 cup/250 ml grapefruit juice
3 tbsp/50 g sugar
6½ tbsp/100 g butter

a little olive oil
1 bunch of chives
salt and freshly ground pepper

In many countries, preparing meat and fish dishes in a sweet-and-sour style has long been common culinary practice. The ancient Romans are said to have delighted in this subtle combination of flavors, which was reintroduced to the West centuries later through the popularity of Far Eastern cuisines. Modern chefs have found many types of fish are amenable to this treatment, as evidence of which we present a very simple recipe using John Dory.

The fish must be fresh, that is firm and stiff, with clear eyes. To cut up the fish neatly, work the blade against the skin between the skin and the flesh, gently pulling the skin away. The skin is tougher than the flesh and the fillets will remain in one piece. Joseph Delphin recommends that you gently pound the fillets flat with a mallet, so that they do not shrink when they are pan-fried.

Watch the sauce carefully as it cooks, and under no circumstances let it boil, which could cause the butter in it to break. Keep the sauce warm after it has thickened to preserve its consistency and flavor.

For this recipe, the best choice of mushroom is the oyster mushroom, which is widely cultivated nowadays.

1. Fillet the John Dory and skin the fish by inserting a knife between the skin and flesh and pulling away the fskin. Separate the fillets into three and trim. Pour some olive oil onto a plate and marinate the fish in it.

2. Place the sugar in a saucepan with 2 tbsp grapefruit juice and cook until caramelized. Pour in the remaining grapefruit juice. Reduce for 10 minutes until you have a syrup. Strain into a bowl. Whisk in the butter and keep warm.

with oyster mushrooms

3. Wash and drain the mushrooms and pat dry. Cut off and shred the stalks. Melt half of the butter in a skillet and brown the mushrooms. Season with salt. Place the fish fillets in a very hot, salted pan. Cook over high heat for 2 minutes on each side, then drain on paper towels.

4. Arrange the mushrooms in the center of each plate. Top with the fish (3 pieces per person). Pour the sweet-and-sour sauce over the John Dory and garnish with a little finely chopped chives.

Preparation time: 45 minutes
Cooking time: 15 minutes
Difficulty: ★★

Serves 4

14 oz/400 g Dover sole fillets
5½ oz/160 g thin green beans
salt and freshly ground pepper

For the fritter batter:
2¾ oz/80 g all-purpose flour
scant tsp/4 g baking powder
4 tbsp water
2 scant tsp/8 g salt

For the béarnaise sauce:
3 egg yolks
¼ cup/60 g clarified butter
2 tbsp/ 15 g chopped shallot
leaves from 1 bunch of fresh tarragon leaves
4 tsp white vinegar
4 tsp white wine
generous 2 tsp/12 g coarsely ground black pepper

For the pastry:
1¾ oz/50 g flour
3½ tbsp/50 g butter
2 egg whites
1 pinch of confectioners' sugar
chives (optional)
salt

The Italian influence in Provençal cooking has inspired Philippe Dorange to create his own version of the classic *fritto misto*, which he prepares with Dover sole.

When choosing a Dover sole, check to see that it is good and firm. Its skin should be shiny and stick tightly to its flesh. To skin the fish, make a shallow incision near the tail between the skin and flesh and remove the skin with one sharp tug, repeating for the other side. Any other method might damage the delicate fillets. The more modest and readily available lemon sole, whose flesh is not as mediocre as it is sometimes made out to be, may be used in place of the Dover sole in this recipe.

For an exceptionally light, crisp result, you can use a tempura batter: Vigorously whisk ice-cold water into the fritter batter and set it aside for about 20 minutes.

If you ordinarily serve fried fish with tartar sauce, you will find that béarnaise sauce makes an interesting change of pace. When preparing this sauce, you must ensure that the egg yolks are well emulsified with the vinegar mixture and that they are warm, but not too hot, when the butter is whisked in. These precautions are essential to prevent the sauce from collapsing. The béarnaise sauce tends to congeal quickly on the surface, but a short, vigorous whisking will bring back its color and consistency.

1. Scale and fillet the Dover soles. Cut the fish into strips and dip in the batter (prepared according to the recipe for "fritter batter" on page 318). Trim and wash the beans and dip these in the batter.

2. To make the béarnaise sauce, combine the finely chopped shallot, coarsely ground pepper, vinegar, ¾ of the tarragon, finely chopped, and the white wine in a saucepan over low heat and simmer until reduced by half. Allow to cool somewhat, then add 3 egg yolks and 1 tbsp water.

# of Dover sole

3. Whisk until foamy. Slowly add the melted clarified butter, whisking vigorously. Strain through a fine strainer. Add the remaining tarragon, chopped, and correct the seasoning. Make the pastry by working the flour into the butter, adding the salt and sugar, and mixing in the egg whites one at a time. Spread the mixture in ovals on a greased baking sheet, sprinkle with chopped chives and bake for 5 minutes at 400 °F/200 °C.

4. Deep-fry the battered sole and beans until golden brown. Drain on paper towels and season. Place some béarnaise sauce on the center of each plate, mound the fried fish and beans on top and crown with a piece of pastry.

Broiled sea bass with mozzarella

Preparation time: 1 hour
Cooking time: 50 minutes
Difficulty: ★★★

Serves 4

One 1¼ lb/600 g sea bass
5½ oz/160 g fresh mozzarella
3 tbsp/60 g basil
1 tbsp/20 g each chervil, tarragon, parsley
2½ tbsp/40 ml olive oil
a few celery leaves for garnishing

For the fish stock:
generous 1 lb/500 g fish bones
1 celery rib

1 small onion
1 medium leek, white part only
1 cup/250 ml white wine
1 bouquet garni
3½ tbsp/50 ml olive oil

For the vegetable mixture:
½ cup/20 g each diced carrot, cauliflower, turnip, celery root, new potatoes, peas, zucchini, mushrooms
6 large cloves garlic
4 cups/1 l fish stock
5 tbsp/75 g basil
10 tbsp/150 g butter
6½ tbsp/100 ml olive oil

Teaming sea bass fillets with a herbed mozzarella topping constitute a delicious and unusual treatment for the highly prized fish as well as for the supple young cheese, which is more frequently eaten uncooked in its native Italy.

Sea bass has firm, white flesh, to which this topping adds a fine note of flavor. The fish should be handled very carefully and boned completely: Its thick bones could spoil the fillets as well as the dining ppleasure of your guests. The skin of fillets should be scored in several places in order to prevent curling during cooking.

If bought packed in liquid, mozzarella should be drained before being puréed along with olive oil, salt, garlic and basil. The resulting delicate green mixture is spread on the pan-fried fillets, which are broiled briefly just before serving to crisp the topping. Philippe Dorange confesses to a weakness for basil, and admits to sometimes preparing a variation on this recipe with that herb alone. Basil is also the main flavoring for the vegetable accompaniment, basil and olive oil being whisked into the vegetable juices at the last moment to make a *pistou*.

1. Cut the vegetables for the accompaniment into ⅛ in/3 mm dice. Prepare the fish stock: soak the fish bones in cold water, then sweat in oil with the finely sliced celery, onions and leek. Moisten with the white wine and add sufficient water to cover the bones. Add the bouquet garni, lightly season with coarse salt and cook for 20 minutes. Strain.

2. Sweat all the vegetables in butter without allowing them to color. Pour over the fish stock and adjust seasoning. Cook for about 30 minutes. Keep warm; add basil and olive oil.

and basil-scented vegetables

3. Purée the mozzarella with the remaining basil, chervil, tarragon and parsley in a food processor. Spread the mixture on a baking tray and set aside . Cut into 3 x 1-in/8 x 3-cm rectangles.

4. Clean and fillet the sea bass, leaving the skin on. Cut into 5 oz/150 g pieces and pan-fry skin side down in olive oil. Top with the soft mozzarella mixture, and pass under the broiler to glaze just before serving on a bed of the vegetables, garnished with the celery leaves.

Whiting with scallop

Preparation time:	30 minutes
Cooking time:	5 minutes
Difficulty:	☆

Serves 4

2 whitings weighing a generous 1 lb/500 g each
8 sea scallops
2 tomatoes
2 shallots

1 lemon
1 sprig of thyme
6½ tbsp/100 g butter
1 cup/250 ml dry red wine (preferably Pomerol or other Bordeaux)
6½ tbsp/100 ml veal stock
6½ tbsp/100 ml fish stock
chives, chopped
salt and freshly ground pepper

In the 18th century, powdered wigs were all the fashion, and the wigmakers, not surprisingly, were generally covered in powder themselves—like a whiting which has been dredged in flour before frying. This, at least, is the explanation given by the French poet Chateaubriand for the fact that all representatives of this profession in his day were called *merlans* or "whitings" themselves, a term later applied by extension to all hairdressers in general in the wake of the novel *Hôtel du Nord* by the French writer Eugène Dabit.

Apart from its literary career, the whiting is a modest but thoroughly decent fish from the same family as pollack and cod. It lives in cold waters and has beautiful silvery blue, scaly skin. Available year-round, its inexpensive, nutritious flesh is suitable for many attractive preparations.

As an example, its scales can be "reconstructed" from sea scallops carefully cut into thin rounds. The scallops must be very fresh—live, if possible—and are ranged along the length of the whiting fillet like scales. The dish is then cooked quickly, so that the scallops do not dry out and the flavor of the fish is completely preserved.

Claude Dupont is a great advocate of Pomerol, a popular Bordeaux produced in the growing region between Libourne and Saint Émilion. The sauce, based on veal and fish stock, should only be made from a fine wine with a perfect bouquet.

1. Clean the scallops and soak in plenty of water for at least 2 minutes. Clean and fillet the whiting, taking care to remove all of the small bones. Place the fillets in a buttered ovenproof dish and season with salt and pepper. Cut the scallops into thin slices.

2. Arrange the scallop slices side by side and slightly overlapping on the fish fillets, like scales. Moisten with fish stock, bring to a boil, then transfer to the oven and continue to poach for a further 3 minutes.

"scales" in Pomerol

3. Place the chopped shallots and the thyme in a pan, moisten with red wine and reduce by a quarter. Add the veal stock and the liquid in which the whiting were poached. Reduce by half. Remove from heat and whisk in the butter bit by bit.

4. Correct the seasoning, add a few drops of lemon juice and put through a fine strainer. Arrange the whiting fillets on 4 plates, pour the hot sauce all around and place some peeled, roughly chopped tomatoes down the middle of the fish. Garnish with chives.

Lemon sole with a mussel

Preparation time: 30 minutes
Cooking time: 20 minutes
Difficulty: ★★

Serves 4

8 small lemon sole fillets
2¼ lb/1 kg mussels
1 tomato, 1 medium carrot, 1 leek
2 shallots
3½ oz/100 g celery root
2 cloves garlic
a few saffron threads

3½ tbsp/50 g butter
6½ tbsp/100 ml white wine
1 bay leaf
1 sprig of thyme
8 sheets rice paper

For the pike stuffing:
1¾ oz/50 g pike fillet
3½ tbsp/50 ml Noilly Prat (French white vermouth)
1 tbsp whipped cream
2 tbsp heavy cream
salt and cayenne pepper

Brill, plaice and lemon sole are trusty standbys of German fish cookery. These flatfishes, also known as "poor man's sole," have fine flesh in their own right that can be used in the preparation of exquisite dishes, as Lothar Eiermann demonstrates here.

The lemon sole, which is found in the Atlantic Ocean, the English Channel and the North Sea, can be recognized by its smooth skin and its tiny head, which looks disproportionately small for its body. Other good flatfish may also be used in this recipe.

The quality of the stuffing will determine how big a hit this dish is. Two instructions must be followed out without fail: first, place the pike (or pikeperch) fillet in your freezer compartment briefly before processing it; secondly, don't add the cream before the proper time. All the raw ingredients must be well chilled to survive the blending process unscathed. Using pikeperch avoids the risk of ending up with too dry a mixture.

The mussel sauce, responsible to a large extent for the originality of this recipe, benefits both from the freshness of the mollusks (which should preferably be small) and from the flavor of the saffron and the subtle hint of bay leaf. Do not be tempted to replace the mussels with scallops, as the flavor of the latter would not be set off to its best advantage here.

1. First prepare the pike stuffing: Cube the pike fillet, season with salt and pepper and place briefly in the freezer. Process with the heavy cream to form a stuffing. Season with the Noilly Prat, salt and cayenne pepper. Press the mixture through a sieve and fold in the whipped cream.

2. Skin the fish fillets, spread with the stuffing and wrap in a piece of rice paper. Clean and trim the vegetables and cut into sticks; blanch and refresh in ice-cold water.

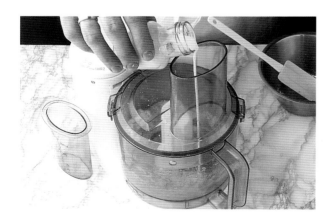

and vegetable *pot au feu*

3. Heat some oil in a pan and lightly sauté the remaining vegetables with the chopped shallots. Add the mussels, seasonings and white wine. Cook, covered, for 5 minutes. Lift out the mussels and remove from their shells. Strain the mussel liquor and reduce. Add the saffron. Whisk in the butter.

4. Pan-fry the fish fillets in some butter and let rest for 4 minutes off the heat. Heat the blanched, refreshed vegetables in the saffron-mussel liquor. Spoon the mussel-vegetable sauce into a shallow bowl and place the lemon sole fillets on top.

Preparation time: 10 minutes
Cooking time: 20 minutes
Difficulty: ✷✷

Serves 4

14 oz/400 g brill fillets
6 oz/180 g mushrooms
2 heads of Belgian endive
lemon thyme
4 tsp/20 g butter
6½ tbsp/100 ml white wine
sugar, salt and freshly ground pepper

For the orange butter:
juice of 1 orange and 1 lemon
zest of ½ orange
2 tbsp/30 g sugar
1 tbsp water
⅓ cup/80 g butter
3½ tbsp/50 ml jellied fish stock
2 tsp/10 ml champagne
2 tsp/10 ml vodka

For the onions:
12 pearl onions
1 cup/250 ml dry red wine
½ cup/125 ml dry port wine
⅓ bay leaf
1 sprig of thyme

Brill is one of the very best flatfish. Its delicious, supple-textured white flesh yields fine fillets and fires the imagination of the cook, here inspiring our chef to create a composition in the form of a rose.

The roses are not difficult to assemble. Since each fillet has both a thinner and a thicker portion, we recommend that you place the thinner strips in the center and the thicker ones on the outside when rolling them up. The steam will cause the individual parts of the rose to adhere to one another, making it easier to handle.

The vegetable accompaniment should achieve a balance between the acidity of the orange, the bitter taste of the Belgian endive and the sweetness of the pearl onions. The citrus juices are boiled down to concentrate their flavors, spiked with a dash of vodka, then softened with a little sugar and the addition of butter towards the end. Taste the sauce during preparation, if necessary correcting the seasoning to achieve the desired tartness before finally whisking in the champagne.

Although it is possible to substitute turbot for brill in this recipe, it is far less economical to use and is not easy to manipulate into the rose shapes. There is no substitute for the Belgian endive, but it can be extended by adding a few leeks, sliced and cooked until tender.

1. Prepare the brill rosettes by slicing the fillets lengthwise into 4 thin strips and rolling them up and assembling into rose shapes. Place on buttered waxed paper and steam over some white wine until opaque. Decorate with sprigs of lemon thyme.

2. Separate the leaves of the Belgian endive and slice the mushrooms. Braise the endive in butter and sprinkle with a little sugar. Add the mushrooms and deglaze with white wine. Simmer for 3–4 minutes, reducing the liquid.

braised Belgian endive

3. Prepare the orange butter by reducing the orange and lemon juice by half. Add the sugar, a little water, the orange zest and vodka, and bring to a boil. Simmer for several minutes. Stir in the fish stock and whisk in the butter. Add the champagne.

4. Combine the pearl onions, red wine and port in a saucepan and bring to a boil. Skim, season and reduce to a syrupy consistency. Arrange the endive leaves in the shape of a star on the heated plates, place the brill rosettes in the center, pour the orange butter between the endive leaves and garnish with the glazed onions.

Breaded

Preparation time: 20 minutes
Cooking time: 8–9 minutes
Difficulty: ★★

Serves 4

One 3¼ lb/1½ kg sea bass
7 oz/200 g mushrooms
3 tomatoes
1 onion
2 cloves garlic
3½ oz/100 g shallots

1⅔ cup/400 ml heavy cream
3½ tbsp/50 ml Noilly Prat (French white vermouth)
1⅔ cup/400 ml fish stock
1 sprig of thyme
1 sprig of basil
salt and freshly ground pepper

For the crumb coating:
6½ tbsp/100 g butter
100 g fresh white bread crumbs
1¾ oz/50 g Gruyère, grated

If you prepare sea bass with flavorful tomatoes and a fine *duxelles* (finely chopped mushrooms), and crown it all with a tasty golden brown crust, you have a marriage of flavors made in heaven. This recipe is also suitable for large parties, since it can easily be prepared the day before. The breadcrumb mixture must be covered with plastic wrap and chilled: the butter hardens, which makes future handling easier.

Jean Fleury recommends using a perfectly fresh line-caught sea bass weighing about 3¼ lb/1½ kg for this recipe. In France, they are purchased "clipped," that is with proof of their origin, but elsewhere your guide to

quality and freshness is a fish with bulging eyes, shiny skin and a firm flesh that springs back when pressed with a finger. The Greek poet and gourmet Archestratus referred unhesitatingly to this fish as the "child of the gods." The best sea bass are line-caught around rocky points, but the majority nowadays are simply caught on trawlers: they are an easy mark, since these fish travel in relatively large schools.

If sea bass is not your cup of tea (certain people find it bland, apparently), you can use turbot, salmon, whiting, or cod in this recipe with excellent results.

1. Prepare a duxelles (mixture of finely chopped mushrooms) and, separately, a tomato concassé (mixture of peeled, coarsely chopped tomatoes). Clean and fillet the sea bass, removing all the bones.

2. Prepare the crumb coating by combining thoroughly the 6½ tbsp/100 g butter with the sieved bread crumbs and the grated Gruyère. Chill.

sea bass

3. Spread some crushed tomatoes on each fillet, following with a layer of duxelles. Prepare the sauce by reducing the Noilly Prat, shallot and fish stock. Add the cream and the sprig of basil and reduce once more. Purée the sauce in a blender and strain.

4. Roll the chilled breadcrumb mixture flat between sheets of waxed paper. Cut out 4 rectangles the size of the fish fillets and use to cover the fish. Grease an ovenproof dish, pour in a little fish stock and place the fillets in the dish. Bake for 8–9 minutes, then place under a hot broiler until golden brown. Spoon the sauce onto the plates and place a fish fillet in the center of each.

Preparation time: 45 minutes
Cooking time: 45 minutes
Difficulty: ★★

Serves 4

One 2 lb 10 oz/1.2kg brill
salmon skin
12 pearl onions
16 small carrots
12 large mushrooms
anchovy paste (optional)
6½ tbsp/100 ml *glace de viande* or reduced
veal stock
6½ tbsp/100 g salted butter
a little flour
salt and freshly ground pepper

For the fish stock with red wine:
2¼ lb/1 kg fish bones, salmon trimmings and
bones
3 cups/750 ml full-bodied red wine
1 onion
1 medium carrot
2 shallots
1 leek
sprigs of flat-leaf parsley
thyme, bay leaves
white peppercorns

Some people confuse brill with turbot, but brill has a smooth skin and turbot a rough one. Brill can reach 28 in/70 cm in length, although it is more usually about 12–24 in/30–60 cm. If possible, choose a good-sized fish for this recipe, yielding thick fillets, which need to be cut into largish pieces.

The crucial factor in this recipe is the cooking process, which must be carried out at a temperature of 140 °F/60 °C. Notice, too, that our chef uses the skin, bones and trimmings of a salmon that was prepared and served earlier—hence, nothing goes to waste. When combined with a good, strong red wine (for example, a French red

from the Loire valley), these leftovers yield a particularly delectable fish stock. Take special care when preparing the stock, however—under no circumstances must the red wine be allowed to boil for any length of time.

The crisp *julienne* of salmon skin provides the ideal foil for the tender brill fillet. First, however, the salmon skin must be dried in the traditional fashion, in the warm summer sun. The crisp shreds of skin are not only decorative, but lend a special subtle flavor to the dish.

The mushrooms for the garnish should be perfectly white, firm and of a good size.

1. Clean, wash and dry the salmon skin. Clean the brill; cut off the head and pull off the skin. Cut in two with a knife. Trim and cut into pieces.

2. Sweat the bones and vegetables in some butter. Moisten with the red wine and water, bring to a boil, skim, and simmer for 25 minutes. Let rest for 10 minutes, then strain. Bring to a boil once more, skim and reduce over medium-low heat. Add the glace de viande and the anchovy paste, if using. Thicken the sauce with the butter and pour in a little unreduced red wine. Adjust seasoning.

on the bone

3. Pat dry the pieces of brill and sprinkle with flour. Fry in a nonstick pan in butter or olive oil. Using scissors, cut the salmon skin into thin strips and place under a hot broiler until crisp. Cook the pearl onions, allowing them to brown. Cook the carrots in a little water with the salted butter and sugar.

4. Remove the stalks from the mushrooms; season the caps and wrap them in individual squares of aluminum foil with a little butter. Place in the oven or under the broiler until tender. Ladle some sauce onto the center of each plate and top with a golden brown fish fillet. Arrange the vegetable garnish decoratively all around and top the fish with the crisp salmon-skin shreds.

Navarin of crab

Preparation time: 30 minutes
Cooking time: 1 hour
Difficulty: ★★

Serves 4

4 large live crabs weighing 1¼–1¾ lb/
600–800 g each
white wine or vinegar

For the sauce:
3½ fl oz/100 g shrimp stock
1 tsp tomato paste
3½ tbsp/50 g butter
¾ cup/200 ml light cream
¾ cup/200 ml *vin jaune* from the Jura
1 sprig of tarragon
1 basil leaf

1 sprig of thyme
½ bay leaf
sea salt
cayenne pepper
white peppercorns

Vegetable garnish:
1 turnip
1 medium zucchini
1 medium carrot
3½ oz/100 g celery root

For the seasoning mixture:
1 oz/30 g green part of leek
1½ oz/45 g red carrot powder
½ medium shallot
a few sprigs of parsley

The French are absolutely nuts about crabs, and growing Gallic demand for this crustacean is largely met by imports from Great Britain. Most of the meat of these large crabs is found in their claws, and the creamy substance has an exquisite taste.

Constant Fonk recommends live crabs weighing 1¼–1¾ lb/600–800 g each. They are cooked in boiling water with salt and some white wine or vinegar for 15 minutes. Once the crab meat is removed, the shell must be cleaned carefully, as it will be filled with the vegetable and crab meat mixture. This can be done in advance to distribute the workload before serving.

It is asserted without any formal proof that the term *navarin* derives from the battle of Navarino in 1827, in which Turkish and Egyptian naval forces opposed a British, French and Russian fleet. The large number of different uniforms was the model for the various vegetables of the accompaniment. Each vegetable must be cooked separately in order to retain its own true taste and a bit of bite.

The *vin jaune* ("yellow wine"), which is used to deglaze the seasoning mixture, is a product of the Jura region of France whose fine quality and long aging period make it ideal for this dish. It contains less alcohol than dry sherry, of which its flavor is reminiscent, and its elegance will delight your guests.

1. Pare the vegetables (turnip, zucchini, carrot, celery root) into little olive shapes and cook each kind separately in salted water. Boil the crabs in water with coarse salt and wine or vinegar for 15 minutes. Remove the meat and creamy substance from the bodies and reserve the shells, claws and legs.

2. Sweat the seasoning mixture, thyme and ½ bay leaf in 3½ tbsp/50 g butter. Add the tomato paste and deglaze with the vin jaune. Moisten with the shrimp stock (or fish stock) and the cream, and add the tarragon, basil and white peppercorns. Cook for 20 minutes.

with *vin jaune*

3. Bind with the creamy substance from the crab and put through a fine strainer. Season to taste with sea salt and cayenne pepper.

4. Add the decoratively cut vegetables and the crab meat to the sauce and warm through. Arrange the crab claws and legs attractively on the plates. Fill the shells with the navarin and place on top of the legs.

Lobster fricassée with

Preparation time: 30 minutes
Cooking time: 20 minutes
Difficulty: ✶✶

Serves 4

4 lobsters (generous 1 lb/500 g each)
1 Savoy cabbage
3 tbsp/20 g mixed white, black and green
peppercorns and allspice berries

4 tbsp/60 g fresh ginger root
13 tbsp/200 g butter
6½ tbsp/100 ml olive oil
2 cups/500 ml lobster stock
chervil leaves
salt

Ginger, once a speciality from India and highly prized in Asian cuisines, has been known in Europe since the Middle Ages. Gray ginger is larger and more aromatic than white ginger, but either can be used in this recipe.

The lobster, preferably a female with tender, tasty flesh, should be bought live. According to its size, it should be parboiled for 1–2 minutes before plunging it in ice-cold water to cool. When cooked, lobsters are bright red, which has earned them the nickname of "cardinal of the seas." Our chef serves it here with Savoy cabbage, an attractive vegetable that has helped European peasants survive many

a famine. In rural areas it is known as the "doctor of the poor," as its high vitamin and sugar content coupled with its low price contributed decisively to the balanced diet of the less well-off. Choose a cabbage that feels quite heavy for its size and cook it right after cutting it up, since cut cabbage does not keep well. Remember that leafy vegetables reduce considerably in volume during cooking.

The addition of the different varieties of pepper and the allspice berries, whose strong taste reinforces that of the ginger, provides the ideal finish to this sprightly dish.

1. Clean and wash the cabbage. Remove the leaves, then blanch and refresh. Cut into scant ½ in/1 cm wide strips and braise in butter until crisp-tender. Boil the lobster in salted water for 1 minute, then plunge into ice-cold water. Peel the ginger, cut into tiny dice and blanch three times.

2. Shell the lobsters, reserving the coral. Cut the tail lengthwise into three. Crush the shells, reserving the heads for the garnish. Make a stock from the shells. Sauté the lobster pieces for 2–3 minutes in olive oil, then drain.

pepper and ginger

3. Pour the fat out of the sauté pan, deglaze with lobster stock and reduce by three-quarters. Add the butter a piece at a time. Place the contents of the pan together with the coral in the blender. Blend for 1 minute, then correct the seasoning.

4. Return the sauce to the sauté pan, add the sliced lobster, blanched ginger, and crushed peppercorns and allspice berries, and bring briefly to a boil. Spoon the cabbage onto the plates, top with the lobster meat, place the head upright on top and coat with the sauce. Garnish with chervil leaves.

Turbot baked in clay

Preparation time: 45 minutes
Cooking time: 30 minutes
Difficulty: ✷✷

Serves 4

3¼ lb/1½ kg turbot
8¾ lb/4 kg kaolin clay
generous 1 lb/500 g celery root
1¾ oz/50 g black truffles
2 bunches flat-leaf parsley

2 cups/500 ml milk
1 cup/250 ml cream
1 cup/250 g butter
juice of 1 lemon
salt and freshly ground pepper

In times past, the delicacy of certain types of fish lent a paradoxical luxury to periods of abstinence from meat: hence, the turbot's French nickname of *roi du Carême* or "king of Lent." Over the course of the centuries, this fine fish has inspired numerous brilliant recipes. Today, the great chefs stake their reputations on creating dishes that taste of the true flavors of their ingredients. This recipe is a perfect example of that commitment.

The turbot must be cooked very carefully to preserve its delicate flavor. But instead of merely cooking it *en papillote* (in a paper parcel), which does seal in its flavor very effectively, our chef recommends an additional jacket of kaolin. This soft clay, also known as china clay, is composed primarily of the mineral kaolinite and is used as a main ingredient in the manufacture of porcelain. Once enclosed in its clay jacket, the turbot will survive the cooking process without falling apart.

For this recipe, choose a good-sized fish that will yield good thick fillets; the firmness of the flesh ensures that it will keep its shape. Under no circumstances open the oven door while the fish is cooking: the clay crust could crack at the slightest change in temperature.

The parsley sauce must be prepared with absolutely fresh parsley at the last minute, in order to preserve the beautiful but short-lived green color. This original and spectacular dish will make the biggest hit in winter.

1. Use kaolin for the clay jacket. Roll the clay out into 16 rectangles measuring 8 in/20 cm long by 6 in/15 cm wide by a scant ¼ in/5 mm thick. This is more easily done between two sheets of waxed paper.

2. Strip the parsley leaves from their stalks and blanch. Refresh in ice water, drain, squeeze dry and push through a sieve. Peel the celery root, rub with lemon juice and cut into small pieces. Place in a saucepan, add milk to cover and cook until tender. Add salt and pepper to taste. Blend with the cream and butter and set aside in a double boiler.

with truffles and parsley

3. Spread the turbot fillets with 1 tbsp softened butter. Season. Top with the truffles, arranged in the shape of a rosette. Place the fillet in the center of a square of waxed paper. Fold the paper like a wallet, with the crease on top.

4. Place the turbot in the center of 1 clay rectangle, place another on top and seal the edges with a little water and refrigerate for 1 hour. Bake for 15 minutes at 350 °F/180 °C. Present on a serving plate, cracking open the clay in front of your dinner guests. Arrange the turbot fillets in the center of the plates and pour the parsley sauce all around.

Foamy cream of

Preparation time: 1 hour
Cooking time: 8 minutes
Difficulty: ✶✶

Serves 4

1 dozen large sea scallops
1 oz/30 g sevruga caviar
1 oz/30 g cooked foie gras, terrine or pâté
3½ oz/100 g fennel
6½ tbsp/100 ml white wine

6½ tbsp/100 ml heavy cream
4 tsp/20 ml olive oil
⅓ cup/80 g butter
10 aniseeds
1 star anise
1 sprig of chervil
1 sprig of dill
1 tsp/5 g paprika
1 tsp/5 g sea salt
1 tsp/5 g crushed pepper
2 cups/500 ml water

This recipe makes a virtue of not wasting anything— including the scallop beards, which are often discarded but here are used to prepare a delicious stock.

Although scallops are widely available, they must be chosen with care. Remaining true to his Norman roots, our chef uses scallops from Dieppe. The coral, an orange roe sac, has no particular taste, and might impair rather than improve the flavor and appearance of the white scallop flesh. As scallops are rarely sold live in the United States, this will be of no concern to American cooks.

The success of this dish is entirely dependent upon the consistency of the cream soup, which thickens when the raw scallops have been sieved, reduced to a fine purée and added to the hot stock. The protein contained in the scallops will bind the mixture almost instantaneously.

The combination of green aniseed, star anise and fennel bulb lends an unusual subtlety to the soup. The caviar, which may be replaced by salmon roe, fulfills a primarily decorative function here, but also heightens the flavor and glamour of the dish.

By the same principle, a cream of cauliflower soup may be combined with crab meat, in this case using the coral and claw meat of the crab

1. Finely slice the fennel and sauté in a little olive oil. Open the scallops. Remove the muscle, rinse under cold running water and set aside. Remove and discard the black pouch. Wash the beards ("frills") and place in a pot with the white wine, cream, fennel and aniseed and star anise. Add 2 cups/500 ml water and simmer for 20 minutes. Strain. If the scallops have been purchased shucked, buy an additional five scallops and use them for the soup base.

2. Cut 4–5 scallops horizontally into thin slices and top each with a dollop of caviar and a little chervil. Sprinkle with paprika and sea salt and grind over some pepper.

scallop soup

3. Push the remaining scallops through a fine-mesh sieve, followed by the foie gras and the softened butter. Mix well.

4. Pour the boiling soup into a bowl, then transfer to a blender. Blend with the sieved mixture for 2 minutes at medium speed to yield a foamy cream soup. Ladle the soup into warmed shallow bowls, top with the scallop and caviar garnish. Decorate with a few sprigs of dill.

Whiting with

Preparation time: 30 minutes
Cooking time: 16 minutes
Difficulty: ✳

Serves 4

Four 1¼ lb/600 g whitings (purchased ungutted or gutted through the gills)
2¼ lb/1 kg carrots
8 new scallions

5 oz/150 g slab bacon
2 tbsp/40 g honey
3 tbsp/20 g cumin seed
1 tbsp /25 g Chinese five-spice powder
5 basil leaves
2 sprigs of dill
2 sprigs of flat-leaf parsley
9 tbsp/140 g butter
salt and freshly ground pepper

Whiting is unjustly snubbed by many chefs, despite the fine texture and digestibility of its appetizing white flesh. This fish of the cod family, which abounds along the coasts of Europe and particularly in the Atlantic, certainly deserves better.

Whiting is a very fragile fish, which loses its scales if handled roughly. Choose a whole, glossy, firm fish, and treat it gently while preparing it. Be sure to remove the skin on the belly, which is dark and bitter, and which distinguishes this fish from the blue whiting.

Care is also required when cooking whiting, since exceeding the recommended cooking time could have disastrous consequences. This is why poaching or steaming, which are so difficult to monitor, are unsuitable for this fish. Philippe Groult recommends searing the whitings over high heat, taking care not to let them fall apart. This recipe is also eminently suitable for mackerel, small sea bass, or sardines.

The five-spice mixture and the deep-fried herbs make a very pleasant foil for the tender flesh of the fish.

1. Make an incision along the backbone of each whiting; remove the backbone, cutting it off at the head and tail; remove the entrails and rinse and dry. Cut off the gills and remove the small bones of the fish with tweezers.

2. Score the skin of the fish in a criss-cross pattern and sprinkle with the five-spice powder. Smear with a little butter and pan-fry over high heat for 7 minutes, turning once after 4 minutes.

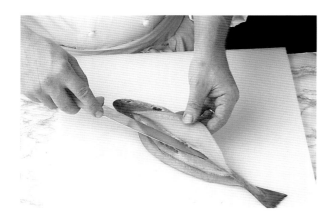

caramelized carrots

3. Slice the carrots on the diagonal and place in a saucepan with the butter, honey, cumin seed and a pinch of salt. Add water to come halfway up the carrots. Cook for 16 minutes, then add the parsley and dill.

4. Finely slice the scallions and stew in a little butter. Cut the bacon into thin strips, and add to the onions; cook until it renders its fat. Spoon the onion mixture onto an oval platter, arrange the carrots decoratively on top, top with the whiting and sprinkle with deep-fried herbs.

Sturgeon with sauerkraut and

Preparation time: 1 hour
Cooking time: 20 minutes
Difficulty: ✳

Serves 4

generous 1 lb/500 g sturgeon fillets
1¾ oz/50 g sevruga caviar
10½ oz/300 g raw sauerkraut
8 *ratte* or other fingerling potatoes

10 tbsp/150 g butter
all-purpose flour
2 tbsp olive oil
¾ cup/200 ml white-wine sauce (see basic recipes)
chives, chervil
salt and freshly ground pepper

The most famous types of sturgeon are the beluga, sevruga and osetrova, all prized for their caviar, on which luxury commodity the countries bordering the Caspian Sea possess a virtual monopoly. The sturgeon itself has succulent flesh, and there are no less than 24 varieties, which have been highly esteemed since the Middle Ages. Although at one time found in all the seas of the world, sturgeon are increasingly rare in Europe, save in the aforementioned Caspian.

In an ideal world, you will buy a whole sturgeon, because it loses flavor when cut into pieces. Marc Haeberlin strongly recommends pan-frying the sturgeon until blood-rare, then wrapping it in aluminum foil so that it continues to cook without drying out.

The flavor of the sturgeon is enhanced by a spicy sauce, bound with a Riesling or other dry white wine. Since caviar is later added to it, it must be seasoned with restraint. Caviar-lovers will want to use sevruga, with its intensely flavored tiny gray eggs, but it is perhaps more appropriate to use pressed caviar, which is considerably less expensive and has a vivid flavor of its own.

The vegetable accompaniment consists of new potatoes and, of course, Alsatian sauerkraut.

1. Cook the potatoes for about 15 minutes in salted water, then peel them. Meanwhile, salt and pepper the sturgeon fillets on both sides; dredge them in the flour and brown in butter for 1 minute on each side.

2. Wrap each fillet carefully and tightly in aluminum foil, and set aside to rest for 10 minutes.

a white-wine and caviar sauce

3. Soak the sauerkraut for 30 minutes, changing the water twice. Rinse thoroughly, then drain completely. Melt a pat of butter in a saucepan and sweat the sauerkraut for 5 minutes. Season. Sauté the potatoes for a few minutes in butter until golden brown.

4. Finish off the white-wine sauce by whisking in the butter. Add the caviar at the last minute, taking care not to let the sauce boil. Mound some sauerkraut in the center of each plate and garnish with caviar. Place the potatoes around the sauerkraut. Pour the white-wine and caviar sauce onto the plates and top with the sturgeon fillets, cut into slices. Garnish with chives and chervil.

Pan-fried monkfish

Preparation time: 30 minutes
Cooking time: 30 minutes
Difficulty: ✶

Serves 4

One 5½ lb/2½ kg monkfish tail
16 cloves garlic, unpeeled
7 oz/200 g piece smoked bacon, cut into strips
generous 1 lb/500 g fresh spinach

2 shallots, chopped
6½ tbsp/100 g butter
¾ cup/200 ml *crème fraîche*
¾ cup/200 ml brown veal stock
1 tbsp extra-virgin olive oil
4 tbsp balsamic vinegar
a little flour
salt and freshly ground pepper

Monkfish tail offers dense, lean flesh and has no bones save for the large central bone. In this recipe, the tail is first pan-fried for about 10 minutes before being baked in a hot oven on the bone, which intensifies the flavor of the fish.

Connoisseurs of the weird and wonderful will be interested to learn that this fish has a very tasty, vitamin-packed liver that can be justly compared with foie gras.

Garlic is the ideal accompaniment for this dish. Highly esteemed in ancient times (to the extent that it was given as payment to the workers who built the Egyptian pyramids), garlic is known for its tonic effect on the circulatory system. When buying, check that the cloves feel firm and plump. Do not peel them before cooking: this gives them a smoother, subtler flavor. Garlic cooked in its skin becomes creamy on the inside while the skin toughens. You need only press the skin to squeeze out the pulp.

The bacon, cut into thickish strips, also "melts" gently when cooked, infusing the other ingredients with its flavor. If you cannot find a monkfish tail, this recipe is also suitable for other fine-fleshed fish, such as baby turbot or salmon.

1. Season the monkfish with salt and pepper and dredge in flour. Heat 1 tbsp olive oil in a pan and sauté the fish on both sides until golden brown.

2. Halfway through the cooking time, add the unpeeled garlic cloves and the bacon strips. Finish cooking in a hot oven (400 °F/200 °C) for 10–15 minutes.

with garlic and bacon

3. Transfer the monkfish to a serving platter and garnish with the bacon and garlic cloves. To prepare the sauce, add the 2 chopped shallots to the pan and deglaze with the vinegar, then moisten with the brown veal stock.

4. Add the crème fraîche, reduce, and whisk in the cold butter. Serve with the blanched fresh spinach.

Salmon "tournedos" with a

Preparation time: 30 minutes
Cooking time: 10 minutes
Difficulty: ✶

Serves 4

4 salmon steaks (4½ oz/125 g each)
7 oz/200 g spinach
1 bunch of watercress
1 bunch of chives

2 sprigs of parsley
1¾ oz/50 g piece smoked bacon
3½ tbsp/50 g butter
1 cup/250 ml cream
2 cups/500 ml fish stock
salt and freshly ground pepper

For many gourmets, the salmon remains the finest fish—rich in protein and omega-3 fatty acids, fairly low in calories and boasting a superb flavor. It is important to know where your fish comes from, since (quite apart from differences between Atlantic and Pacific salmon) Norwegian salmon has a milder flavor than its Scottish cousin. In addition, a distinction should be drawn between wild and farmed salmon. Here, Michel Haquin shows his colors and uses the excellent farmed salmon from his native Belgium.

Although there must be a thousand different ways to prepare this versatile fish, there is at least one constant: the fish must be absolutely fresh, firm and glossy, with clear, slightly bulging eyes. The steaks are cut from the fleshiest part of the salmon, near the head; take care not to overcook them, as you wish to retain their color and tenderness. Next—and Haquin is adamant on this score—the little layer of fat between the skin and flesh must be scraped off so that it does not spoil the flavor of the "tournedos."

Watercress is featured to good effect in the herb sauce. Like spinach, it has an assertive flavor and should be used in moderation.

Fresh pasta or attractively pared potatoes are suitable accompaniments for this springtime dish, which should be served piping hot.

1. Remove the central bone from each salmon steak without separating the 2 fillets. Roll up like a "tournedos" and tie with string.

2. Wash and drain the watercress, chives, spinach and parsley. Chop coarsely with a hand-held blender or knife and set aside. Reduce the cream with the fish stock to coating consistency and pour this mixture over the chopped herbs. Purée with a hand-held blender, pass through a fine strainer and reduce again to a creamy consistency. Whisk in the butter.

chive cream sauce and bacon

3. Cut the bacon into strips and blanch; pan-fry until crisp and set aside. Season the salmon with salt and pepper and brown in butter in a hot pan for 2 minutes on each side. Drain on paper towels.

4. Remove the string from the "tournedos" and pull off the skin. Using a knife, scrape off the thin layer of fat between the skin and flesh. Spoon some hot sauce onto each plate, place the salmon in the center and sprinkle with the bacon strips. Serve piping hot.

John Dory with tomatoes,

Preparation time: 45 minutes
Cooking time: 30 minutes
Difficulty: ★

Serves 4

For the shrimp sauce:
3½ oz/100 g small shrimp
1 carrot, 1 onion and 1 celery rib, all finely diced
¾ cup/200 ml fish stock
3½ tbsp/50 ml white wine
1⅔ cup/400 ml cream
butter

For the pasta dough:
1¾ cup/250 g flour
2 eggs
6½ tbsp/100 ml cuttlefish ink
2½ tbsp/40 ml olive oil
4 tsp lemon juice

Two 2¼ lb/1 kg John Dory
2 tomatoes
12 basil leaves
salt and freshly ground pepper

There are no fewer than 162 different species of shrimp, so what they lack in size, they make up for in sheer variety. Unlike most other crustaceans, which crawl along the sea bed, at times clumsily and with difficulty, shrimp are graceful swimmers.

The Belgians are mad about shrimp. Along the coast, a number of fishermen still fish for them on horseback, according to a centuries-old traditional method. The industrial ports of Zeebrugge, Ostende and Nieuwpoort do a roaring trade in these crustaceans. Millions of shrimp are consumed in Belgium each year, especially the small gray North Sea ones, reputed to be the tastiest. As a rule they should be bought very fresh, live if possible, or if not, at least very firm. A soft, straight shrimp should instantly arouse your suspicions.

The head of the John Dory is as large as the rest of its body. Behind the pectoral fins on both sides is a large black spot, according to legend the finger marks of Saint Peter, patron saint of fishermen, hence the French name for the fish (*Saint Pierre*). This fish is much appreciated for the delicacy of its flesh.

Make sure you allow the pasta dough to rest for an hour before rolling it out. This dish should be served hot and eaten without delay, as it does not keep well.

1. Heat some butter in a pan and gently cook the unshelled shrimp and the diced carrot, onion and celery for 5 minutes. Deglaze with the fish stock and the white wine. Season and reduce. Add the cream and cook for 20 minutes over low heat. Strain through a fine-mesh strainer. Correct the seasoning.

2. Mix together all of the ingredients for the pasta dough, then rest the dough for an hour. Using a pasta maker, roll the dough out thinly, then cut out rectangles measuring 4 x 8 in/10 x 20 cm. Cook for 2–3 minutes in boiling salted water to which a dash of olive oil has been added.

basil and black pasta

3. Peel and seed the tomatoes and cut into quarters. Refresh the rectangles of pasta in cool water and lay on paper towels to dry. Spread with butter, and make 1 tulip per person out of each 2 strips.

4. Remove the fillets from the fish and steam them until their flesh turns opaque. After three-quarters of the cooking time, place the tomato pieces on the fish and steam until done. Heat the tulips in the same steamer. Warm the sauce and add the basil leaves. Arrange the fish on the plates and pour over the sauce.

Cod fillet

Preparation time: *1 hour*
Cooking time: *15 minutes*
Difficulty: ☆☆

Serves 4

Four 5 oz/150 g cod fillets
30 mussels, cooked
12 lettuce leaves
¼ cup/25 g capers
¼ cup/25 g cornichons
1 oz/25 g onions
1 oz/25 g parsley, chopped
1 cup/250 ml vegetable stock

½ tsp heavy cream
2 tbsp/30 g butter
juice of 1 lemon
salt and freshly ground pepper

For the herb and breadcrumb topping:
½ cup/50 g white bread crumbs
1 oz/25 g parsley
1 sprig of thyme
1 sprig of rosemary
1 clove garlic
3½ tbsp/50 ml olive oil
1 pinch of salt

In this recipe, cod fillets are coated with a bread crumb and herb mixture, and the result is a cut above the traditional British fish and chips. Cod fishing is very important to the English, who employ enormous trawlers that can gather in up to 30 tons of fish per hour.

Choose nice, thick cod fillets, which will not fall apart during cooking. Cod is known for its white, delicate flesh, but its taste is not always particularly marked. For this reason, a strong accompaniment based on capers and cornichons is used in addition to the herb and breadcrumb

topping. The thyme and rosemary play a similar role in the crumb coating.

Paul Heathcote finds that the best mussels chosen to accompany the cod are the large specimens cultivated on vertical ropes in the Thau lagoon in the south of France. Other mussels can be used as well. You might also wish to substitute scallops for a more sophisticated result, or a mixture of mussels and oysters, which would allow you to incorporate the oyster liquor in the dish.

1. In a food processor, blend the dry ingredients for the herb and bread-crumb topping, then add the olive oil a little at a time.

2. Broil the cod fillets until the flesh is opaque and flaky but not quite cooked through. Season with salt, pepper and lemon juice. Top the fish with the herb mixture. Dice the onions and cook for 10 minutes in a little water; drain.

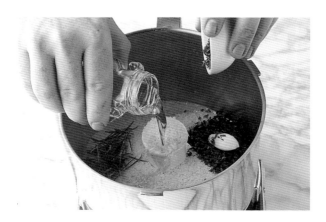

with mussels

3. Bring the vegetable stock to a rolling boil. Dice the cornichons and add to the stock, along with the capers, chopped parsley and onions. Pour in the cream, whisk in the butter and add the cooked, shelled mussels, which have been seasoned with salt and lemon juice.

4. In the meantime, blanch the lettuce in boiling salted water and place 3 leaves in the center of each plate. Just before serving, broil the herb-topped fillets until golden brown. Dish up the fish and pour the sauce all around.

Preparation time: 30 minutes
Cooking time: 20 minutes
Difficulty: ✷

Serves 4

Four 2¾ oz/80 g tuna steaks
7 oz/200 g new potatoes
7 oz/200 g fine green beans
scant 9 oz/250 g tomatoes
7 oz/200 g shallots

1¾ oz/50 g black olives
½ cup/125 ml extra-virgin olive oil
6½ tbsp/100 ml balsamic vinegar
juice of 1 lemon
salt and freshly ground pepper

As a tribute to the *salade niçoise*, the first dish he tasted outside of his native England, Paul Heathcote invented this recipe, made with medallions of fresh bluefin tuna instead of canned tuna fish, and above all without a trace of hard-boiled egg.

The bluefin tuna, which is fished both in the Mediterranean and in the Atlantic, often grows to an impressive size, reaching lengths of almost 10 ft/3 meters and weights of 440–660 lb/200–300 kg. It is still caught by some tuna boats using the traditional bait of herring. Fresh tuna is normally sold in thick slices or steaks; its wonderfully dense, bright-red meat goes a long way.

In order to preserve the flavor of the tuna, the bloody portion of the flesh should be removed, as it turns gray and bitter when cooked. Cooked on one side only, the flesh remains appetizingly tender, but it should not be kept waiting long after it is cooked: prepare it just before serving.

The quantity of balsamic vinegar given here is for ordinary commercial balsamic vinegar, which is less-strongly flavored than the real thing. If you are fortunate enough to have some genuine aged *aceto balsamico tradizionale di Modena* on hand, just a few drops will suffice to correct the flavor of the whole and transform the shallots and new potatoes into an incomparable delicacy.

This recipe may also be prepared with sea bass or red mullet.

1. Cut the tuna meat into medallions weighing about 2¾ oz/80 g each.

2. Finely chop the shallots and combine in a saucepan with the balsamic vinegar, the oil and a pinch of salt. Simmer until the shallots are done. Set aside to cool.

balsamic vinegar

3. Prepare the potatoes and green beans and boil or steam them. Pit the olives. Blanch, peel and seed the tomatoes and cut into petal shapes. Mound the vegetables on the center of each plate and pour a spoonful of sauce over.

4. Heat some olive oil in a skillet and briefly cook the tuna on one side only. Season with salt and lemon juice and place cooked-side-up on top of the vegetable garnish.

Grilled

Preparation time: 30 minutes
Cooking time: 10 minutes
Difficulty: ★

Serves 4

4 medium potatoes
2 potatoes for the chips
1 bunch of young dandelion greens
1 bunch of dill
1 bunch of arugula, 1 small head escarole
1 tbsp *crème fraîche*
3½ tbsp/50 g butter
salt and freshly ground black pepper

For the gravad lax:
1¼ lb/600 g fresh salmon (for four 5 oz/150 g fillets)
¾ cup plus 1 tbsp/200 g sugar
1 bunch of dill, chopped
6½ tbsp/100 ml cognac
7 tbsp/100 g salt, coarsely crushed peppercorns
For the mustard sauce:
2 tbsp Meaux or similarly coarse-grained mustard
1 tsp dark soy sauce
1 tsp light soy sauce
1 tsp mustard seeds
1 tbsp **demi-glace** or reduced veal stock
juice of 1 lemon
1 shallot, chopped
1 tbsp sherry vinegar

Dill and marinated raw salmon are a marriage made in heaven. The highly aromatic herb never fails to flatter, rather than overpower, its delicate, subtly flavored companion. The amount of dill in the marinade should therefore give no cause for concern, as this particular partnership is based on complementarity rather than competition.

The marinade containing both sugar and salt is typically Scandinavian, and can preserve the fish for up to 10 days. In this recipe the salmon is marinated for at least 48 hours.

The *gravad lax* is cooked very briefly, on the skin-side only, leaving the flesh itself very rare. If you wish to do like the Norwegians, you can eat the salmon cold, in thin strips on toast, with mustard sauce. In the Nordic countries, everyone knows this centuries-old dish; and it enjoys the same high reputation that fresh salmon does. Norway, incidentally, plays an important role in salmon farming, being responsible for 70 percent of the world production of this fish.

The marinade may be improved by adding a mixture of fresh fennel and crushed aniseed and coriander.

1. Place the salmon fillet on a platter and sprinkle with all the marinade ingredients. Pour over the cognac and marinate for 48 hours. Bake 4 potatoes in the oven, halve lengthwise and scoop out the flesh, leaving the skins intact. Use a vegetable mandoline to cut the other two potatoes into chips, and fry these in clarified butter.

2. Mash the scooped-out potato with the butter and crème fraîche and season with salt and pepper. Fill the potato shells and keep warm. Cut the salmon into four 5 oz/150 g pieces.

gravad lax

3. Grill the gravad lax on the skin side only, leaving the flesh very rare. Clean the salad ingredients (dandelion, dill, arugula and escarole) and make the mustard sauce by combining the appropriate ingredients.

4. Place a piece of salmon on each plate, remove the skin, and garnish the fish with a small mound of salad, a potato boat studded with chips, and the crisp salmon skin. Pour the sauce all around.

Catfish with

Preparation time: 40 minutes
Cooking time: 30 minutes
Difficulty: ✶✶

Serves 4

Four 7 oz/200 g fillets of catfish
5 oz/150 g large pink shrimp
7 oz/200 g small gray shrimp
2 cups/500 g butter
2 heads of lettuce
1 bunch of fresh basil

½ leek
½ medium carrot
½ onion
fresh thyme
1 sprig of rosemary
2 egg yolks
2 cloves garlic
salt and freshly ground pepper

To garnish:
salmon caviar

A large number of fish—among them the lizard fish, parrot fish, moon fish and saw fish—have names based on purported similarities with other animals or objects. The catfish, however, bears little resemblance to our furry household pet.

The catfish, a freshwater predator, was introduced from its native North America into France at the end of the 19th century, and immediately displayed such voracious eating habits that it was feared that the newcomer would upset the aquatic ecological balance.

The physical appearance of the catfish, with its whisker-like barbels (hence, perhaps, its name) and slimy skin, could well put off potential buyers. That would be a pity, since it has very fine white flesh. It is farmed on a large scale in the United States.

If catfish is unavailable, sea bass or monkfish can be substituted with equal success in this recipe; steam or pan-fry the fish, or poach it in a court bouillon, according to your own preference, before serving with the flavorful shrimp butter.

The shrimp butter, which requires careful preparation, is made from small raw shrimp. Here, too, substitutions are possible; for example, a langoustine and shrimp butter would also flatter the catfish.

1. *Finely chop the ½ carrot, ½onion, ½ leek, garlic, rosemary and thyme and sweat in a little butter. Add the small gray shrimps, including heads and shells, and the butter. Purée the mixture with a hand-held blender, then bring it to a boil, skim, and simmer for about 30 minutes. Pass through a fine strainer and keep warm in a double boiler.*

2. *Cook the lettuce in boiling salted water; drain and spin dry. Prepare a sabayon by whisking together the 2 egg yolks and a little water over the heat.*

shrimp butter

3. Gently sauté the lettuce in a little butter. Add the chopped basil, salt, pepper and the shelled pink shrimp. Finally, fold in the sabayon and keep warm.

4. Cut the fish into pieces and season with salt and pepper, top with basil leaves and steam. Arrange the fish on a bed of sabayon, shrimp and cooked lettuce. Place the salmon caviar in the middle of the fillet and drizzle with the shrimp-butter sauce.

Sea bass

Preparation time: 2 hours
Cooking time: 1 hour
Difficulty: ✶✶

Serves 4

One 3¼ lb/1½ kg sea bass
generous 1 lb/500 g San Marzano or other
ripe plum tomatoes
1 eggplant
1 zucchini
1 green bell pepper
1 onion

3¼ cups/800 ml olive oil
4 slices nettle bread
4 basil leaves

Ingredients for the nettle bread:
Nettles
4¼ cups/500 g all-purpose flour
2 tsp/10 g sugar
1 tbsp/16 g baking powder
1 tbsp/16 g yeast
2 tbsp oil
⅔ cup/150 ml water
2½ tsp/12 g salt

In the Campania region in southern Italy, *acqua pazza* is a one-dish fisherman's meal containing generous quantities of fish, tomatoes, and olive oil. This cooks down into a sort of aromatic soup that is served ladled over stale bread; the sort of dish that fishermen fed to their families with the unsold fish left over from their catch.

For his version of this humble recipe, our chef has chosen sea bass, a quick-cooking fish. In keeping with Mediterranean traditions, he adds a clever vegetable accompaniment. The nettles in the bread lend piquancy to the dish. The fearsome-sounding stinging nettle is often unfairly banned from the kitchen, in spite of its agreeable taste and copious iron and vitamin content. Either the greater or the lesser stinging nettle can be used.

If the thought of nettles leaves you cold or if you are unable to obtain them, you should in any case serve toasted country bread, rye or pumprnickel with the *acqua pazza*. It makes no difference whether the loaf is a little old or has been frozen.

The Greek poet and gourmet Archestratus was singing the praises of the sea bass, whose taste he found delectable, back in the middle of the 4th century B.C. There is nothing new under the Mediterranean sun.

1. Sweat the finely chopped onions and finely diced tomatoes in olive oil until you have a even-textured sauce. Place the ingredients for the nettle bread in a food processor and process for several minutes. Let rise for 1 hour, place in a loaf pan and let rise for another hour. Bake for 1 hour at 275 °F/140 °C.

2. Finely dice the other vegetables and sauté gently in the remaining olive oil. Add the basil and keep warm.

acqua pazza

3. Transfer the sauce, vegetables, 4 oz/1 glass of water and the sea bass fillets to an ovenproof dish. Cook for 5 minutes in a 325 °F/160 °C oven.

4. Cut the nettle bread into slices. Place a slice of bread on each warmed plate, lean the fish fillets up against it, and spoon over the sauce and vegetables. Garnish with a basil leaf.

Scorpion-fish ragout with

Preparation time: 40 minutes
Cooking time: 1 hour
Difficulty: ★★

Serves 4

One 2¼ lb/1 kg scorpion fish
2¼ lb ripe tomatoes
1 green bell pepper
2 leeks
⅔ cup/150 ml white wine

6½ tbsp/100 ml extra-virgin olive oil
a few leaves chervil
salt and freshly ground pepper

For the pasta dough:
¾ cup plus 1 tbsp/400 g flour
4 egg yolks
1 tbsp olive oil
2 tbsp water
pinch of salt

Paccheri are one of the countless varieties of pasta consumed in record quantities in Italy. Alfonso Iaccarino has fond memories of his Neapolitan childhood, in which these noodles were a particular favorite. There is a reason why they are made into tube shapes: the sauce is meant to fill as well as cover them.

Gragnano, a little town on the Sorrento peninsula on the Gulf of Naples, is home to a museum of pasta, among other curiosities. And what better tribute could there be to the deep-rooted tradition of pasta making?

The other main ingredient in this recipe is the scorpion fish, an essential component of *bouillabaisse* and

renowned for its firm flesh. Both the highly prized small brown scorpion fish and the more common large red scorpion fish live in rocky sea beds, feeding on small crustaceans. Don't forget that the head of the fish, which contains a good quantity of flesh, is crucial for the consistency of the ragout. Incidentally, the tastiest morsel of the scorpion fish is deemed to be the so-called "king's piece": the cheek.

To make the most of the flavors and colors of the fresh fish and the green bell pepper, Alfonso Iaccarino strongly recommends that you prepare this ragout at the very last moment.

1. To prepare the sauce, finely chop the leeks in a food processor or with a knife, and sweat with the fish head in olive oil. Deglaze with the white wine. Add the quartered tomatoes, and cook for about 1 hour. Pass through a fine strainer.

2. Place the green bell pepper under a hot broiler until black and blistered all over. Peel and cut into very thin strips. To prepare the pasta, place the flour on a work surface, making a well in the center; gradually incorporate the other ingredients into the flour, kneading through thoroughly. Rest the dough for 1 hour. Roll out thinly, cut into rectangles and form into tube shapes.

paccheri di Gragnano pasta

3. Fillet the scorpion fish and cut the flesh into cubes. Place the green bell pepper strips, chopped chervil, sauce and fish cubes in a pan and cook for about 10 minutes.

4. Cook the paccheri in plenty of boiling salted water until al dente. Mix the noodles with the sauce and the fish and serve.

Pikeperch strips on *rösti*

Preparation time: 45 minutes
Cooking time: 20 minutes
Difficulty: ✲

Serves 4

1 pikeperch (1¾ lb/800 g)
2 potatoes
1¾ oz/50 g soybean sprouts
3½ oz cucumber (1¾ oz in small sticks,
1¾ oz in cubes)
1 tbsp capers
1 tbsp shallot
6½ tbsp/100 g butter

pinch of Chinese five-spice powder
chives
salt and freshly ground pepper

For the sesame-cream sauce:
3½ oz/100 g white of leek
1 shallot
6½ tbsp/100 g butter
¾ cup/200 ml *crème fraîche*
¾ cup/200 ml chicken stock
6½ tbsp/100 ml white wine
6½ tbsp/100 ml Noilly Prat (French dry
vermouth)
3½ tbsp/50 ml sesame oil
salt and freshly ground pepper

Rösti is a typically Swiss dish originally eaten by farmers and manual laborers at breakfast to fortify themselves for the forthcoming day's work. It consists of potatoes boiled in their skins, shredded when cold, and formed into little pancakes that are fried quickly. Main crop, rather than new, potatoes are used because the latter do not contain enough starch. In the past, a little lard was added to make the *rösti* more substantial; nowadays, however, this is a lighter dish which Swiss chefs serve alongside bratwurst or the ever-popular Zurich-style veal.

Pikeperch contains very few bones, which makes it easier to prepare than some other fish. Like all other fish, it must,

of course, be absolutely fresh, and should be scaled and gutted in the usual way. Then it needs to be cut into even-sized pieces thick enough to stand up to the cooking process.

If you wish to give this dish an Asian touch, as André Jaeger usually does, you may replace the Noilly Prat with *shaoxing*, a Chinese wine with a taste slightly reminiscent of sherry. The *shaoxing* lends character to the nutty tasting sesame cream. The soybean sprouts are used for much the same reason. This everyday food of the Orient has long been popular in Western cuisnes.

1. Finely chop the leek and shallot. Sweat in the butter, then deglaze with the white wine and Noilly Prat. Reduce by half. Add the crème fraîche and chicken stock. Season and reduce once more by half. Add the sesame oil at the last minute and purée in a blender.

2. Boil the potatoes in their skins. When cool, peel and grate. Form into small cakes. Fillet the pikeperch, remove the skin and any remaining bones and cut the fish into ½ in/1 cm slices. Finely chop the capers and shallot. Season with a little salt and the Chinese five-spice mixture, and let stand for a few minutes.

with a sesame-cream sauce

3. Fry the 4 small rösti pancakes in oil and butter until golden brown and crisp. In another pan, heat a little butter until it foams, then add the capers, shallot, chopped soybean sprouts and the cucumber sticks.

4. Add the pikeperch strips and sauté for 1 minute. Spoon some sesame-cream sauce onto each plate, top with a rösti pancake and arrange the fish on top. Sprinkle over the finely diced cucumber and the chopped chives.

Red mullet with

Preparation time: 20 minutes
Cooking time: 20 minutes
Difficulty: ★★

Serves 4

Two 10½-oz/300 g red mullet
2 potatoes
6½ tbsp/100 g butter, clarified
2 tbsp wheat starch
1 egg yolk
some olive oil
salt and freshly ground pepper

For the sauce:
7 oz/200 g shallots
juice of 1 orange
3½ tbsp/50 ml Noilly Prat (French white vermouth)
3½ tbsp/50 ml dry white wine
2 cups/500 ml fish stock
4 tsp/20 g butter
1⅔ cups/400 ml *crème fraîche*
1 sprig of rosemary

"Superb" was the simple comment with which Paul Bocuse greeted the results of Roger Jaloux's research, conducted in the Bocuse test kitchen at Collonges-au-Mont-d'Or, with a view to tailoring a new coat of scales. Rather than talk of tailoring, it would be more apt to speak of "sculpture" when presented with this attractive dish, in which the tender flesh of the fish and the crisp potatoes combine marvelously to produce a dish of inimitable refinement.

Choose waxy potatoes free from spots and bruises to make the thin scales, which will be blanched, then brushed with some starch dissolved in boiling water and a drop of clarified butter, to stop them from turning black and to

make them easier to handle. Our chef prefers the thin-skinned Bintje potatoes from Holland, which are available year-round in France, where they have become a highly regarded kitchen staple. Arranging the potato "scales" on the fish is not difficult, but the subsequent handling requires some care.

This is indeed regal attire for the "prince of the Mediterranean", the little red mullet, which tastes of iodine when very fresh. The only disadvantage of this fish are its numerous bones, so that you must budget enough time for boning the mullet thoroughly. If this puts you off, or if red mullet are unavailable to you, you may replace them with a small sea bass.

1. Clean the red mullet, taking care to remove all of the small bones. Cut the potato into thin rounds with a vegetable mandoline, then stamp out small scales. Blanch the potatoes in boiling water and allow to cool; drain and brush with a mixture of wheat starch and clarified butter.

2. Brush the fish fillets with egg yolk and cover with the potato rounds, overlapping to form scales.

potato "scales"

3. To make the sauce, gently sauté the shallots in butter; deglaze with the white wine and Noilly Prat and pour in the fish stock. Reduce to a syrupy consistency and add the crème fraîche. Reduce to coating consistency. In a separate saucepan, reduce the orange juice with the rosemary sprig, then add to the cream sauce; bring to a boil and pass through a fine strainer.

4. Fry the mullet fillets in a nonstick pan until the potatoes are golden brown (about 7–8 minutes). Spoon about 2 tbsp sauce onto each plate and top with the fish fillets. Decorate according to preference.

Spiced cod with

Preparation time: 30 minutes
Cooking time: 20 minutes
Difficulty: ★★

Serves 4

One 2 lb 10 oz/1.2 kg cod
1 lemon
1 mango
2 tomatoes
1 each red, green and yellow bell pepper
1¾ lb/800 g cauliflower
1 onion
3½ tbsp/50 g butter
6½ tbsp/100 ml olive oil
6 bunches of mâche
2 sprigs of cilantro

For the mango chutney:
3½ tbsp/50 ml vinegar
6½ tbsp/100 ml water
1 pinch of sugar

Spices for the cod (¾ oz/20 g)
1 orange, 1 lemon
1 vanilla bean
2 cinnamon sticks
saffron, curry powder, aniseed, ground coriander

For the salad dressing:
1 ginger root
3½ tbsp/50 ml vinaigrette

For the sauce:
6½ tbsp/100 ml soy sauce
2 cups/500 ml fish stock
lemon juice and water

The Portuguese proudly boast a thousand different ways of cooking salt cod alone; not to be outdone, the French and Germans seem to have a similar number of names for this fish, depending on its age and maturity, the waters in which it is caught and whether it is the fresh salted sort. Though English has fewer synonyms in common use for cod, this should by no means be taken to imply a lack of appreciation for the fish in the United Kingdom and North America. The following dish would in any case delight the most jaded palate, whatever the nationality of its owner.

In this recipe, the fish is accompanied by a complex spice mixture that will demand a bit of advance preparation. The orange and lemon zest, for example, must be dried near a

heat source to render them brittle so that they can be crushed more easily. All of the other spices, measured out carefully, are likewise processed to a fine powder; they should be stored in a tightly closed container, and sprinkled on the cod only at the last moment.

Mangoes are imported from many exotic locations, but do not always reach their destination ripe. You should therefore select a fruit that yields to the pressure of a finger, applied to the most brightly colored part of the fruit, which has received the most sun. The heavier mangos, incidentally, are not necessarily the most aromatic or the richest in vitamins. Poaching the mango in vinegar water imparts a sweet-sour taste to the flesh.

1. Zest the orange and the lemon and dry the zest. Crush or grind the spices and the dried citrus peel to a powder. Fillet the cod and cut into 4 portions of equal size; salt and set aside. Peel the remaining lemon and cut the zest into a fine julienne; blanch twice.

2. Peel the mango and cut the flesh into very thin strips. Gently poach in the vinegar, water and sugar mixture for about 10 minutes. Peel, seed and dice the tomatoes. Cut the red, yellow and green bell peppers into thin strips, and divide the cauliflower into florets.

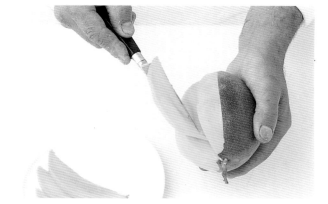

sweet-and-sour mango

3. Sprinkle the pieces of cod with the ground spices and begin cooking in very hot olive oil, then place the fish on a baking sheet covered with baking parchment and bake at 350 °F/180 °C for 4–5 minutes. Whisk together the water and soy sauce, then add a little fish stock and the lemon juice.

4. Carefully clean the mâche and drain. Grate the ginger root over the salad and top with the vinaigrette. Sweat the cauliflower and tomatoes quickly in butter, then dry a few thin rings of onion. Arrange the fish with its fruit and vegetable accompaniments on plates and garnish with cilantro leaves.

Pikeperch with soft

Preparation time: 40 minutes
Cooking time: 10 minutes
Difficulty: ☆

Serves 4

One 1¼ lb/600 g pikeperch
5½ oz/160 g soft carp roe (milt of the male carp)
9 oz/260 g white of leek

11 oz/320 g shiitake mushrooms
juice of ½ lemon
oil
1 shallot
4½ tbsp butter, clarified
2½ tbsp/40 ml strong reduced veal stock
flour
salt and freshly ground pepper

The pikeperch or zander is found both in North America and Europe, including in Alsace. A close cousin of the perch and pike and the North American walleye, this voracious predator hunts by night, which makes catching it a hit-and-miss affair. If luck is on your side, you will be rewarded with beautiful soft white fillets that make very good eating.

The carp also abounds in Alsatian rivers and lakes. This fish was highly prized in the Middle Ages, appearing on royal tables in the form of pâtés. In the 19th century, Brillat-Savarin was mad about its soft roe, which he used to garnish omelets. The soft roe is absent during the spawning season from April to June. This creamy food must stay soft when cooked; it should be pan-fried just until golden brown. If you cannot get hold of soft carp roe, which is considered to be an Alsatian specialty, this recipe may also be prepared with monkfish or cod liver, whose fine qualities often go unrecognized.

Use only the white part of the leeks, which are beautifully mild and ideally complement the flavor of the fish. This combination achieves perfection when vegetables of the best quality are used.

1. Finely chop and blanch the whites of leek. Cut the pikeperch fillets into 4 equal portions of about 5 oz/150 g each, leaving the skin on. Salt and pepper the fish, pan-fry in olive oil until golden brown and finish cooking in the oven.

2. Finely slice the mushrooms and sauté in butter with the chopped shallots. Add a pinch of salt.

carp roe and leeks

3. Drain the soft roe on paper towels and dredge in flour. Fry them in a little oil in a nonstick pan until golden brown, turning them carefully.

4. Drizzle the plates with the clarified butter, mixed with the juice of ½ lemon and the veal stock. Arrange the mushrooms, pikeperch and leek in the center and surround with the soft roe.

Salmon trout

Preparation time: 30 minutes
Cooking time: 3–5 minutes
Difficulty: ★

Serves 4

2¼ lb/1 kg salmon trout
1 bunch turnip tops (arugula may be substituted)
2 tbsp/30 g butter

1 tsp/5 g wheat starch
1 cup/250 ml fish stock
1 cup/250 ml vegetable stock
6½ tbsp/100 ml *crème fraîche*
salt and freshly ground white pepper

Turnip tops are sort of halfway between herb and vegetable. One of the few fresh greens available after the Second World War, turnip tops are nowadays somewhat neglected in Germany. Low in price, they are known there as a poor man's vegetable.

This rather fragile cruciferous plant should be handled with care, and prepared quickly but carefully. When chopped in the food processor it must not turn into a mush, but retain some body and chunkiness. Since the turnip tops contain a great deal of water, the sauce should be prepared just before serving, as it might separate if left to stand too long.

Salmon trout poses no insurmountable problems with regard to preparation. Just take care to poach it briefly, so it will keep its lovely pink color; the contrast with the deep green turnip tops will delight your dinner guests. A salmon trout weighing about 2¼ lb/1 kg should yield decent-sized fillets that can then be cut into attractive slices.

Other river fishes may be substituted for the salmon trout, but could lack its delicate color. A sea trout, with its even tastier flesh, would make an unexpected change of pace. And if you are unable to get hold of turnip tops, this recipe may be made with arugula, mustard greens or young leaf spinach.

1. Fillet and skin the salmon trout and cut into 4 equal pieces about 2½ in/6 cm in length. Halve each piece and place in an ovenproof dish that has been greased with butter and sprinkled with salt.

2. Wash the turnip tops thoroughly, then cut up coarsely and blanch the white parts. Process with some of the fish stock in a blender or food processor, taking care not to reduce to a mush. Bring the rest of the fish stock to a boil and bind lightly with the wheat starch.

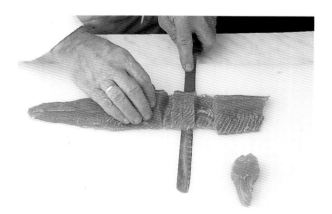

with turnip tops

3. Place the salmon trout in a low oven and cook gently so as to preserve its natural color.

4. Combine the crème fraîche with the vegetable stock. Add the turnip tops and bring to a boil. Whisk in the butter a bit at a time, then season with salt and pepper. Place the cooked salmon trout on heated plates, surround with the turnip tops, top with the sauce and serve at once.

Vasa Museum

Preparation time: 40 minutes
Cooking time: 40 minutes
Difficulty: ✲

Serves 4

10½ oz/300 g salted salmon
10 potatoes
2 onions
3 eggs

1⅔ cup/400 ml milk
3½ tbsp/50 g butter
3½ oz/100 g dill
salt and freshly ground pepper

The *Vasa*, the superb flagship of the 17th-century Swedish fleet, named after Sweden's ruling dynasty of the time, went down with all hands on its maiden voyage. Wonderfully preserved by the salt water, it was refloated in the 1960s and turned into a museum, where Örjan Klein opened his restaurant "K.B."—the perfect "laboratory" for both traditional and haute cuisine, as this salmon and potato gratin so eloquently demonstrates.

Scandinavian salmon is among the best in the world, and this is hardly surprising when one thinks of the ice-cold waters of Sweden and Norway. Salmon abound here, and it is easy to find good specimens 9–13 lb/4–6 kg. Pink salmon is primarily Norwegian, while the white-fleshed salmon is found in the Baltic.

Once you have chosen your salmon and cut it into thin slices, it only remains to assemble a *gratin*, quite soft and not too thick. If too thick, it would take too long to cook, which would dry out the potatoes, whose primary task is to moderate the temperature around the fish.

Although savory rather than sweet, this pudding can be served at the end of a meal. Some melted butter should be passed around separately for each guest to "customize" the top layer of potatoes in terms of flavor and texture.

1. Gently sauté the finely sliced onions in some butter for a few minutes until soft and reduced in volume. Boil the potatoes whole in their skins, then peel and cut into slices. Cut the salmon into slices.

2. Butter a gratin dish and cover the bottom with a layer of potatoes. Top with half of the onions, dill weed and salmon. Repeat the layering process, finishing with a layer of potatoes.

salmon pudding

3. Whisk together the eggs and milk and pour over the pudding. Grind some pepper over the top.

4. Dot the top with butter and bake for 20 minutes at 375–400 °F/190–200 °C. Remove from the oven and garnish with melted butter and chopped dill.

Skate wing fried in sesame

Preparation time: 20 minutes
Cooking time: 40 minutes
Difficulty: ★★

Serves 4

1¼ lb/600 g skate wings
40 leaves flat-leaf parsley
½ white cabbage
1 ginger root
¼ cup/60 ml sesame oil
peanut oil for deep-frying
pinch of sea salt
freshly ground white pepper

For the sauce:
⅓ cup/80 ml concentrated fish stock
2 tbsp/30 ml soy sauce
¼ cup/60 ml maple syrup
2 tbsp/30 ml red-wine vinegar
4 cups/1 l grapeseed oil

For years the soybean has been increasingly popular in European and American cooking, appearing in appetizers, entrées and even desserts in the form of texturized vegetable protein, tofu, soy sauce, and even the beans themselves. Soybeans are low in fat and high in protein, and the subtle flavoring properties of soy sauce are prized by gourmets.

Japanese soy sauce or *shoyu* is a highly savory condiment made from crushed soybeans and wheat that are fermented for several months in salt water. The sauce for this dish can be prepared the day before, so that you can devote yourself entirely to the skate the following day.

Skate is best in winter, a season that suits this large, flat-bodied creature that can reach several yards in length, and that moves along in a fascinating gentle wavelike motion. A voracious carnivore, it possesses small, sharp teeth capable of causing great damage.

If you are not buying your skate already filleted, carefully wash the fish before preparing it, as it can sometimes smell of ammonia. The fillets are always taken from the thickest part. Since they are fragile, they should be monitored closely as they cook. Handle them as little as possible, as they fall to shreds with disconcerting ease.

1. Prepare the sauce by mixing together the fish stock, soy sauce, maple syrup and red-wine vinegar. Reduce to a syrupy consistency. Whisk in the grapeseed oil and keep warm.

2. Wash the cabbage leaves; slice coarsely and wilt in a little butter. Stir with a fork on which you have speared the peeled ginger.

oil with soy sauce

3. Clean, skin, trim and fillet the skate wing. Season with salt and fry in very hot sesame oil.

4. Deep-fry the parsley leaves in peanut oil. Just before serving, arrange the skate wing, cabbage and fried parsley on the plates. Spoon some sauce to the side as a finishing touch.

Dover sole strips

Preparation time: 45 minutes
Cooking time: 20 minutes
Difficulty: ✶

Serves 4

1¼ lb/600 g Dover sole fillets
14 oz/400 g potatoes
1 tsp chopped shallot

scant 3¼ cups/800 ml fish stock
1 tbsp Champagne vinegar
2 tbsp peanut oil
1¾ oz/50 g lean bacon
3½ tbsp/50 g butter
1 sprig of thyme
8 fresh bay leaves
pinch sea salt
4 black peppercorns

In order to convince polite society that the potato, until then used only as animal fodder, was a choice foodstuff, the French horticulturist Parmentier obtained secret authorization from the king for a huge plantation in Neuilly. In 1785, the secrecy surrounding this field fueled peoples' imaginations: what on earth was going on behind the fences? When the tubers were ready for harvest, people flocked to the fields from all over. One had only to surround the potato with an air of mystery in order to increase its value.

The two centuries that separate us from Parmentier have by no means rid us of our gullibility: advertizers still use the same tricks with the same success. Still, we have gained the potato. In this recipe, our chef celebrates the humble spud in a light dish similar to a meat *pot-au feu* but made with sole.

The greater the depths at which the Dover sole is caught, the tastier its flesh usually is. A fresh sole can be recognized by its firm, stiff body and rough skin, which can only be pulled off with difficulty. In this recipe, it may be replaced by other white-fleshed flatfish, such as turbot.

The potatoes and bacon can easily be prepared in advance. The julienned bacon cooks very quickly, and should be watched carefully so that it doesn't burn.

1. Cut the potatoes into ⅛ in/2 mm slices and cut out rounds 1¼in/3 cm in diameter from these. Sauté the finely chopped shallots and the thyme, bay leaves, peppercorns and salt in some oil. Moisten with half of the fish stock. Bring to a boil, add the potatoes, and poach until completely cooked.

2. Fillet and skin the Dover sole. Cut the fillets on the diagonal into 1¼ in/3 cm long strips. Brush with melted butter and place in an ovenproof dish.

with sour potatoes

3. Cut the bacon into fine strips and fry in its own fat. Drain on paper towels. Heat the remaining fish stock with the bay leaves.

4. Moisten the sole fillets with a few drops of fish stock and bake in a 350 °F/180 °C oven for 7 minutes. Divide the potatoes among 4 shallow bowls. Place the sole fillets on top and garnish with the julienned bacon. Add a few drops of vinegar, a bay leaf and the stock.

Sea urchins with

Preparation time: 20 minutes
Cooking time: 15 minutes
Difficulty: *

Serves 4

12 sea urchins
3 tbsp each celery root, carrot and leek, cut into tiny dice
1 shallot, chopped

1 tsp tomato paste
juice of 1 lemon
6½ tbsp/100 ml fish stock
1 tbsp Noilly Prat (dry French vermouth)
1¼ cup/300 ml cream
salt and freshly ground pepper

You would be hard pressed to find a less appealing looking creature than the sea urchin. In France, most of these echinoderms come from Erquy in Brittany. There are also good quality ones from Ireland. In certain parts of the world—Sicily for example—there are varieties of this creature that are not edible.

Fresh sea urchins taste best between November and March. Choose rather large specimens, with firm prickles and a generally robust appearance.

The only edible part of the sea urchin is its coral, the five crimson or orange-colored little "tongues." It is essential that they be cleaned carefully in cool water.

The same is true for their shells, which will be later filled with the cream sauce. Since the coral has a very strong iodine taste, we recommend that you use fish stock in the accompaniment, the subtlety of which is capable of taming this wild flavor. For the same reason, mild-tasting vegetables are used, cut into tiny dice and flavored with vermouth. The mixture of vegetables given here, incidentally, is just a suggestion and can equally well be replaced by other varieties, such as asparagus.

An ideal cream sauce implies a perfect blending of all of the constituent flavors. This can only be achieved with a long cooking time of up to 3 hours.

1. With a pair of scissors, cut a circular opening into the slightly concave side of the sea urchins. Pour their juices through a fine sieve into a bowl. Scoop out the crimson coral with a teaspoon and rinse in cold water. Carefully wash out the shells, turn upside down to drain, and reserve.

2. Transfer the sea urchin juices to a saucepan with the diced vegetables, chopped shallot, tomato paste, fish stock and Noilly Prat and reduce by half.

a vegetable cream

3. Add the cream and simmer for 10–15 minutes to allow all the flavors to blend. Correct the seasoning and add the juice of ½ lemon.

4. Place the corals in the shells and heat under the broiler. Fill the shells with the vegetable cream and serve at once.

Trout "surprise"

Preparation time: 20 minutes
Cooking time: 5 minutes
Difficulty:

Serves 4

One 4 lb 6 oz/2 kg trout

For the parsley butter:
⅓ cup/80 g butter
½ bunch flat-leaf parsley
½ bunch curly parsley
2 tsp finely chopped shallot
1 tsp lemon juice
2 tbsp *glace de viande* or reduced veal stock
salt and freshly ground pepper

The Ancient Greeks ranked parsley above all other herbs, weaving it into crowns for the winners of the Isthmian and Nemean games, much as they later did with laurel. This simple little herb was also reputed to be capable of reinvigorating the dying, and was called *petroselinon*, "plant that breaks stones."

This recipe uses a mixture of flat-leaf and curly parsley, both of which are rich in vitamins A and C. To prevent the parsley from oxidizing, it should be processed with the butter and other ingredients at the last minute. The resulting parsley butter is identical to that used for snails except that omits the garlic.

The parsley butter is used to stuff the fish. Choose a fine plump lake trout with shiny skin, weighing around 4½–5½ lb/2–2.5 kg. The fillets must be thick enough to open out and absorb the parsley butter well. If you are unable to get hold of a lake trout, avoid smaller river trout and choose another fish instead.

The fish must be cooked gently, so that the flesh stays appetizingly supple while the butter melts completely. This dish should be served immediately, while it is piping hot, with, for example, new potatoes. As a variation, our chef recommends chive butter, or even better, sea urchin or anchovy butter mixed with capers.

1. Fillet the trout and divide into 4 equal-sized portions. Cut these horizontally through the center and open out. Place the butter, two types of parsley, 2 tsp finely chopped shallots, 1 tsp lemon juice and 2 tbsp glace de viande in a blender or food processor. Blend, season and set aside.

2. Season the inside of the trout fillets and stuff with the parsley butter.

with parsley butter

3. Close the trout fillets and carefully seal the edges, so that the butter will not ooze out too quickly when it is cooking. Lightly season the fish.

4. Melt some butter in a skillet and sauté the fillets over low heat for about 2 minutes, depending on thickness. Arrange on plates or a platter and garnish with a bouquet of fried parsley.

Arctic char with

Preparation time: 45 minutes
Cooking time: 30 minutes
Difficulty: ★★

Serves 4

Two 1¾ lb/800 g arctic char
20 baby carrots with green tops
juice of 2 lemons

1 cup/250 g butter
2 cups/500 ml carrot juice
3½ oz/100 g flat-leaf parsley
salt and freshly ground black pepper

Optional:
1 leek (for garnishing)

The arctic char is a large, sturdy, salmon-like fish which lives in cold waters. It is becoming increasingly rare in the lakes of Burgundy in southeastern France, where a few melancholy fishermen meet with dwindling success in catching it—to the extent that there are worries about its very survival in the wild. Farmed arctic char have now, however, become fairly common.

The tasty flesh of this fish can be appreciated at its best when it is prepared fresh. Check for a rounded belly and bulging eyes; these criteria do not apply to farmed char.

Jacques Lameloise is quite open about his fondness for carrots with their green tops still on, those early, small,

thin-skinned root vegetables with their attractive bright color. Highly rated nowadays, carrots were somewhat scorned in the past. Now the carrot is the second most popular vegetable in France, which explains its constant availability and numerous preparation methods. This recipe is a fine example, combining the little glazed roots with the juice of freshly squeezed carrots, strongly reduced and seasoned with a little lemon juice. You'll be amazed at how well this juice goes with the fish.

It is said that carrots were white in days gone by. If this is true, we should be grateful that their color changed to orange, ot this dish might never have been created.

1. Blanch the carrots in salted water and refresh. Glaze in clarified butter for 20 minutes over a low heat. For the final garnish, cut the leek into thin julienne, blanch, drain and fry for a few minutes in hot oil. Drain and set aside.

2. Prepare the char by cutting off the fins and filleting the fish. Remove the bones, trim the fillets and score the skin of the fish. Season with salt and pepper.

glazed carrots

3. With a centrifugal juicer, squeeze 2 cups/500 ml juice from raw carrots. Add the lemon juice. Reduce by half and whisk in the butter. Adjust seasoning.

4. Melt some butter in a pan and sauté the char fillets for 2 minutes on each side without allowing to brown. Drain on paper towels. Pour some of the carrot juice onto each plate and arrange the char and the glazed carrots on top. Sprinkle with flat-leaf parsley.

Cape Skagen

Preparation time: 45 minutes
Cooking time: 20 minutes
Difficulty: ✶✶

Serves 4

2 whole plaice (dabs) (brill may be
substituted),
2¼ lb–3¼ lb/1–1½ kg each, or 4 small ones,
1¼ lb/600 g each
a little butter
2 sprigs of thyme
lemon slices
2 large leeks
6½ tbsp/100 ml heavy cream
salt and freshly ground pepper

For the celery-root gratin:
1 lb 10 oz/750 g celery root
juice of 1 lemon
2 tbsp oil
2 tbsp mustard

For the cucumber salad:
½ large cucumber
2 cloves garlic
2 tbsp olive oil
6½ tbsp/100 ml vinegar
juice of ½ lemon
1 bunch of curly parsley
a few lettuce leaves

Those well versed in geography will have heard of Cape Skagen, the northernmost tip of the Jutland Peninsula of Denmark. This maritime region abounds in all sorts of fish, and is visited by fishing boats of several nationalities.

The flatfish are divided into two groups: the upper crust, led by Dover sole, turbot and John Dory, and the more ordinary lemon sole, brill and the (European) plaice or dab. Although gourmets tend to look down their noses at the second group of fish, chefs in the know are at pains to rehabilitate their reputation. Brill and plaice are similar in appearance, with their little mouths and orange-spotted top sides. The gray sole perhaps has somewhat firmer flesh than the plaice, but this difference can be offset by adjusting cooking times accordingly. To prevent the fillets

from drying out and to preserve the delicate taste of the fish, Erwin Lauterbach recommends cooking the plaice whole: the thin layer of fat under its skin melts from the heat of cooking, penetrating the flesh with its moisture and flavor. You will need a suitable pan, capable of holding this large fish whole and cooking it quickly over a high heat.

The Danes are very fond of cucumber, both as an hors d'oeuvre and as an accompaniment to main dishes. The cucumber is sliced into rounds and sprinkled with salt to draw out the excess moisture, then used to garnish the fish generously. The addition of cream to the ample pan juices of the leeks renders the preparation of a more elaborate sauce unnecessary.

1. Halve and seed the unpeeled cucumber and cut into small dice. Marinate in a dressing made of the oil, finely chopped garlic, vinegar, lemon juice, salt and pepper.

2. Scale, fillet and bone the fish, leaving the skin on. Pan-fry in hot butter with a few sprigs of thyme and some lemon slices. Clean the celery root and cut into ½ in/1 cm thick slices. Mix together the mustard and lemon juice. Correct the seasoning.

plaice

3. Gently sauté the celery root in oil and place in an ovenproof dish. Brush with the mustard and lemon mixture and place under the broiler for a few minutes. Strip the parsley leaves from their stalks. Clean, trim and halve the leeks. Rinse and dry the lettuce leaves and cut into small pieces.

4. Cook the leeks in a very little water until the water has completely evaporated. Add the cream and cook until done. Mix the lettuce, parsley and cucumber with the dressing and serve this salad separately. Serve the plaice with the leeks and the celery root au gratin.

Pan-fried mackerel fillets

Preparation time: 40 minutes
Cooking time: 10 minutes
Difficulty: ✻

Serves 4

Two 10½ oz/300 g mackerel
3½ oz/100 g peas
½ large cucumber

2 onions
juice of 1 lemon
2 tbsp aquavit
3½ tbsp/50 ml olive oil
1 bunch of dill
freshly ground pepper
1 tbsp salt

In Denmark, it is not enough to be an accomplished chef, capable of preparing all of the various ingredients in a recipe according to the rule book. The Danes place equal emphasis on the art of food presentation and table decoration, and in this they excel. These details, characterized by harmony and good taste, are of the utmost importance for our chef, Erwin Lauterbach.

Next in importance is the absolute freshness of the mackerel, whose spindle-shaped bodies and shiny, silvery, striped skin are easy to recognize at fish counters. Mackerel pass close to the Danish coasts twice yearly, in spring and fall, in the course of their migrations, traveling through the seas in huge schools from which miraculous harvests are made. Their flesh is very firm and a bit on the fatty side: this can be balanced by judiciously chosen vegetables, or with a shot of brandy or spirits—here, flavored with caraway.

Aquavit, the potato-and-caraway drink traditional in Denmark and other Scandanavian countries, not only lends a lovely color to the sauce, but also is an effective aid to digestion.

We recommend vegetables such as onions and cucumbers in a dressing, or celery, and potatoes.

1. Fillet and bone the mackerel. Leaving the skin on, cut the fillets into 2 in/5 cm pieces.

2. Halve the cucumber lengthwise and scoop out the seeds, then cut into ¼ in/5 mm thick slices. Place in a sieve over a bowl and sprinkle with salt. Weight for at least 1 hour to eliminate excess juices.

with salted cucumber

3. Cut up the onions, pod the peas, strip the dill from its stalks and put the stalks to one side. Sweat the onions in olive oil without allowing them to color. Add a little water and the dill. Braise,covered,then reduce, mixing in the peas and cucumber last. When the vegetables are cooked, remove the dill and add the aquavit, lemon juice and oil, to create a dressing.

4. Heat some oil in a nonstick pan and brown the mackerel fillets on the skin side. Divide the dressed onion-cucumber mixture among the plates, placing the pieces of mackerel on top. Garnish with sprigs of dill and spoon some peas in the center.

Halibut with white

Preparation time: 40 minutes
Cooking time: 25 minutes
Difficulty: ★★

Serves 4

One 17½ oz/500 g halibut
12 white asparagus spears
2 shallots

3 dandelion leaves
2 tbsp chopped parsley or tarragon
a little butter
1 tbsp black peppercorns
1 tbsp olive oil
¾ cup/200 ml balsamic vinegar
salt

Halibut is the largest flatfish, with specimens almost 13 ft/4 m in length and 660 lb/300 kg in weight recorded. As you will hardly be wanting to prepare this recipe in such quantity, however, choose a more modest-sized fish. A deep-dwelling fish, halibut has fine, delicate flesh. We recommend that you fry it only just before serving to counteract its tendency to dry out during cooking.

The asparagus spears should be as thick as possible and very white. Their taste is wonderfully preserved by the balsamic vinegar and the dressing in which they are marinated before they are heated and served. It cannot be stressed enough that the whole point of this recipe lies in the balance between the seasonings and herbs, including the dandelion. Native to Europe and Asia, this plant, so commonly despised as an invasive weed, has long been known for its medicinal properties and is often used in special diets. In this recipe, however, you should also juggle with parsley, lime and garlic—a choice mixture even without further additions.

1. Cook the peppercorns in water for 25 minutes, then remove and crush. Chop the shallots, seasonings and 2 tbsp of herbs. Reserve a small amount of each for garnishing, mixing the rest together. Peel the asparagus and cook in boiling salted water until tender. Refresh and set aside.

2. In a saucepan, reduce the balsamic vinegar by a third. Add a little oil and pour over the asparagus.

asparagus and herbs

3. Wash, fillet and bone the halibut. Cut into four 4½ oz/125 g medallions and pan-fry in butter until golden brown on both sides. Remove from the pan and place on a warm plate to rest.

4. Reheat the asparagus in its marinade; set 3 asparagus spears on each plate, slightly fanned out with the tips pointing in the same direction. Place a halibut medallion to the side and sprinkle over a few drops of balsamic vinegar and the remaining mixture of seasonings and herbs.

Broiled gilt-head sea bream

Preparation time: 1 hour 30 minutes
Cooking time: 2 hours
Difficulty: ✳

Serves 4

Two 14 oz/400 g gilt-head sea breams
4 purple artichokes
scant 9 oz/250 g fennel
scant 9 oz/250 g tomatoes
2 cloves garlic

2 anchovy fillets
¾ cup/70 g white bread crumbs
¾ cup/200 ml extra-virgin olive oil
1 cup/250 ml white wine
1⅔ cup/400 ml water
½ bunch of flat-leaf parsley
2 tsp/10 g coriander seed
2 bay leaves
1 sprig of thyme
salt and freshly ground white pepper

The gilt-head sea bream is the pearl of the sea breams. Caught on the high seas by pelagic trawlers, it can be recognized by the golden half-moon between its eyes. Its delicate, fine, supple flesh makes this large, 12–20 in/30–50 cm fish one of the best eating fish of the Mediterranean, with the added advantages of having few bones and being quite easy to prepare.

Our chef recommends patting the sea bream dry, brushing it with olive oil and broiling it before finishing it off in the oven, taking care not to overcook it as this might toughen its flesh. The fish is served with a light vegetable sauce. This may be prepared the day before and whisked with the oil just before serving; in fact, advance preparation makes the sauce even more interesting, giving the flavors time to meld with one another.

The purple artichoke, which is well known in the south of France, is eaten both raw and cooked. Cooked in a covered pot, purple artichokes stay supple and firm, and their hearts are ideal for filling with a stuffing of tomatoes seasoned with thyme, garlic and bay leaf. Don't forget the olive oil, whose fine flavor is absorbed by the artichokes and whose subtle nuances contribute to the success of this delicious summer dish, which should be served piping hot.

1. Peel and seed the tomatoes, then blend to a purée. simmer with the finely sliced fennel, pepper, coriander, white wine and 1⅔ cup/400 ml water for 2 hours.

2. Purée the mixture, then reduce and whisk in the olive oil. Trim the artichokes, removing the hairy choke, then cut them in half.

with Greek vegetable *jus*

3. Cook the artichokes in a covered pot with the thyme, bay leaves and garlic in a little olive oil. Mix the bread crumbs with the parsley, a little garlic and the chopped anchovy fillets.

4. Heat the artichokes in some olive oil and fill with the breadcrumb stuffing. Broil the sea bream fillets and finish in the oven until just cooked. Arrange the sauce and the stuffed artichoke hearts on the plates. Place a fish fillet on top of the sauce and garnish with some flat-leaf parsley.

Sea bass with Swiss

Preparation time: 1 hour 15 minutes
Cooking time: 40 minutes
Difficulty: ★ ★

Serves 4

One 3¼ lb/1½ kg sea bass
1¼ lb/600 g Swiss chard
7 oz/200 g smoked bacon

2¾ oz/80 g shallots
2 cloves garlic
2 oz/60 g Parmesan, freshly grated
scant 1¼ cups/300 g butter
¾ cup/200 ml olive oil
2½ cups/600 ml chicken stock
6 sprigs of flat-leaf parsley
fleur de sel

Sea bass is sometimes criticized for being too fatty. On the other hand, it is rich in protein, iiodine and phosphorus. Found in both the Mediterranean and the Atlantic, the sea bass feeds on many marine species. Shiny skin and clear eyes are reliable indicators of freshness. It has white, flaky, very delicate flesh; watch it like a hawk while it cooks, because it will become bland and mushy if overdone.

As a departure from the traditional pairing of bass and fennel, Dominique Le Stanc uses Swiss chard in this recipe, making the most of the two-toned vegetable. The

chard is washed, then the stalks are peeled to remove their fibers. It is then cooked in salted water—10 minutes for the ribs, 2 minutes for the leaves—and refreshed under cold water. The process of wrapping the vegetable parcels may be best accomplished the day before, as it requires a bit of patience.

Just before serving, the sea bass fillets are sprinkled with *fleur de sel*. Harvested from the surface of the water, it is much finer than coarse sea salt crystals. Its taste, slightly reminiscent of violets, has even earned it the flattering nickname of "caviar of salts."

1. Sweat the shallots. Add the sliced smoked bacon. Pour in the chicken stock and simmer gently for 20–30 minutes over low heat.

2. Cook the Swiss chard in boiling salted water. Finely chop 7 oz/200 g of the leaves and the ribs. Mix with the chopped garlic, grated Parmesan and a little olive oil. Season with salt and pepper.

chard and *fleur de sel*

3. Wrap the stuffing in the remaining chard leaves, forming little triangular parcels. Fillet the sea bass. Halve the fillets. Pan-fry briefly in hot olive oil on the skin side. Finish cooking in the oven.

4. Reduce the poultry-bacon stock and whisk in the butter. Briefly sauté the Swiss chard parcels. Spoon the sauce onto the plates, top with the sea bass and sprinkle with fleur de sel. Arrange the chard parcels all around, alternating with parsley leaves.

Roast herbed salmon

Preparation time: 30 minutes
Cooking time: 20 minutes
Difficulty: ★★

Serves 4

2¼ lb/1 kg salmon
½ celery root
1 potato
1 oz/30 g chopped truffle

¼ cup/60 g butter
¾ cup/200 ml cream
⅔ cup/150 ml beef stock
⅔ cup/150 ml reduced brown veal stock
⅔ cup/150 ml olive oil
flour (for dusting)
¾ oz/20 g chives
pinch grated nutmeg
2 tsp/10 g coarse sea salt
salt and freshly ground black pepper

Celery is edible in its enirety: ribs, leaves, seeds and root are all rich in vitamins and minerals, and are known for their calming effect.

Celery root, or celeriac, is a thick, knobby ball that feels quite heavy for its size. Any specimens sounding hollow when tapped should not be used. In this recipe, it is combined with potatoes to make a fine, creamy, not too thick purée. The butter and cream should not be added until the last minute.

And now to the salmon. Choose a piece cut from a fish weighing 8¾–11 lb/4–5 kg, which will yield thick, meaty fillets. Monitor the cooking process very carefully: if cooked at too high a temperature, the fish will dry out and the dish will be spoiled. Three to four minutes cooking time on the skin side is sufficient, followed by a few seconds on the other side, just enough to color it. Between the skin and the flesh of the salmon lies a layer of fat: in this recipe it is removed.

The flavor of this dish is further enhanced by sprinkling the plate with chives that have been heated in butter. Choose the fine-bladed variety if possible, and chop the chives at the last moment before cooking, to retain the most intense flavor.

1. Peel the celery root and potato. Cut into chunks and cook in boiling salted water for 20 minutes. Drain and press through a sieve or put through a food mill.

2. Reheat the celery root and potato purée, adding 8 tsp/40 g butter, the cream, nutmeg, salt and pepper. Mix and keep warm. Bone and trim the salmon. Cut 4 good rectangles from the fillets and dust the skin side with flour.

with a Périgord-style *jus*

3. Sweat the chopped truffle in butter. Deglaze with the truffle juice from the can. Add the veal stock and reduce slightly. Whisk in the butter. Keep warm. Cook the salmon pieces on the skin side for 3–4 minutes in hot oil: turn and fry for just a few seconds on the other side. Keep warm.

4. Lift the skin from the salmon and remove the layer of fat. Sprinkle on a few grains of coarse sea salt and some chives that have been warmed in butter. Replace the skin. Spoon a circle of celeriac purée onto the plates and top with the salmon, skin-side up. Pour the sauce around the purée.

Quick-smoked salmon

Preparation time: 30 minutes
Cooking time: 12 minutes
Difficulty: ★★

Serves 4

17½ oz/500 g salmon fillet, cut from the
thicker side
2 slices smoked bacon
scant 9 oz/250 g small *ratte* or other fingerling
potatoes
sea salt

For smoking the fish:
1 stovetop smoker
sawdust

For the dressing:
1 leek
1 shallot
2 tomatoes
4 tsp/20 ml wine vinegar
3½ tbsp/50 ml peanut oil
1 tsp mustard
¾ oz/20 g capers
chives, chopped
tarragon, chopped
salt and freshly ground black pepper

This is not your typical smoked salmon, which is first salted, then smoked. Léa Linster's recipe uses fresh salmon, quickly smoked in a stovetop smoker. Pictured in the second photograph below, the smoker is a simple gadget. It is filled with sawdust and then left to heat up; as soon as it starts to smoke, the salmon is placed on the top rack and the box is closed. The heat under the smoker must not be too high, because the sawdust must only smolder, not burn. You may use sawdust or shavings from various types of wood, each of which imparts a different flavor: fruit trees, vine shoots, old wine barrels, and so forth. Make sure you don't use wood that has been treated with toxic chemicals.

On the advice of a Finnish fisherman, our chef recommends choosing the piece of salmon from the thickest part of the fish, right under the head. To prepare the salmon for its brief sojourn in the smoker, it should be salted very lightly and brushed with a little olive oil. After it has finished cooking, you may wish to sprinkle it with some *fleur de sel* and chopped chives.

The finished dish presents a subtle combination of colors, with the cooked salmon sitting prettily on a bed of potatoes. Léa Linster prefers the *ratte* variety. Small and waxy, they hold their shape well when cooked and are thus perfect for this recipe.

1. Select the thickest part of the salmon. Fillet the fish, cut into pieces and season with salt and pepper. Cook the potatoes in their skins.

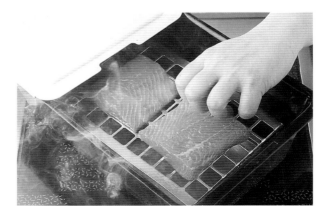

2. Smoke the salmon fillets for 3 minutes, then transfer to an ovenproof dish and continue cooking in a 300 °F/150 °C oven for about 8 minutes.

with a leek dressing

3. To prepare the dressing, cut the leek, shallot and tomatoes into tiny dice and chop the tarragon. In a small bowl, whisk together the mustard, vinegar, salt and pepper. Add the oil, followed by the capers, diced vegetables and tarragon. Peel the potatoes and cut into rounds.

4. Arrange the potato rounds in the center of the plate and top with the smoked salmon. Spoon over some dressing and decorate with chopped chives.

Arctic char with blue

Preparation time:	*30 minutes*
Cooking time:	*30 minutes*
Difficulty:	☆

Serves 4

Four 17½ oz/500 g arctic char
1 oz/30 g *bleu de Trizac* (or other blue cheese)
7 oz/200 g celery

½ cabbage
1¾ oz/50 g bacon
5 eggs
1 cup/250 ml chicken stock
3½ oz/100 ml heavy cream
8 tsp/40 g butter
¾ oz/20 g parsley
salt and freshly ground black pepper

Unlike the American brook char, which, as its name implies, is found in flowing waters, the arctic char lives in the cold waters of Alpine lakes. This salmonlike fish, increasingly rare in the wild, is distinguished by its delicate, soft, and fragile flesh. Once gutted, the flesh must be carefully patted dry; on no account should it be rinsed under running water.

The cooking time of Arctic char must be strictly limited, since overcooking would dry out its flesh and spoil its texture. This difficulty can be avoided by cooking the arctic char whole and filleting it only afterwards.

Alternatively, you may wish to substitute salmon or even trout.

Bleu de Trizac is the only raw-milk blue cheese made in the Auvergne. It has a very strong flavor, making it ideal for heightening the somewhat insipid taste of freshwater fish. The butter-and-blue-cheese cream, although not particularly difficult to make, must be perfectly smooth, so it can be incorporated into the sauce and the scrambled eggs without any lumps. The sauce and the eggs will retain their creamy consistency if you follow the instructions precisely.

1. Clean the char and carefully pat dry, then fillet and bone it. Cut the bleu de Trizac into pieces and cream with the slightly softened butter. Dice the bacon.

2. Season the fish fillets and pan-fry on the skin side for 5 minutes. Transfer to an ovenproof dish, dot with butter and bake in a preheated 250 °F/120 °C oven for 8 minutes.

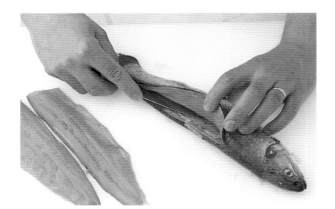

cheese and scrambled egg

3. Bring the chicken stock to a boil. Remove from the heat and whisk in half of the blue-cheese butter. Add half of the parsley and keep warm. Cut the celery into thin sticks, wash, and blanch in boiling salted water. Do the same with the cabbage leaves.

4. Melt some butter over low heat. Pour in the beaten eggs and whisk slowly until cooked to a creamy consistency. Stop the cooking process by adding the cream. Sprinkle with the remaining chopped parsley. Incorporate the remaining blue-cheese butter. Reheat the cabbage and celery in a little butter, plate the fish, vegetables and egg, and serve.

Pan-fried red mullet with deep-

Preparation time: 45 minutes
Cooking time: 2 minutes
Difficulty: ★★

Serves 4

Four 12 oz/350 g red mullets
4 celery leaves
4 basil leaves
1 fennel bulb

1 small potato
scant 2½ oz/70 g celery root
1 tomato
1 medium eggplant
1 medium zucchini
1 red bell pepper
6½ tbsp/100 ml olive oil
1 slice country bread
salt and freshly ground pepper
coarse sea salt

Red mullet is caught from February to June along the coasts of the Atlantic and the English Channel, where it is sometimes also knnown as surmullet. Sea bream may also be used

Every part of the red mullet is tasty. In this colorful, very Mediterranean recipe, Guy Martin even makes use of the liver, reduced to a paste and spread on toasted bread.

For this recipe, choose red mullet as broad as your open hand. Make sure that your fish seller does not gut the mullet, since it is the liver that accounts for the originality of this dish.

Red mullet has many bones, which should be removed carefully. It also has fragile flesh, and so should be quickly pan-fried, leaving the skin crisp. The fennel underscores and complements the distinctive taste of the fish. Use either firm, white bulbs, puréed with a little potato, or small stalks of wild fennel, which should be braised.

Guy Martin recommends accompanying this dish with a mixture of Mediterranean vegetables, simply sautéed, gently and briefly, in olive oil to retain their crunchiness.

1. Scale and fillet the mullets. Reserve the livers and push them through a sieve. Set aside.

2. Finely dice the tomatoes, eggplant, zucchini and red bell pepper and sweat in olive oil. Cook the fennel and the potato in boiling water and mash to a purée.

fried celery and basil leaves

3. Cut the celery root into thin slices and deep-fry in olive oil, along with the basil and celery leaves. Pan-fry the red-mullet fillets.

4. Toast the bread and cut out six 1½ in/4 cm circles. Spread them with the mullet-liver paste. Heat the fennel purée and the diced vegetables. Spoon the purée onto the plates and top with the mullet fillets. Arrange the diced vegetables, the deep-fried celery and basil leaves and the liver toasts on top.

Portuguese

Preparation time: 40 minutes
Cooking time: 30 minutes
Difficulty: ★★

Serves 4

14 oz/400 g monkfish
14 oz/400 g skate
14 oz/400 g conger eel
14 oz/400 g eel

14 oz/400 g squid (or cuttlefish)
14 oz/400 g onions
1¾ lb/800 g ripe tomatoes
1¾ lb/800 g potatoes
3 cloves garlic
2 green bell peppers
1 small chile
1 bunch of parsley
1 bay leaf
¾ cup/200 ml white wine
¾ cup 200 ml olive oil

Caldeirada à portuguesa is the name given in Portugal to this fish soup, of which there are almost as many versions as there are towns claiming its invention. From the Costa Verde in the North to the tip of the Algarve in the South, it is prepared with the most varied sauces, which are more or less hot with chile, and a variety of ingredients such as pasta or potatoes. In spite of this diversity, however, the basis of the dish always remains the same: it is always a soup made from a wide variety of fish.

If you were a stickler for tradition, you would slice the fish in pieces, bones and all. Our chef departs from custom here, and recommends removing the bones in order to spare your guests this unpleasant chore. Depending on what is available at the fish market, you can prepare this

dish with sea bream, red mullet, John Dory or any other flavorful fish—as well as with shrimp, clams and other seafood. Moreover, it is also possible to make this soup with just one type of fish—grouper, for example. We should also mention the *caldeirada* from Aveiro on the west coast of Portugal, which combines both ocean fish and freshwater fish.

By alternating layers of fish and vegetables, you ensure that the flavor of each penetrates the other as the *caldeirada* cooks. In addition, the vegetables trap the heat, so the fish remains firmer. It is essential to the success of the dish that your dinner guests be offered sufficient quantities of strongly seasoned broth (*caldo*).

1. Clean the fish. Cut into pieces and season.

2. Slice the onions into thin rings. Slice the garlic thinly. Peel and seed the tomatoes and cut into rounds. Peel the potatoes and cut into ⅜ in/1 cm thick slices. Halve and slice the green bell peppers. Place the vegetables in separate small bowls.

"bouillabaisse"

3. Starting with the vegetables, alternate layers of vegetables and fish in a pot until you have used up all the ingredients, seasoning as you go. Add the parsley, bay leaf and a crushed chile.

4. Pour over the white wine and the olive oil. Season, and cook, covered, over low heat for about 30 minutes. Serve in the same pot if possible.

Salt cod

Preparation time: 15 minutes
Cooking time: 20–30 minutes
Difficulty: ★

Serves 4

2¼ lb/1 kg thick salt cod
8 potatoes
2 heads of broccoli
4 cloves garlic

1 lemon
2 eggs
2 tbsp/30 g butter
1⅔ cups/400 ml olive oil
¾ cup/200 ml milk
2 sprigs of parsley
1 bay leaf
white bread crumbs
salt and freshly ground pepper
coarse salt

The word *lagareiro* comes from the Portuguese *lagar* or oil press, bringing to mind the rich olive orchards found by the Romans when they conquered Lusitania. Maria Ligia Medeiros chose this description for the potatoes rather than the salt cod (*bacalhau* in Portuguese), which, her compatriots claim, can be prepared in as many different ways as there are days in the year: Made into fritters (*pastéis*), served *à Miquelina*, pan-fried, braised...

This recipe, which is fairly common in the east of the country, requires thick salt cod fillets, which are cooked in plenty of oil. First, though, you must set about the ritual task of de-salting the cod, which takes no less than 30 hours. The aim is to get rid of most, but not all, of the salt; otherwise it would lose a great deal of its flavor.

You can release your pent-up aggression on the potatoes. Once you have ascertained that they are done, place them on a flat surface and split them open by giving them a good punch with your fist. No kitchen gadget could produce a similar result. To accompany the cod, our chef recommends cooked turnip greens. A last word of advice on the salt cod: do not use thin fillets.

1. De-salt the cod by soaking it in several changes of fresh water for about 30 hours. Drain, remove the skin and cut the fish into 4 thick 3 x 6 in/8 x 15 cm pieces. Place the cod in a flat, fairly shallow container with the chopped garlic, lemon juice, pepper, parsley and bay leaf. Pour on milk to cover. Allow to marinate for 3 hours.

2. Dry the pieces of cod in a kitchen towel. Place the potatoes on a bed of coarse salt, drizzle a little olive oil over them and bake for 20 minutes.

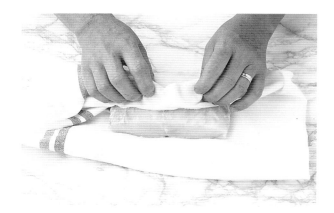

lagareiro

3. Dip the fish in beaten egg and place in an ovenproof dish from which you will serve the cod. Top each piece of fish with two small pats of butter and the bread crumbs, pour over the oil, sprinkle with the chopped garlic and moisten with a couple of spoonfuls of milk from the marinade. Bake for 15 minutes at 350 °F/180 °C, basting frequently.

4. Cook the broccoli in boiling salted water. As soon as the potatoes are done, remove them from the dish and split them open them with a punch of the fist. Garnish the dish in which you have cooked the fish with potatoes and broccoli, and pour boiling oil over the vegetables.

Lemon sole with celery

Preparation time: 45 minutes
Cooking time: 15 minutes
Difficulty: ☆

Serves 4

Four 10½ oz/300 g lemon sole
2 ribs celery
2 tomatoes
6½ tbsp/100 g butter
1 cup/250 ml fish stock
a little white wine

10 saffron threads
a little lemon juice
tarragon, thyme
salt and freshly ground white pepper

For the celery root mousse:
¼ celery root
3½ tbsp/50 g butter
2 tbsp/30 ml cream
salt and freshly ground white pepper

Dieter Müller is always on the search for something new. Here, he recommends recreating the scales of a fish with overlapping slices of celery, whose shape makes it well suited for this purpose. For the fish, he has chosen lemon sole, which has thicker fillets than Dover sole.

Lemon sole is easy to recognize by its brown spots, which distinguish it from other varieties of flatfish, which tend toward pinkish-gray. The fillets are well-sutied to poaching. If they are too thin, fold them over. If lemon sole is not available, Müller suggests fillets of brill or turbot, or as a freshwater alternative, pikeperch.

Two varieties of celery serve as a garnish: the celery root is made into a light mousse, which acts as a base for the scales, and the scales themselves are made from celery ribs blanched in boiling water. As soon as the celery "scales" are in position, Dieter Müller suggests that you may want to fix them in place with a second layer of celery mousse.

For the saffron sauce, use only high-quality threads, rather than the powdered form of this precious spice.

1. Cook the celery root in boiling salted water. Process to a purée, transfer to a saucepan and stir over medium heat to dry the purée. Add the butter and the stiffly beaten cream and set aside. Thinly slice the celery ribs on a slight diagonal. Blanch briefly in boiling salted water and refresh immediately.

2. Fillet the fish and season with salt and lemon juice. Spread a thin layer of celery root mousse on the fillets and top with overlapping pieces of celery to form "scales."

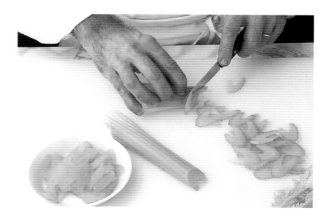

on a saffron-tomato *fumet*

3. Prepare the sauce: Stir the saffron threads into the fish stock. Reduce by half, whisk in the butter and add the peeled, diced tomatoes and the chopped herbs. Season to taste with salt and freshly ground pepper.

4. Place the fish fillets in an ovenproof dish and pour in the white wine and fish stock. Bake for about 8 minutes in a 375 °F/190 °C oven. Ladle some sauce onto the warmed plates and top with the fillets. This dish may be served with fresh noodles, buttered spinach or boiled potatoes.

Pikeperch roulade

Preparation time: 1 hour
Cooking time: 15 minutes
Difficulty: ✷✷

Serves 4

One 3¼ lb/1½ kg pikeperch
7 oz/200 g salmon fillet
2 beets
16 large spinach leaves
¾ cup/120 g wild rice, uncooked weight (as an accompaniment)

juice of ½ lemon
2 tbsp fish stock
2 tbsp riesling
1 cup/250 ml heavy cream
salt and freshly ground pepper

For the sauce:
6½ tbsp/100 ml Riesling
1 cup/250 ml fish stock
1¼ cups/300 ml heavy cream
⅓ cup butter
1 tbsp whipped cream
salt

Riesling is an exceptional grape that makes a noble, aromatic wine. It is cultivated by vintners on both sides of the Rhine. In this recipe, it lends the necessary finishing touch to the pikeperch-salmon duo. In the opinion of Dieter Müller, no other white wine could take its place in this sauce.

Pikeperch, also known as zander, is found in rivers and lakes. This member of the perch family also has a certain affinity with the pike, as its composite name indicates. Choose a very fresh specimen of decent size. If you are put off by the fragility of its flesh, you could replace it with, say, John Dory, of which our chef is very fond.

In this recipe, the stuffing is enriched with the salmon trimmings: before these are added, they should be puréed with the cream. Care should be taken when puréeing the salmon in the food processor, as the heat of the rotating blades can cause the salmon to lose color, which may have to be restored by adding a little beet juice to the mousse.

Spinach and rice are common accompaniments for fish. Wild rice lends a bit of variety, in terms of shape, color and flavor. It should be brought slowly to a boil and cooked until tender. Traditionally harvested by Native Americans, this highly nutritious grain lends a New World touch to an otherwise Central European dish.

1. Fillet and skin the pikeperch; remove all remaining bones. Divide into 7 oz/200 g portions. Cut the remaining pikeperch flesh and a generous 5 oz/150 g salmon fillet into cubes. Season with salt and pepper and refrigerate for 40 minutes. Process this chilled mixture and add the cream until you have a mousse. Press through a sieve.

2. Add the lemon juice and the remaining scant 2 oz/50 g of cubed salmon to the mousse. Add a little beet juice to intensify the color, and season to taste. Blanch the spinach leaves in boiling salted water, refresh, drain and spread out on a cloth. Season the pikeperch fillets and spread them with the stuffing.

with riesling sauce

3. Place the pikeperch fillets, topped with the stuffing, on the spinach leaves and roll up. Transfer the roulades to an ovenproof dish, adding the riesling and fish stock. Bake for 6 minutes, or until done.

4. Pour the fish stock and riesling into a saucepan and reduce by half. Add the heavy cream and reduce to a creamy consistency. Remove from the heat and whisk in the butter and the whipped cream. Correct seasoning. Cut the fish roulades into slices. Spoon some sauce onto the heated plates, top with the sliced roulade and mound some wild rice to the side.

Gurnard with sautéed

Preparation time: 45 minutes
Cooking time: 15 minutes
Difficulty: ★★

Serves 4:

3¼ lb–4½ lb/1½–2 kg gurnard
4½ lb/2 kg vegetables in season, such as
artichokes, green beans, turnips, green
asparagus, carrots, leek, celery, tomatoes

8 slices of fatty serrano ham
1 leek
1 clove garlic
4 bay leaves
a few leaves flat-leaf parsley
olive oil
1⅔ cup/400 ml brown veal stock
salt and freshly ground pepper

With its superb flavor and key role in bouillabaisse, the gurnard or sea robin deserves occasional star billing, which our chef gladly gives it in this dish. In order to obtain a really fresh fish, Jean-Louis Neichel always goes to the little ports on the Costa Brava and deals direct with the fishermen.

The unusual name of this fish comes from the Old French *gornart* or "grunter," referring to the sound it is said to make when hauled out of the water. If gurnard is unavailable, you may substitute scorpion fish or other rock fish.

Tasty fish demands flavorful vegetables that are in season, which will support the fish in its starring role without stealing the scene. It is appropriate for the color green to dominate, but be sure to include turnips and carrots as well. A julienne of Spanish serrano ham is used here, which flavors the vegetables beautifully. This ham comes from a breed of white, black-legged pigs, free-range and acorn-fed. Serrano ham is at its best after two years' drying. Producers test the ham at regular intervals with the help of the *calado*, a traditional instrument carved from the bone of a horse.

1. Clean and trim the vegetables, peeling them where necessary. Cook each type separately until al dente. Allow to cool.

2. Fillet the fish and cut into four 5½ oz/160 g pieces. Place 1 bay leaf between the skin and flesh of each piece. Bake the seasoned fish with the olive oil and 1 clove garlic for 10 minutes.

vegetables and serrano ham

3. Cut half of the ham into fairly thin strips and sauté with the vegetables in a little butter. Add the veal stock and parsley and simmer, covered, for 2 minutes. Deep-fry the julienned leek.

4. In a skillet, sauté the remaining 4 slices of ham. Place a nest of vegetables on each plate, top with the fish and finish off with the fried leek and the ham. Drizzle with a little olive oil and serve.

Baby squid and octopus

Preparation time: *50 minutes*
Cooking time: *40 minutes*
Difficulty: ☆

Serves 4

10½ oz/300 g baby squid or cuttlefish
10½ oz/300 g tiny baby octopuses
(approximately ¾–1¼ in/2–3 cm long)
1 slice of fatty serrano ham
7 oz/200 g white kidney beans (ganxet beans)

1 red bell pepper
1 green bell pepper
1 yellow bell pepper
1 carrot
1 tomato
1 onion
3 cloves garlic
flat-leaf parsley
thyme
a little olive oil
salt and freshly ground pepper

The finest Catalan dishes owe a great debt to the *ganxet* or white kidney bean: small, flat, and easy-to-cook with a creamy consistency, it lends depth, body and flavor to cream soups and broths alike. In one famous recipe, *butifarra con judías*, the beans are sautéed in rendered ham fat and served with a large sausage. This filling winter dish inspired Jean-Louis Neichel to create a recipe that brings together the flavors of the land and sea.

There is virtually no difference between the small squid anbd the small octopus, bith of which are known by different names in the various regions where they are caught. They are simply diminutive members of a family that contains some real monsters, a number of which can grow to even more than 6 ft/2 m in length.

The tiny squid and octopus should be deep-fried without being washed first, exactly as is done for the famous tapas, dispensed by the thousand in the bars along the Ramblas in Barcelona.The small octopus, which is somewhat rarer than other varieties, may be a bit more expensive, but boasts a creamier consistency.

The flavor of the typically Sopanish serrrano ham really enriches this dish.

1. Peel, core and seed the 3 bell peppers and cut into strips. Gently sauté the finely sliced onion, peppers, thyme and a crushed clove of garlic in some olive oil for 15 minutes. Cook the white beans in unsalted water for 40 minutes.

2. Sauté the squid and the octopus in separate pans with an unpeeled, crushed clove of garlic in some hot olive oil.

with white kidney beans

3. Remove the beans from their cooking water. Cut the serrano ham into small pieces. Peel and carefully seed the tomato and cut into small dice. Sauté all the ingredients in olive oil.

4. Place a spoonful of the mixed peppers and a spoonful of beans on each plate. Top with the squid and octopus and garnish with a little chopped parsley.

John Dory with deep-fried

Preparation time: 45 minutes
Cooking time: 15 minutes
Difficulty: ★★

Serves 4

One 1¼ lb/600 g John Dory
6 medium-thin leeks
1¾ oz/50 g cornstarch
4 cups/1 l oil for deep-frying

For the sauce:
4 ripe Roma or other plum tomatoes
¾ cup/200 ml tomato juice
4 tsp/20 ml olive oil
1 tbsp sherry vinegar
1 tbsp sliced tarragon
salt and freshly ground pepper

The voracious John Dory, which goes by the Latin name of *Zeus faber*, is found in both the Atlantic and the Mediterranean, and inhabits rocky coasts for preference. The homeliness of this fish is largely due to its head and huge mouth; when filleted it offers only fine, succulent flesh. At the end of the meal the John Dory will be showered with compliments.

Choose a decent-sized, fresh fish and cook it slowly and evenly, finishing it in the oven.

The deep-fried leek nests require a bit of advance preparation. The julienne (a French term meaning very thin strips) of leek should be prepared the day before, plunged into ice water and drained thoroughly. If they are dusted in a little cornstarch just before frying, any remaining water is absorbed and the result will be crisper.

Aromatic tomatoes such as the Roma variety reach their peak in September and October. Although lovely and juicy, they remain firm when cooked. They must be sun-ripened and full of flavor, as they will be served lukewarm and virtually raw. The flesh of these tomatoes should be nice and tender. If they are to your liking, it is a good idea to preserve them for later use; they will bring a taste of sunshine to the winter months.

1. Peel, seed and dice the tomatoes. Drain in a sieve. Pour the tomato juice into a saucepan with the salt and pepper. Add the diced tomatoes, olive oil and sherry vinegar. Heat to lukewarm. Stir in 1 tbsp tarragon, cut up at the last moment. Correct the seasoning.

2. Finely julienne the white of the leeks and place in a bowl of ice water. Heat the oil for deep-frying in a small saucepan. Drain and dry the julienned leek.

leeks and tarragon tomatoes

3. Dust the leek julienne with cornstarch, then plunge one-quarter of the mixture into the hot oil in 1 clump. Turn as soon as the leeks hold together. When both sides are cooked, drain on paper towels. Salt lightly and keep warm. Repeat the process until you have 4 deep-fried leek "nests."

4. Divide the fish into 4 equal portions of about 5 oz/150 g, leaving the skin on; then bone the fish. Heat a few drops of olive oil in a nonstick pan. Place the fillets skin-side down in the pan, brown over medium-low heat and turn. The flesh should remain pink. Arrange the fillets on warmed plates, decorate with a border of lukewarm tomato sauce and place a "nest" of leek next to the fish.

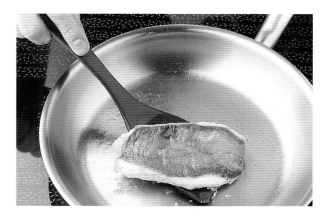

Pan-fried pikeperch with bone

Preparation time: 30 minutes
Cooking time: 1 hour
Difficulty: ✷

Serves 4

1 large pikeperch (3¼ lb/1½ kg)
16 pieces of beef marrow bone, 1½ in/4 cm
long
4 shallots
1 clove garlic
1 bouquet garni
1¾ oz/50 g smoked bacon

2 cups/500 ml red gigondas wine
1 cup/250 ml veal stock
6½ tbsp/100 ml olive oil
3½ tbsp/50 g butter
chervil leaves
sea salt
freshly ground pepper

For the onion–black currant marmalade:
1 onion
1 tbsp black currant preserves
6½ tbsp/100 ml wine vinegar
¾ cup/200 ml red wine
2 tsp/10 g sugar

Since eastern France is landlocked, it is primarily river fish that are eaten in this region. The lack of coastline also explains the *marinière de poisson* traditional to this area, prepared with carp, catfish and gudgeon, and seasoned with white wine and onions. This recipe is based on the same principle, but contains only one type of fish, chosen for its delicacy: the pikeperch or zander.

The best pikeperch is fished in the spring, when the water level of streams and rivers sinks. After you have filleted the fish, pan-fry it over moderate heat, taking care not to overcook it. Thicker fillets may need to be finished in the oven.

The beef marrow should remain in the bone until you are ready to prepare it, so it does not dry out. It should be soaked for at least 24 hours in ice-cold water, so refrigerate it and change the water at regular intervals. After removing the marrow from the bones, you should then poach it for a few minutes.

The wine sauce is similar to the base of a *matelote* or eel stew. Gigondas is a powerful red wine from the Rhône valley whose alcohol content is somewhat above average and thus stands up well to the brisk reduction that is essential before the veal stock is added. Finally, the sweetish, slightly tart black currant preserves contrast marvelously with the somewhat more pungent sauce.

1. Scale the pikeperch. Divide into fillets of about 5 oz/150 g and remove all bones. Lightly fry the smoked bacon in a pan until the fat runs. Chop the shallots and clove of garlic and sauté until golden. Pour off the fat and moisten the contents of the pan with the gigondas. Reduce to a syrupy consistency. Prepare the onion-black currant marmalade by sweating the onions and adding all the other ingredients. Stew, covered, over low heat for 40 minutes.

2. Add the veal stock and bouquet garni. Reduce, adjust seasoning and pass through a fine strainer. Set aside in a hot-water bath to keep warm. At the last minute, whisk in 3½ tbsp/50 g butter.

marrow and Gigondas sauce

3. Poach the beef marrow for a few minutes in salted water at 195 °F/90 °C. Pour a few drops of olive oil into a nonstick pan. Sauté the fish fillets until golden on both sides, removing as soon as they are just done.

4. Drain the bone marrow and place around the pikeperch fillets. Pour the very hot gigondas sauce all around. Sprinkle a little sea salt on the marrow. Make the onion and black currant marmelade by sweating the onions and adding all the other ingredients. Stew, covered, over low heat for 40 minutes.

Champigny-steamed

Preparation time: 35 minutes
Cooking time: 55 minutes
Difficulty: ★★★

Serves 4

One 4½ lb/2 kg brill
8 cups/2 l Champigny (Loire Valley red wine)
6 shallots
1 onion
6 medium carrots

⅓ cup/40 g flour
1¾ oz/50g *glace de viande* or reduced meat stock
13 tbsp/200 g butter
parsley sprigs
thyme
1 bunch of flat-leaf parsley
black peppercorns
crushed black pepper
whole cloves
fine salt, coarse salt

Champigny and Saumur-Champigny are light, fresh red wines produced in the area around Saumur, bordering the vineyards of Touraine and Anjou in the Loire valley. These wines should be drunk well chilled, and do not age well. Champigny is rich in tannin and is ideally suited for sauces, as it loses some of its acidic tang, but not its bouquet, during cooking.

Brill is a large flatfish that is caught in the English Channel and the Atlantic. Although it disdains the bait of the angler, it falls prey to the trawlers' nets. Unlike the turbot, which it resembles to a certain extent, it has very smooth skin. Its fine, highly nutritious flesh is at its best in the months of May and June.

Choose a decent-sized fish if possible, since smaller fish mean more waste and less flavor. Moreover, thick fillets divided into individual-sized portions are preferable to small, thin fillets. Cooking time should be kept to a bare minimum, so that the Champigny steam does not eclipse the flavor of the fish.

The *glace de viande* is essential for the consistency of the sauce, which should be have a good consistency but should not be too thick; it must be subtle enough in flavor to enhance the brill without overpowering it.

1. Fillet the brill and divide into 4 equal pieces. Remove the skin from both sides of the fish, and carefully rinse the head and bones. Chop up the bones and head and sweat in ⅓ cup/80 g butter; add the shallots and 3 carrots, finely diced.

2. Dust the preceding ingredients with flour. Stir well and add two-thirds of the Champigny. Reduce over low heat for 45 minutes. Pour the remaining one-third of the Champigny in the bottom of a steamer. Add 3 whole peeled carrots, the parsley sprigs, the onion studded with the cloves, and the thyme.

fillets of brill

3. Sprinkle the 4 pieces of fish with coarse salt and crushed pepper and place on a steamer rack. Cover and steam the fish for about 10 minutes.

4. Strain the sauce. Reduce and correct seasoning. Whisk in the butter and add the glace de viande. Pass the sauce through a fine-mesh strainer one more time and divide among 4 plates. Place a piece of brill in the center of each plate and garnish with the flat-leaf parsley.

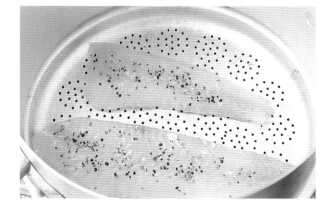

Braised monkfish

Preparation time: 55 minutes
Cooking time: 35 minutes
Difficulty: ★★★

Serves 4

One 3¼ lb/1½ kg monkfish tail

1 generous lb/500 g snow peas
12 pearl onions

2 lemons
6⅔ tbsp/50 g flour
10½ oz/300g unsliced white sandwich bread
3½ tbsp/50 ml white wine
2 cups/500 ml heavy cream
13 tbsp/200 g butter
salt, freshly ground pepper and sugar

Though the head of the monkfish is generally reckoned to be too hideous to display at the fish counter, it has an exquisite-tasting tail, meaty and delicious. It spends most of its time perched on the rocks, waiting for its prey. This it attracts with a sort of "fishing rod" located on its head that terminates in a fleshy "bait"—hence its other name, "anglerfish."

The monkfish tail consists of fine, firm flesh that is completely free of bones, apart from the central bone. Just be sure to remove all of the membrane under the skin so that this does not shrink and toughen while the fish is cooking. Provided that you follow this advice, the monkfish will delight your dinner guests with its tender, tasty white flesh.

We recommend snow peas as an accompaniment for the monkfish. Unlike other varieties of peas, which must be shelled, snow peas have small, thin edible pods with immature seeds, which are always eaten whole (hence their French name, *mangetout* ("eat-all"). Watch them carefully as they cook, because they should be served *al dente*.

The julienne of lemon zest must be blanched long enough to rid it of any bitterness. The crunchy white-bread *croûtons* should serve as a contrast to the soft fish: prepare them at the last moment, making sure they do not absorb too much melted butter.

1. Fillet the fish and remove all the membranes. Cut the zest of 2 lemons into thin julienne; blanch for 5 minutes and drain. Trim and blanch the snow peas.

2. Cut the fish fillets into 12 chunks. Dredge the fish in seasoned flour and pan-fry in ¼ cup/60 g hot butter. Pour off the fat. Quickly sauté the snow peas in ¼ cup/60 g butter.

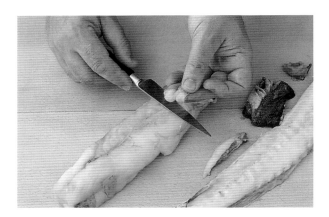

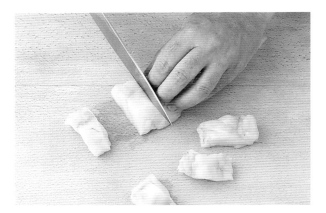

with snow peas

3. Deglaze the pan with the white wine and add the cream. Simmer for about 5 minutes. Cut off the crusts of the bread, slice and cut into heart-shaped pieces and brown in butter. Glaze the pearl onions by cooking in butter with a little water and sugar.

4. Put the sauce through a fine strainer and whisk in the remaining butter. Arrange the snow peas in fan shapes on each plate. Place the monkfish in the center and mask with the sauce. Garnish with the glazed onions, the bread hearts and the julienne of lemon.

Monkfish medallions with

Preparation time: 15 minutes
Cooking time: 15 minutes
Difficulty: ★★

Serves 4

One 3¼ lb/1½ kg monkfish tail
10½ oz/300 g foie gras
10 tbsp/150 g butter
a little flour for dusting

2 cups/500 ml Bonnezeaux (sweet white Loire valley wine)
1 tbsp cognac
2 cups/500 ml heavy cream
salt and freshly ground pepper

According to Paul Pauvert, the common monkfish is more suitable for this dish than the smaller black-skinned variety, the so called *lotte rousse*. Just how does one go about checking monkfish for freshness? Because it is generally sold without its head, you can't rely on its eyes or gills as indicators. Just make sure that its firm, shiny, slightly iridescent flesh is entirely free from yellow fibers.

Once in "tail" form, preparing monkfish is a pleasant job: there are no bones to deal with save the central one, and when cooked appropriately its flesh is marvelously tender. Here, the fish is cut into medallions, which are gently browned in butter for several minutes on each side. The main thing here, however, is not the extremely simple cooking process to which the fish is subjected, but the accompanying sauce, in which our chef makes an inspired combination of cognac and Bonnezeaux wine.

Flambéing the monkfish medallions in cognac lends them greater sumptuousness and depth of flavor. Deglazing their pan juices with Bonnezeaux, a sweet Anjou wine deserving of greater recognition and that makes an elegant pairing with foie gras, imparts a mellow yet slightly acid note. Using these two ingredients one after the other produces a subtle and inimitable effect. Take care, however, to add them in moderation; too much cognac would irrevocably overpower the fish.

Serve this dish piping hot, and don't even dream about leftovers: there won't be any.

1. Fillet the fish and cut into 4 good medallions of equal size. Flatten these slightly, season, and dust with a little flour.

2. Brown the fillets in butter over low heat for about 10 minutes. After about 7 1/2 minutes, flambé with the cognac and deglaze with the wine. Reduce by a quarter and add the cream. Lift out the medallions and keep warm.

Bonnezeaux and foie gras

3. Prepare the foie gras butter by blending half of the foie gras and one-third of the butter in a food processor. Reduce the sauce by half. Using a potato peeler, finely shave the remaining foie gras.

4. Whisk the foie gras butter into the sauce a little at a time. Season with salt and pepper and strain. Place the monkfish medallions in the center of the plates, pour around the sauce and top with the foie gras shavings. Garnish and serve hot.

Pikeperch with Belgian

Preparation time: 30 minutes
Cooking time: 5 minutes
Difficulty: *

Serves 4

One 2¼ lb/1 kg pikeperch
4 plump heads of Belgian endive

3 cups/750 ml Saumur-Champigny (French red wine)
6½ tbsp/100 ml sherry vinegar
2 tbsp/30 g sugar
1 tsp cornstarch
2 tbsp/30 g butter
2 sprigs of chervil
salt and freshly ground pepper

The pikeperch can grow to a very large size and weight (up to 40 in/1m in length and 33 lb/15 kg in weight). It is particularly prized for its fine flesh and low number of bones. The fish should be filleted and skinned just before the fillets are flattened slightly to make them even more tender.

Saumur-Champigny is one of the lightest of the Loire-valley reds, drunk cool in the Anjou region. A fresh, robust wine, its bouquet grows in strength over the years, but this is not a wine to lay down for decades. Take care to reduce the sauce gently in order to preserve the aroma and flavor of the wine.

Belgian endive owes its existence to the oversight of a Belgian botanist, whose chicory plants produced the tasty shoots when accidentally allowed to sprout in the cellar. Choose plump specimens (class 2 or 3) that are firm and free from brown spots, and cut them into very thin strips.

The pikeperch should be removed from the oven before it is fully cooked, and placed at once on a very hot plate: this allows the fillets to continue cooking slowly while resting, so that they will be perfectly soft when it is time to serve them.

1. Remove and discard the outer leaves of the Belgian endive and cut the remaining leaves into strips the size of bean sprouts.

2. Melt some butter in a pan and gently sauté the endive strips. Sprinkle with a little sugar and lightly caramelize. Season with salt and pepper.

endive in Champigny

3. Prepare the sauce by caramelizing the remaining sugar and deglazing the pan with the vinegar. Add the wine, reduce by one-third, season and bind lightly with the cornstarch.

4. Clean and fillet the pikeperch. Flatten the fillets lightly and cook them in a 300 °F/150 °C oven for 5 minutes. Transfer the fillets to hot plates, then pour the sauce all around and decorate with a few chervil sprigs before serving.

Perch fillets with

Preparation time: 45 minutes
Cooking time: 15 minutes
Difficulty: ★★

Serves 4

Generous 12 oz/350 g young perch fillets
½ cup/50 g bread crumbs
2 eggs
butter, flour
salt and freshly ground pepper
4 zucchini with blossoms still attached
olive oil (for frying)
3½ tbsp/50 ml heavy cream

1 tsp chopped thyme
salt and freshly ground pepper

For the *confit* tomatoes:
8 fleshy tomatoes
½ garlic clove, finely chopped
pinch of sugar
a few drops of balsamic vinegar
a few drops of red-wine vinegar
6½ tbsp/100 ml extra-virgin olive oil
1 tsp rosemary
salt and freshly ground pepper

Perch abounds in the rivers and lakes of Switzerland, along whose shores it is customarily served fried, with tartar sauce. This fearsome predator, which ruthlessly pursues and devours smaller fish, particularly eel fry, can reach up to 14 in/35 cm in length and 4½ lb/2 kg in weight. Greenish brown with wide, dark stripes, it is less colorful than its American cousin, the aptly named rainbow perch.

As a food, it is a deservedly popular fish with delicate flesh. The pan-fried fillets will be done in a trice; longer than 1–2 minutes cooking time could adversely affect their fine flavor.

Although tomatoes are available all year, for the *confit*-tomato accompaniment, try to buy firm, fleshy summer tomatoes, which are sweeter and more fully flavored, and use a highly aromatic olive oil. The tomatoes should be cooked very slowly with aromatic herbs. Your patience will be rewarded by a delicious result, especially if you have used genuine balsamic vinegar from Modena, with its divinely subtle flavor.

Horst Petermann is all in favor of these *confit* tomatoes accompanying other kinds of fish such as Dover sole or red mullet, which can be prepared exactly like the perch.

1. Salt and pepper the perch fillets. Dredge in flour, then coat in beaten egg. Press bread crumbs into the flesh-side only. Scald the tomatoes and plunge in ice water. Peel and seed them and let drain on paper towels.

2. Sprinkle the bottom of a large pan with sugar. Arrange the quartered tomatoes on top, season with salt and pepper and sprinkle with the chopped rosemary and garlic. Gently heat the pan to melt the sugar. Sprinkle the tomatoes with a few drops of balsamic and red wine vinegar and drizzle with the olive oil. Cook over moderate heat. Separate the zucchini flowers from the zucchini. Carefully rinse the blossoms and dry on paper towels.

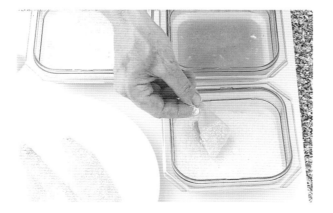

confit tomatoes

3. Wash the zucchini and slice into rounds. Heat the olive oil in a pan and add the zucchini. Season with salt and pepper and sprinkle with thyme. Simmer over moderate heat until tender. Pour over the cream. Shake the pan until the vegetables have absorbed all the cream.

4. Pan-fry the fish fillets in the butter-oil mixture until golden brown, starting with the breaded side. Arrange the tomatoes in a semicircle on heated, flat plates. Mound the zucchini in the center and top with the fish fillets. Garnish with the deep-fried zucchini flowers.

Turbot and anise potatoes

Preparation time: *1 hour*
Cooking time: *30 minutes*
Difficulty: ★★

Serves 4

One 4½ lb/2 kg turbot
2 tsp/10 g black peppercorns
2 tsp/10 g mustard seeds
2 tsp/10 g juniper berries
a few drops olive oil
2 lemons
sea salt

For the anise potatoes:
10½ oz/300 g potatoes
cumin seed

a little olive oil
a little anise-flavored vinegar
salt, freshly ground pepper

For the white sauce:
6½ tbsp/100 g homemade mayonnaise
6 ½ tbsp/100 ml heavy cream
salt and freshly ground pepper
vinegar

For the green sauce:
2 shallots, 2 bunches of basil
1 bunch of chervil
1 bunch of flat-leaf parsley
2 tsp pine nuts
6½ tbsp/100 ml olive oil
a few drops of red-wine vinegar
salt and freshly ground pepper

A member of the flatfish family, turbot is found in cold waters such as the English Channel and the Atlantic. Long prized for its fine flesh, the turbot is so delicate that it usually requires an accompaniment that will enhance, not mask, its flavor. Look for a large European turbot, which should yield good fillets without too much waste.

The fillets are smoked using a method similar to that passed down by the indigenous peoples of the Caribbean and Oceania. This is one of the first methods successfully used by humans to preserve perishable meat and fish.

For this recipe, Horst Petermann strongly recommends the Charlotte potato, a small winter variety with a fine, very smooth skin. Its firm, yellow flesh lends itself well to the creation of a light, soft purée, particularly if you are able to buy the early, shorter potatoes, which are preferable to the longer variety intended for storage. Although relatively new, Charlottes are gaining an ever-growing following among both producers and consumers. Yukon golds are a good alternative.

It is the herbs and other seasonings that make this subtle dish really shine, provided these are prepared properly and used in the quantities stated. Once cooked, the turbot should be served immediately, accompanied by a few flavorful greens such as radicchio, arugula or dandelion.

1. Fillet the turbot. Separately crush the peppercorns, juniper berries and mustard seeds in a mortar with a pestle, then mix together. Add grated lemon peel, a little lemon juice and the olive oil and stir together to make a marinade.

2. For the white sauce, make a mayonnaise with an egg yolk, mustard, salt and vinegar. Add the same quantity of heavy cream to the mixture. For the green sauce, make a dressing by blending together the olive oil and vinegar, then add the basil, chervil, parsley, finely minced shallots and the pine nuts.

with two sauces

3. Season the fish with sea salt and brush with the marinade prepared in step 1. Wash the potatoes and cook them in their skins in boiling salted water to which some cumin seeds have been added. Cut the potatoes into small rounds and season with anise-flavored vinegar and olive oil.

4. Smoke the fish quickly over high heat in a stovetop smoker. Finish by sautéing in a nonstick pan in some oil. Arrange the potatoes in a semicircle in the center of the plates. Pour over the white sauce. Top with a chunk of fish. Pour the green sauce over and garnish with the salad leaves.

Cockle and mussel

Preparation time: 1 hour
Cooking time: 45 minutes
Difficulty: ✶

Serves 4

1½ lb/650 g small cultivated mussels
1½ lb/650 g cockles
3½ oz/100 g fresh spinach
2 small tomatoes
2 shallots

scant 2½ oz/70 g chervil
¾ cup/200 ml white wine
1 tbsp heavy cream
5 tbsp/70 g butter
salt and freshly ground pepper

For the garnish (optional):
1 potato

This first course should be served covered, with the contents of the little pot unveiled only at the last moment. Of all the shellfish, it is the cockle that yields the best broth; and the chervil butter that accompanies it here is also a delight for the taste buds.

As with all shellfish, you must first rid the cockles and mussels of their sand. Cockles open only if you manage to mimic their marine habitat, thus deceiving their natural filter. This you do by heating salted water in a pot with an egg. As soon as the egg rises to the surface, tip the cockles into the water. Gourmets prefer their cockles cooked.

There are several varieites of this bivalve, those from Normandy being the mostly highly prized: the large

cockle, and the prolific common cockle (*Cardium edule*), which gives itself away by the little piles of sand it leaves behind when it burrows.

Choose medium-sized mussels: the very small ones cook too quickly and the larger ones don't have as fine a flavor.

Roland Pierroz has conjured up a dish of contrasting colors, tastes and textures. As a foil for the shellfish he has chosen chervil and spinach, which should be fresh and crisp, and whose flavor discretely enhances the iodine tang of the cockles and mussels. This invigorating dish with its sea flavors can lose some of its sparkle when it comes in contact with the air, and so should be left covered until the last moment.

1. Prepare the chervil butter by processing the softened butter with the chervil (washed, drained and stripped of its coarse stalks), then pushing through a fine-mesh sieve. Refrigerate. Wash the shellfish under running water. Cook the spinach in boiling salted water.

2. Cut a cross in the tops of the tomatoes, then scald and peel them. Halve the tomatoes vertically, scoop out the seeds and juice and cut into ¼ in/5 mm wide strips.

stew with chervil

3. Chop the shallots and simmer half of them with the mussels and half of the wine until the mussels open. Repeat the process with the cockles. Remove the cockles and mussels from their shells, straining and reserving their juices. Reheat the spinach in a little butter. Drain the shellfish. For the garnish, cut a potato into matchstick strips and form into a latticework circle. Sauté in a little hot oil until golden brown.

4. Bring 1¼ cups/300 ml of the cooking water to a boil; add the cream and whisk in the chilled chervil butter. Adjust the seasoning. Heat the shellfish in the sauce without boiling. Arrange the spinach in shallow bowls, top with the shellfish and sauce, garnish with tomato slices and chervil sprigs and decorate with the potato disk.

Langoustine, shellfish

Preparation time:	1 hour
Cooking time:	30 minutes
Difficulty:	★★

Serves 4

One 7 oz/200 g red mullet
1 sea bass
4 langoustines (size 18/24)
7 oz/200 g mussels
7 oz/200 g cockles
white part of 1 leek

1 tomato
½ medium carrot
4 cloves garlic
4 shallots
1 tbsp tomato paste
1 tbsp ground turmeric
1¼ cups/300 ml white wine
3½ tbsp/50 ml olive oil
flat-leaf parsley
salt
croûtons
rouille
freshly ground pepper

The combination of shellfish and crustaceans is always a winner. This soup draws its inspiration from traditional fish soups and celebrates fish, mussels, cockles and langoustines with equal enthusiasm. This choice is not meant to be proscriptive, and you could equally well include some clams, or replace the langoustines with shrimp or lobster.

There is one cardinal requirement for preserving the tender flesh and special aroma and flavor of the langoustines: a short cooking time. For this reason, Roland Pierroz has opted for steaming, which treats them with the necessary respect and allows the cook to monitor progress. Another useful tip to ensure success: before cooking, cover the langoustines with ice cubes and refrigerate; this will keep them fresh and firm up their flesh.

The mussels used in this recipe should be shiny, moist, and live. Any mussels that are open before cooking should be discarded, to avoid the risk of food poisoning. The freshness of the shellfish is obviously the best guarantee of quality for your soup.

The subsequent steps yield a beautifully smooth soup sufficiently concentrated by reduction, but not overly strong. Garlic, shallot and turmeric subtly enhance the flavor. Turmeric, incidentally, belongs to the ginger family. A traditional ingredient in curries and other Indian dishes, it is seldom available fresh, but is usually bought in dried, powdered form.

1. Shell the lagoustines. Refrigerate the tails, together with the pieces of fish. Set aside the shells for garnish. In separate covered pots, steam the mussels and cockles with ⅓ cup plus 1½ tbsp/100 ml white wine and half of the chopped shallots until they open. Drain, and strain the cooking liquid.

2. Finely chop 2 shallots. Peel and crush the garlic. Finely slice the white of leek and the half carrot. Heat the oil in a saucepan and sweat all the ingredients together with the tomato paste, stirring constantly. Add ⅓ cup plus 1½ tbsp/100 ml white wine, the shellfish cooking liquid, turmeric, and 4 cups/1 liter water and continue cooking.

and fish soup

3. Bring to a boil and simmer for 20 minutes, uncovered. Press through a strainer and reduce the liquid to 2¾–3½ cups/600–700 ml. Season and reserve. Cut the tomatoes into small cubes for a garnish.

4. Bring some water to a boil in a steamer, and steam the langoustines and the fish pieces for 2 minutes. Steam the shellfish for 30 seconds to reheat. Ladle the soup and the fish into shallow bowls. Garnish with tomatoes and parsley, croûtons and rouille.

Roast turbot fillet with

Preparation time: 45 minutes
Cooking time: 10 minutes
Difficulty: ⋆

Serves 4

One 4½ lb/2 kg turbot
1½ lb/650 g miniature squid
2 red bell peppers

2 tomatoes
juice of 1 lemon
½ head of garlic
7 tsp/35 g butter
¾ cup/200 ml olive oil
½ bunch flat-leaf parsley
salt
freshly ground pepper

This recipe brings together a number of quintessentially Mediterranean products: bell peppers, garlic, squid, and, of course, olive oil. Our chefs have chosen Italian olive oil, whose fruity flavor harmonizes marvelously with the fish, provided it is used with discretion.

Baby squid are particularly prized in Spain, and are available all year round. The squid are first pan-fried in smoking-hot oil until they brown: their juices will caramelize, producing a crisp coating that intensifies their flavor. The squid will shrink as they are frying. Once they are the size of garlic cloves, the red bell pepper, garlic and parsley should be added to the pan. Leave the garlic cloves whole and unpeeled, so that they hold their shape when cooked and look more attractive on the plate. None of these ingredients are particularly robust and care should be taken not to overcook them; try to use a nonstick pan.

The Pourcel brothers are great fans of "noble" Mediterranean fish. Here, they have opted for turbot, but you could substitute Dover sole or sea bass in this recipe. Remember that turbot is a very fragile fish, and should be cooked gently to avoid a disappointing taste and texture.

To give this dish an even stronger Mediterranean bias, other herbs, such as thyme or basil may be used.

1. Break up the garlic into individual cloves. Place the unpeeled cloves in a small saucepan with ⅓ cup plus 1½ tbsp/100 ml water and ¾ cup/200 ml oil and simmer until the cloves are tender inside and yield easily to thumb pressure.

2. Peel the bell peppers and cut into rings. Peel and seed the tomatoes and cut into small dice. Reserve. Sort through the squid; clean and wash thoroughly. Coarsely chop the parsley. Remove the ink sacks from the squid and drain the squid on paper towels.

pan-fried baby squid

3. Pour some olive oil into a pan and sauté the squid over high heat. Halfway through the cooking, add the red bell pepper and a little butter. Fry until the mixture is nicely colored. Add the parsley leaves and the cooked garlic cloves. Season and remove from the pan.

4. Fillet and skin the turbot and cut into 5½ oz/160 g portions. Pan-fry the fillets and season. Add the diced tomato and lemon juice to the squid, along with ¾ cup/200 ml of the oil in which the garlic was simmered. Arrange this mixture on plates and top with the turbot. Pour over the squid cooking juices.

Cod topped

Preparation time: 1 hour 30 minutes
Cooking time: 30 minutes
Difficulty: ✲✲

Serves 4

3¼ lb/1½ kg cod or pollack
7 oz/200 g sea salt
⅔ cup/150 ml fish stock
olive oil, juice of 2 lemons

For the ratatouille topping:

4½ oz/120 g mushrooms
4½ oz/120 g small onions
4½ oz/120 g zucchini
3½ oz/100 g red bell peppers
3½ oz/100 g yellow bell peppers
1 tbsp chopped flat-leaf parsley

For the sauce:
1 cup/250 g raw tomato purée
2 tsp cooked red bell pepper
2½ tbsp/40 ml lemon juice
2½ tbsp/40 ml sherry vinegar
3½ tbsp/50 ml extra-virgin olive oil
salt, freshly ground white pepper, cayenne pepper

For the sauce garnish:
16 black Niçois olives
16 small green olives
12 cloves preserved garlic
12 cherry tomatoes
tarragon, basil, chervil

To finish:
Assorted salad leaves (mesclun), chives, deep-fried thyme sprigs, fleur de sel, extra-virgin olive oil, olive oil for frying the thyme

Ratatouille is the surely the most famous example of Provençal cuisine, especially of the Nice area. A number of different versions exist, all of them evocative of the south of France. Here, Stéphane Raimbault commends to you his ratatouille, together with another southern French tradition: *aïoli*, the Provençal garlic mayonnaise, which he has given an interesting twist.

The basic concept of this recipe is to use the fresh cod to evoke salt cod by "marinating" it in sea salt. Cod is a fairly lean fish with very little waste.

The fish is filleted and "dry-marinated" in plain salt for about 15 minutes, depending on the size of the fillets. This process not only firms up the flesh of the cod, which tends to be flaky, but also ensures that the fish will be well seasoned.

Cut into tiny dice, the vegetables for the ratatouille do not take long to cook. They should remain crisp-tender and hold their shape, delighting the eyes as well as the palate.

The ratatouille topping envelops the cod fillets in a cloak of contrasting colors, aromas and flavors. The sauce, which contains bell peppers, garlic and olives, adds a final, distinctively Provençal touch to this substantial dish.

1. Fillet the cod and remove any stray bones. "Marinate" the fillets for about 15 minutes in sea salt. Rinse the fillets and cut into portion-sized pieces.

2. Cut the ingredients for the ratatouille into very small dice. Lightly sauté the vegetables in olive oil, beginning with the onions and bell peppers, then adding the mushrooms and zucchini. Add the parsley and correct the seasoning. Place in a covered container and refrigerate until needed.

with ratatouille

3. Season the cod fillets, cover with the ratatouille and place in an ovenproof dish. Pour in fish stock and lemon juice to half-cover. Bake for 5–6 minutes at 350 °F/180 °C.

4. For the sauce, purée the red bell peppers and mix with the other sauce ingredients. Add the garnish and spoon the sauce onto the plates. Place a cod fillet in the center of each plate and garnish with the mesclun, tied together with a chive.

Deep-fried hake with

Preparation time: 45 minutes
Cooking time: 10 minutes
Difficulty: ★

Serves 4

1¾ lb/800 g hake fillet
4 tbsp all-purpose flour
1 tbsp cream
1 tbsp egg white

For the garnish:
4½ oz/125 g mushrooms
¼ Savoy cabbage

½ tsp finely chopped garlic
½ tsp finely chopped fresh ginger root
1 tbsp vegetable oil

For the dressing:
½ oz/15 g fresh ginger root
2 tbsp wine vinegar
1 tbsp mushroom-flavored soy sauce or dark
soy sauce
1 tbsp chile sauce
2 tbsp vegetable oil
1 tbsp Asian sesame oil
½ bunch of cilantro
salt and freshly ground white pepper

Like whiting and herring, hake is a common fish of the North Atlantic and the Irish Sea, so it is hardly surprising that it once occupied a special place in the cuisine of the British Isles.

Try to buy fillets from a hake weighing 6½–8¾ lb/3–4 kg. A larger fish would be difficult to cook evenly, and the flavor of smaller fillets would be overpowered by the crispy skin during cooking.

The garnish consists of vegetables that are especially popular in Ireland: Savoy cabbage and cultivated mushrooms. Although local tastes do not run to cèpes or porcini, Paul Rankin still thrills at the memory of picking an incredible 66 lb/30 kg of cèpes there in just two hours.

Other green vegetables such as Swiss chard or spinach would also go well here.

The use of ginger in this vegetable accompaniment may come as something of a surprise. Measure the chopped ginger exactly, as its strong taste can eclipse the more subtle flavors of the other ingredients. Combine it sparingly with the soy and chile sauces and the sesame oil to add lightness to the dish.

Other spices may be used to flavor the dressing: cayenne pepper, black and white sesame seeds, garlic powder or curry powder. Use them with discretion, because it is really the fish that has the starring role in this recipe, and its delicate flavor should remain recognizable.

1. First, prepare the dressing. Put the ginger, cilantro, wine vinegar, soy and chile sauces into a small bowl, season with salt and pepper and whisk until the salt has dissolved. Add the vegetable and sesame oils in a thin stream, whisking constantly. Adjust the seasoning.

2. Shred the cabbage and blanch in boiling salted water for 1 minute; drain and refresh in cold water. Heat 1 tbsp oil in a pan, add the garlic and ginger and stir-fry over high heat. Add the cabbage and the sliced mushrooms and cook for 1 minute. Season with salt and pepper, remove from the heat and keep warm.

sesame-ginger dressing

3. Cut the hake fillets into 5 oz/150 g pieces and score the skin decoratively. Mix together the cream and egg white in a shallow bowl. Coat the fish with this mixture, then dredge with flour.

4. Heat the oil to 350 °F/180 °C. Add the fish and fry for 3 minutes on each side. Drain on paper towels. Divide the vegetables among 4 warm serving plates, top with the fish and pour the dressing around.

Sautéed pike fillets

Preparation time: 50 minutes
Cooking time: 30 minutes
Difficulty: ★

Serves 4

Four 6 oz/180 g pike fillets
2¼ lb/1 kg live crayfish
2 tbsp oil
2 tbsp butter
salt and freshly ground white pepper

For the sauce:
2 tbsp diced carrots
2 tbsp diced onions

2 cloves garlic
3 tbsp oil
1 tbsp tomato paste
2 tbsp cognac
6½ tbsp/100 ml white wine
1¼ cups/300 ml heavy cream

For the dressing:
¾ cup/200 ml vinaigrette
2 tomatoes
1 tsp crushed garlic
1 tsp chopped tarragon
1 tbsp chopped parsley
salt and freshly ground pepper
a few tarragon and chervil sprigs to garnish

In Canada, the home of our chef Paul Rankin's wife Jenny, pike is held in especially high esteem. It is also common in Ireland, where it is known as a "poor man's fish." In this recipe, Paul Rankin pairs the pike with crayfish to produce a fresh, flavorful dish, accompanied by a subtle dressing and a sauce with Mediterranean overtones.

The pike is recognizable by its green back and its almost pointy jaw. Among the most delicate of freshwater fish, it has very fine, firm, white flesh, which, however, can be somewhat bland-tasting. It can therefore be served with a well-seasoned sauce intended to "lift" the flavor of the fish. This sauce should be prepared with great care, following the instructions to the letter.

Enthusiastic crayfish breeders will recommend the Australian variety of this freshwater crustacean, the large, brown and rather fine-flavored *Cherux tenuimanus*. Others swear by the Louisiana crayfish.

If you can't get hold of any presentable pike, you can substitute any other freshwater fish that yields nice fillets.

1. Wash the crayfish and plunge into boiling salted water. Bring the water back to a boil and allow to simmer for barely 30 seconds. Remove from the heat and let rest for 4 minutes. Drain the crayfish, set aside the heads and crush them with a pestle in a bowl. Peel the tails and reserve.

2. Lightly brown the crushed heads for 3 minutes, then add the diced vegetables and garlic and cook for a further 2 minutes. Stir in the tomato paste, cognac and wine. Reduce by half. Add 4 cups/1 l water and simmer for 20 minutes. Press through a strainer and reduce the liquid to 1 cup/250 ml. Stir in the heavy cream and reduce to a creamy consistency.

with freshwater crayfish

3. Cut the fish into four 6 oz/180 g fillets, season, and pan-fry in a mixture of oil and butter for 3 minutes on each side. Peel and seed the tomatoes and cut into small dice. Pour the vinaigrette into a saucepan and whisk in the garlic and herbs. Add the diced tomato and mix well.

4. Reheat the crayfish tails in the dressing. Spoon some dressing onto heated plates, arrange the crayfish tails in a circle and spoon over some of the creamy sauce. Place a pike fillet in the center of each plate and garnish with tarragon and chervil.

Pike studded

Preparation time: 45 minutes
Cooking time: 20 minutes
Difficulty: ☆

Serves 4

One 3¼ lb/1½ kg pike
One 1¾ lb/800 g eel
2 gray shallots

½ cup/120 g butter
¾ cup/200 ml white Chinon wine
⅓ oz/10g *fleur de sel*
freshly ground pepper

An adaptable fish, pike has been on the menu for centuries in a great many guises. Medieval gourmets, fascinated by the voracity of this freshwater predator, nicknamed it "the great water-wolf." It was very much in vogue in the 16th century, frequently gracing the table of the French king.

Choose river pike for preference, since pike from ponds or lakes spends most of its life buried in the mud, and can taste accordingly.

Eel was at one time considered to be unhealthy. It is still wise to steer clear of excessively large specimens, which will have spent more time than younger eels migrating bteween the sea and freshwater, passing through swamps and possibly polluted ares in the process. These days, a

number of talented chefs have created complex and subtle dishes featuring eel.

In addition to cutting a fine figure in the famous fish stew, *matelote tourangelle*, eel can be very successfully paired with pike. As it is a highly perishable fish, eel should be kept alive until the last moment. Here it is sliced into short, thin strips that can be inserted into the pike fillets with a larding needle. This recipe combines some of the finest specialties of the Loire valley, enhancing the fish with the lively Chinon wine of which Rabelais was so fond.

Cook the pike carefully so it stays tender, and serve it piping hot on a bed of stewed white of leeks.

1. Fillet and skin the pike and remove all of its bones. Skin the eel, then fillet it and cut it into strips.

2. Divide the pike into 4 equal pieces. Using a larding needle, thread the pike fillets with the eel strips.

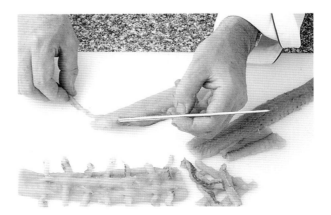

with eel

3. Melt some butter in an ovenproof dish and sweat the finely chopped shallots. Moisten with the wine. Place the pike fillets in the dish, sprinkle with fleur de sel, grind over some pepper and bake for about 6 minutes at 350 °F/180 °C, basting frequently.

4. Lift out the pike and transfer the cooking juices to a saucepan. Reduce by half. Whisk in the remaining butter. Dish up the pike fillets and pour over the sauce.

Sautéed langoustines with

Preparation time: 30 minutes
Cooking time: 3 minutes
Difficulty: *

Serves 4

24 langoustines
2 zucchini
8 cloves garlic
pinch of thyme
1 tsp/5 g chopped chives
1 tbsp/15 g butter
salt and freshly ground pepper

For the stock:
the langoustine heads
1 onion
1 medium carrot
1 bouquet garni
1 tbsp/15 g butter

For the marinade:
2 pinches of Madras curry powder
3½ tbsp/50 ml olive oil

Curry powder is not a single spice, but a mixture of various ones chosen according to the meat, fish or vegetable it will be used to season. It can consist of cardamom, turmeric, cumin, mustard seed, cloves and a good dose of cayenne pepper, ground together into a fine orange-yellow powder.

The proportions of the spices in curry powders vary a great deal, so you should give some thought as to which curry powder to use for a particular dish. This is particuarly important when preparing *desmoiselles*, as langoustines are called in Cherbourg. Jean-Claude Rigollet recommends the subtle but strong Madras curry powder.

Langoustines should really only be cooked live. If this is not possible, make sure that they are absolutely fresh and translucent. There should be 8-10 langoustines to the pound/15–20 langoustines to the kilo to yield the right size of tail.

Zucchini, with their delicate flesh and subtle taste, make a suitable accompaniment for these different nuances of flavor. A dish like this, however, seems to cry out for yet another piquant element. Our chef has therefore hit on a garlic *jus* whose potent aroma and flavor are unleashed by pounding the cloves in a mortar. Just follow the instructions, and you'll have no trouble in creating this light, aromatic dish.

1. Separate the langoustine heads from the tails. Dice the onion and carrot and gently brown them in butter with the langoustine heads. Pour in enough water to cover, add the bouquet garni and reduce by a quarter. Pass through a fine strainer and keep warm.

2. Meanwhile, shell the raw langoustine tails. Wash the first zucchini and cut into thin strips. Roll each langoustine in a zucchini strip and fasten with a toothpick.

curry and garlic juices

3. Lightly salt and pepper these kebabs. Marinate for 15 minutes in olive oil and Madras curry powder. Lightly sauté the crushed garlic cloves in 1 tbsp butter and moisten with the langoustine stock. Cook this garlic jus over low heat for 10 minutes.

4. Cut the second zucchini into fine julienne and sauté together with the thyme in some olive oil. Heat a little olive oil in another pan and sauté the langoustine tails over high heat. Place a mound of zucchini in the center of each plate and surround with the langoustine kebabs. Pour over some garlic jus and sprinkle with chives.

Bourride with Dover sole

Preparation time: *1 hour*
Cooking time: *2 hours*
Difficulty: ✫✫

Serves 4

3¼ lb/1½ kg Dover sole fillets
12 langoustines

For the Dover sole and langoustine stock:
heads and bones of the Dover sole
heads and bones of the langoustines
1 onion, 1 carrot and 1 leek
½ fennel bulb
1 rib celery
1 bulb garlic
3½ tbsp/50 g butter
3½ tbsp/50 ml olive oil

For the sauce:
2 cloves garlic, 6½ tbsp/100 g butter
3½ tbsp/50 ml cream
3½ tbsp/50 ml olive oil

For the vegetables:
7 oz/200 g carrots, celery, zucchini
14 oz/400 g potatoes

For the honey caramel:
4 tsp/20 g honey
8 tsp/40 g butter
4 tsp/20 ml sherry vinegar

For the garnish:
chives
chervil leaves

Despite hailing from the Ardèche in southern France, Michel Rochedy wasn't always a devotee of olive oil. This recipe, however, would convert all but the most hardened skeptics. Used in conjunction with the butter that subtly underscores the sweetness of the langoustines, olive oil makes its mark in this recipe, adding a distinctly Mediterranean flavor.

As ever, the success of this dish is dependent upon the quality of the ingredients used. Rochedy always prepares this bourride with freshly landed Dover sole, and with langoustines from the bassin d'Arcachon, which he rates highly. He strongly recommends that if you are not planning to cook them immediately, you separate the langoustine heads from the tails, wrap the latter in plastic wrap and place them in the freezer for up to 3 days.

To caramelize the langoustine tails, melt the butter very slowly in a nonstick pan, then raise the heat to high and sear the crustaceans. The process is quickly finished off by adding the honey and deglazing the pan with sherry vinegar.

The Dover soles are done in no time at all. They should be cooked until barely done, so their flesh will stay nice and tender. Special care should be taken in preparing the stock, which has the task of setting off the individual components of this dish to best effect without overpowering them. Don't forget the garlic, which lends this dish a genuinely Provençal touch.

1. Fillet the Dover soles and shell the langoustines. Melt the olive oil and butter in a pan and gently brown the shells and fish bones together with the finely cut-up stock ingredients. Pour in enough water to half-cover and cook over low heat for 2 hours. Strain. Cut the carrot, celery and zucchini into sticks. Peel the potatoes and trim into olive shapes. Cook the vegetables separately and keep warm.

2. Place the sole fillets in a buttered dish and season. Moisten with half the stock and poach the fish (it should be just barely done).

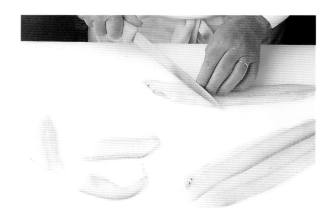

and caramelized langoustines

3. Prepare the sauce: Reduce the remaining stock by half, then add 2 garlic cloves and the cream. Boil for 1 minute, then whisk in the butter, followed by the olive oil. Purée and strain the sauce. Correct seasoning.

4. Pan-fry the langoustine tails in butter until they are golden. Add the honey and deglaze with 1 tbsp sherry vinegar. Serve the soles and langoustines in shallow bowls, adding the vegetables. Pour over the sauce and garnish with a few chives and chervil leaves.

John Dory fillet

Preparation time: 10 minutes
Cooking time: 10 minutes
Difficulty: ✶

Serves 4

Two 1¾ lb/800 g John Dory
4 artichokes
4 large potatoes (optional)

¼ cup/60 g butter
¼ cup/60 ml cream
3½ tbsp/50 ml cognac
2 cups/500 ml oil
2 tsp/10 g white peppercorns
salt and freshly ground pepper
a few chervil leaves

John Dory, a maritime fish of the *Zeidae* family, prefers rocky coasts in European latitudes and in Africa, and is caught by trawlers in fairly deep waters. It is much prized for its supple, firm and flavorful white fillets. It is occasionally imported to the United States.

Unlike black peppercorns, which are the dried immature fruit of the pepper, white peppercorns come from the ripe fruit. They are soaked after harvesting and their outer coat is rubbed off. In ancient times, pepper was brought to Europe by Arab traders from Malabar, and was literally worth its weight in gold. Its heyday came toward the end of the Middle Ages, after the Portuguese discovered new centers of cultivation in Sumatra. This valuable commodity even served as the dowery for Isabella of Spain when she married Charles V of Spain.

The artichoke started out its illustrious career as a medicinal plant and then switched to the gastronomic fast track. The sliced artichoke hearts take on the most amazing shapes when fried, which can then be arranged on top of the largest leaves to delight your dinner guests.

1. Fillet the fish. Peel the potatoes (if using) and cut into French fries. Deep-fry the potatoes or toss with oil and oven bake.

2. Coarsely crush the peppercorns. Place the fish fillets on top and press down firmly. Repeat for the other side. Season with salt.

with cracked pepper

3. Pan-fry the fish fillets in clarified butter for 4–5 minutes on each side. Remove from the pan and keep warm. Blanch the artichoke leaves and refresh under cold running water. Using a vegetable mandoline, shave the artichoke hearts into wafer-thin slices.

4. Deglaze the sauté pan with cognac. Add the cream and butter and allow to thicken. Strain the sauce and correct the seasoning. Deep-fry the artichoke chips for several minutes. Heat the plates, spoon on some sauce and top with the fish fillets. Garnish with the artichoke chips, reheated artichoke leaves and chervil leaves.

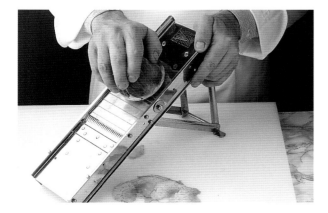

Pikeperch-and-frog

Preparation time: 15 minutes
Cooking time: 20 minutes
Difficulty: ★★

Serves 4

1 pikeperch
20 pairs frogs' legs
2 oz/60 g fresh goat cheese

1 shallot
15 spinach leaves
2 tbsp/30 g butter
16 cups/4 l light cream
4 cups/1 l heavy cream
3½ tbsp/50 ml white wine
salt and freshly ground pepper

One method of preparing food in little parcels is a specialty of Marseilles, there known as *pieds et paquets* ("feet and parcels"). The traditional dish, popular in the Rhône valley, consists of lamb's feet and little parcels of tripe. The trick is to seal these parcels in such a manner that they do not burst open during their long simmering period in white wine and stock.

The similarities with the traditional dish, however, begin and end with the presentation of the ingredients in parcels. For this recipe we use pikeperch, which is common in the watercourses of southern France. If you are not buying the fish in fillets, choose a good stiff specimen covered by a thin, slippery film, a guarantee of freshness. Filleting the fish is not difficult, as it has relatively few bones.

In our version of this recipe, frogs' legs take the place of tripe as the filling for the parcels. Look for very firm, stiff legs, once more an indicator of the freshness that will guarantee the success of this dish. They should be cooked initially just long enough to allow them to be boned, because they will receive a second cooking in the pikeperch parcels.

The pikeperch fillets, which are stuffed and held together in a little parcel with toothpicks, will surprise and delight your dinner guests. The effect is enhanced by cream sauce of some character, enriched with goat cheese.

1. Melt some butter in a braising pan and stew the finely chopped shallot until transparent. Add the frogs' legs and sweat them briefly. Add the white wine and cream to cover. Cook, uncovered, for 4–5 minutes. Remove the frogs' legs and bone them, reserving the meat.

2. Fillet the pikeperch and slice into cutlets. Sweat the spinach in butter for 2 minutes only, so that it keeps its bright green color.

parcels with goat cheese

3. Lay the cutlets out on the work surface and season with salt and pepper. Place a spoonful of frog meat onto each cutlet. Draw up into a parcel and close carefully with toothpicks. Bring the light cream to a boil and, off the heat, and the fish parcels. Place in the oven for 4–5 minutes. Beat the heavy cream until it forms soft peaks.

4. Remove the parcels from the oven and keep warm. Mix the goat cheese (in pieces) and the whipped cream into the cream in which the parcels were cooked. Lay 3 spinach leaves out flat in the center of each plate and place a fish parcel on top of each. Pour the cream sauce all around. Place under the broiler until the sauce turns an appetizing golden brown.

Sea bream in salt

Preparation time: 35 minutes
Cooking time: 20 minutes
Difficulty: ★★

Serves 4

One 2¼ lb/1 kg sea bream
1¾ lb/800 g coarse salt
4 sprigs thyme

For the sauce:
3½ oz/100 g salt-cod entrails, boiled and cut into ⅜ in/1 cm lengths
4 pieces blood sausage
1 tbsp *sofrito* (tomato, onion and thyme softened in olive oil)

¾ cup/200 ml entrail cooking-water
¾ cup/200 ml water

For the *picada*:
blanched almonds
1 clove garlic
a few leaves flat-leaf parsley

For the *sanfaina*(Catalan ratatouille):
1 onion
1 green bell pepper
1 small eggplant
1 zucchini
2 ripe tomatoes

To our knowledge, Catalonia is the only place in the world where salt-cod entrails (*tripas de bacalao*) are eaten. The intestines are first desalted, then boiled. Their gelatinous texture, together with the cooking water, yields an unusual but very flavorful substance. But this is not the end of the gastronomic surprises in store for you. After you have discovered the delights of *tripas de bacalao*, you will have the pleasure of tasting *picada* and *sanfaina*, two specialties that are virtually unknown outside their native Catalonia.

In principle, the quick cooking process to which the sea bream is subjected is simplicity itself. The fillets, laid skin-side down on a bed of coarse salt, are gradually penetrated by the cooking heat, while their own juices mingle with and partially dissolve the salt. The result is extremely flavorful. Only certain kinds of fish—those with a tough enough skin—can withstand this treatment. If you can't get hold of sea bream, then sea bass will fit the bill nicely. On no account forget the sprig of thyme, whose flavor unfolds beautifully in the covered casserole.

The *picada* has a few points in common with *sofrito*, but in addition contains ground roasted almonds and often pine nuts as well, yielding a piquant mixture of unusual flavors. As for the *sanfaina*, there cannot be a single Catalan chef or home cook in Barcelona who doesn't make his or her own version of this relative of ratatouille.

1. Desalt the cod intestines for 10–12 hours in a sieve. Drain and bring to a boil in liquid consisting of ½ fresh water and ½ desalting water. Fillet the sea bream and cut into 7 oz/200 g portions. Cover the bottom of a covered casserole with a layer of lightly moistened coarse salt. Place the fillets on top.

2. Place a sprig of thyme on each fillet. Cover the casserole and cook over high heat for 7 minutes. Remove from heat and wait 3 minutes before lifting off the lid.

with Catalan *sanfaina*

3. For the sanfaina, finely slice the onion and sauté until golden brown. Add the peeled, seeded tomatoes. Roast the green bell pepper, then peel and cut into thin slices. Do the same with the zucchini and eggplant. Season the mixture and cook over low heat. To make the picada, roast the blanched almonds, then pound in a mortar with the garlic clove and parsley.

4. For the sofrito, heat some olive oil in a pan and add the onions, whole tomatoes and thyme, sautéing until the mixture is very soft. Purée, and add half of the water in which the intestines were cooked, plus the picada and cubed blood sausage. Serve the sea-bream fillets in the casserole in which they were cooked, and the sanfaina and the sauce separately as accompaniments.

Gurnard with cumin

Preparation time: 15 minutes
Cooking time: 8 minutes
Difficulty: ✶

Serves 4

One 4½ lb/2 kg red gurnard
4 artichokes
1 large zucchini
a little extra-virgin olive oil
salt and ground cumin

For the parsley sauce:
2 cups/500 ml extra-virgin olive oil
a few sprigs of flat-leaf parsley

The gurnard, or sea robin, which makes a grunting noise when landed, is one of the 8–10 varieties in the *Triglidae* family (so called because of the triangular shape of its members). The most common variety is the pink-bellied red gurnard, whose ease of preparation makes it a boon to cooks. It can also be prepared Catalan-style, accompanied by a *sofrito* of garlic, onions and tomatoes.

The recipe presented here by Santi Santamaria is so simple: The fish is grilled and finished in the oven, and the artichokes are sautéed. The most unusual thing about the dish is the light sprinkling of cumin powder over the fish fillets. According to Spanish tradition, it is the Moors who, occupying portions of the Iberian peninsula until its reconquest at the end of the 14th century, were responsible for introducing this distinctive-tasting spice to Europe. Frequently found in Indian, North African and Latin American cuisine, cumin seed is less commonly used to season fish dishes. Its relative, caraway, is very popular throughout the Netherlands, the German-speaking countries and Scandinavia.

Cumin is quite a pungent-tasting spice, and should be used sparingly so as not to mask the true flavor of the fish. Sprinkle it over the fillets just before they are done to impart a subtle flavor. Extra parsley may be added to the sauce to give it a brighter color; substitute tarragon if you prefer.

1. Clean the fish and cut into four 9 oz/250 g portions. Trim the artichokes and cook in water acidulated with lemon juice until al dente. Drain upside down. Cut the artichoke hearts into small pieces and sauté in olive oil until golden brown.

2. To make the sauce, strip the parsley leaves from their stalks, then wash the leaves and spin dry. Transfer to a blender and purée to an emulsion with 2 cups/500 ml olive oil.

and artichokes

3. Salt the fish fillets, sear on a hot grill and transfer to the oven for 8 minutes. Sprinkle with the ground cumin just before they are done.

4. Thinly cut the zucchini on the diagonal. Just before serving, dip in a light batter and deep-fry in hot oil until golden brown. Arrange several pieces of artichoke and a fish fillet on each plate and pour the parsley sauce around. Garnish with fried zucchini slices.

Preparation time:	25 minutes
Cooking time:	40 minutes
Difficulty:	✶✶

Serves 4

4 sea-bass fillets
4 turbot fillets
4 John Dory fillets
4 crayfish
4 langoustines
generous 1 lb/500 g mussels

2 large potatoes
2 cloves garlic
1 large onion
2 anchovy fillets preserved in salt
6 tbsp extra-virgin olive oil
1 cup/250 ml water
2 tbsp white wine
1 bunch of parsley
1 tomato, diced
garlic *croûtons* (made by rubbing a clove of
garlic on toasted slices of baguette)
salt and freshly ground pepper

One fish does not a teeming ocean make, so Ezio Santin has no scruples about mixing different species, especially when it is a question of delighting our taste buds while celebrating the beneficence of the sea. His *burrida* or Italian seafood stew is packed with fish, crustaceans and mollusks and brilliantly revives the old traditions of the Ligurian and Sardinian fishermen whose honorable pursuit dates back to ancient Roman times.

Burrida was once a fisherman's dish, consisting of whatever fish he set aside to feed his family rather than sell. Its composition would thus vary substantially depending on the day's catch. Its Provençal cousin, the *bourride*, almost always contained monkfish.

Mussels do not appear in the original recipes, but Ezio Santin accords them quite a special role, since their cooking liquor is used as the basis for the rest of the dish. The method recommended here preserves the distinctive flavor of each ingredient: Each fish is prepared separately—which is only logical when you consider their widely varying textures. Be sure that the anchovies are rinsed thoroughly so that they are not too salty.

Although the combination of turbot, sea bass and John Dory is not written in stone, it does make for a well-balanced range of flavors, which you could supplement according to taste with slightly fattier fish such as mackerel.

1. Cut the fish fillets into 1½ oz/40 g pieces; remove all bones and trim and clean the fish. Cook the crayfish and langoustines in boiling salted water and shell. Reserve the cooking water.

2. Cut the anchovy fillets into small pieces and gently sauté with a crushed clove of garlic in 2 tbsp olive oil for 2–3 minutes over low heat. Add the chopped onion and the diced potato and continue to sweat. Moisten with water and cook for 5–6 minutes or until the potatoes are nearly done.

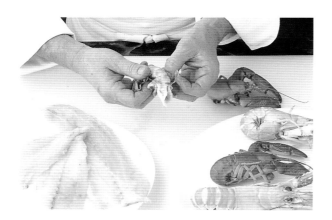

pesce misto

3. In another saucepan, heat 2 tbsp olive oil with a clove of garlic and the parsley. Add the mussels and the white wine. Cover and cook for about 2–3 minutes, or until the mussels open. Strain the mussel liquor over the potatoes and onions. Correct seasoning. Brown the fish fillets in the remaining oil.

4. Add all the ingredients except for the mussels to the stock in which the crayfish and langoustines were cooked. Raise the heat and cook until done. Serve the burrida in shallow bowls with garlic croûtons, the mussels and some finely diced tomato.

Sea bream with lime

Preparation time: 15 minutes
Cooking time: 4–6 minutes,
     according to fillet thickness
Difficulty: *

Serves 4

Four 9 oz/250 g sea bream fillets
20 cherry tomatoes
2 medium zucchini
capers

3½ tbsp/50 ml extra-virgin olive oil
2 tbsp butter
1 sprig of rosemary, chopped
1 clove garlic
1 lime
1 lemon
dried oregano and fresh mint
salt
freshly ground pepper

The best recipes aren't necessarily those with the most ingredients. Rather, it is the judicious combination of a few top-quality raw materials that creates the really memorable dishes. This is why Nadia Santini has decided on a simple accompaniment to the sea bream.

Highly rated by the Roman epicure Apicius, who devoted numerous recipes to it, sea bream abounds in the Mediterranean, and is prized by gourmets of this region for its delicate white flesh and distinctive flavor. It should be remembered, though, that this is a very fragile fish, which requires careful cooking to preserve its fine flavor and keep it intact.

Capers, a quintessentially southern European seasoning, harmonize beautifully with sea bream, as with most white fish. If possible, use capers that have been preserved in salt rather than vinegar, to avoid a clash of tastes with the butter in which the fish is browned. A little chopped fresh rosemary sprinkled on top of the fillets as they cook will pleasantly bridge the gap between the delicacy of the fish and the tartness of the capers.

Like other citrus fruits, limes are richj in vitamin C. Choose small firm ones for optimum freshness and tang. The cherry tomatoes lend a bright flavor as well as color to the dish. There are red, yellow and orange varieties available.

If your fishmonger cannot get sea bream for you, this dish could also be made with another variety of white fish, such as a sea bass.

1. Cut off the very top of each cherry tomato. Sprinkle the tomatoes with some oregano and salt and drizzle with a little olive oil. Place in the oven for 5 minutes.

2. Cut the zucchini lengthwise into thin slices and sauté in olive oil until golden brown. Roll up each slice and place a mint leaf on top of each. Keep warm.

zest and capers

3. Melt a little butter in a nonstick pan. Add the chopped rosemary, grated lemon zest, garlic, capers and fish fillets. Season with salt and pepper.

4. Turn the fish and cook for 3 minutes on the other side. Place a fillet in the center of each plate, arranging 5 cherry tomatoes and a few zucchini rolls around it. Top the fish with a few strips of lime zest and some capers.

Salt cod with cilantro

Preparation time: *15 minutes*
Cooking time: *45 minutes*
Difficulty: ✶✶

Serves 4

Four 10½ oz/300 g slices salt cod (desalted
for 48 hours)
7 oz/200 g small potatoes
2 tbsp/30 g butter
2½ cups/600 ml olive oil
1 cup/250 ml milk
6½ tbsp/100 g coarse salt
salt and freshly ground pepper

For the vegetable topping:
2 cloves garlic
2 small onions
3 ripe tomatoes
1 bunch of cilantro
1 bunch of flat-leaf parsley
salt and freshly ground pepper

No one knows who first thought of preserving cod in salt, although the matter has been hotly disputed for centuries. The Portuguese and Spanish winegrowers certainly began to make use of this method a very long time ago, drying and salting this fish for later use.

Your first task will be to acquire the salt cod most suited for this recipe. Although, generally speaking, it is customary to serve modest-sized portions of this fish, this recipe requires as large a piece as possible, since the thicker it is the better it will taste. The Portuguese have literally hundreds of different ways to cook salt cod, and this is one of the more substantial ones.

How to explain the manner in which the Portuguese deal with the *a murro* (literally, "punched") potato? First, it is baked in coarse salt. Then, however, the cook deals it a vicious blow with the fist as soon as it emerges from the oven. Choose small varieties of potato such as "Charlotte" or "Roseval," which will stand up best to this heavy-handed treatment.

The vegetable and herb topping, which should taste strongly of garlic and cilantro, will enhance the flavor of the fish admirably, provided that the ingredients are measured carefully rather than being thrown together in random quantities.

1. Soak the cod for 48 hours to remove excess salt, changing the water several times during this period. Pat the fish dry and place in a high-sided dish. Pour the milk over and set aside for 1 hour.

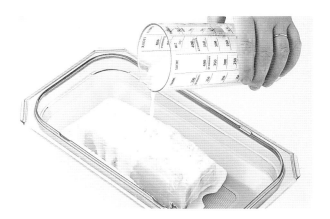

2. Remove the fish from the milk and pat dry with a cloth. Place the olive oil and the fish in an ovenproof dish. Bake the potatoes at 400 °F/200 °C for 30 minutes on a bed of coarse salt. Remove from the oven, brush off the salt and punch each potato flat with a single blow.

and *a murro* potatoes

3. To make the vegetable topping, chop the garlic, cilantro, parsley, onion and tomatoes, combine in a bowl and season with salt and pepper.

4. Top the fish with the vegetable mixture and dot with 2–3 tbsp butter. Bake at 400 °F/200 °C for 45 minutes. Place a portion of fish in the center of each plate and surround with the potatoes.

Fillet of Dover sole

Preparation time: 30 minutes
Cooking time: 35 minutes
Difficulty: ★★

Serves 4

3 Dover soles
10½ oz/300 g littleneck clams
14 oz/200 g pink shrimp
3½ oz/100 g rice
⅔ cup/150 ml *crème fraîche*

For the sauce:
1 onion
1 tomato
3½ oz/100 g small gray shrimp
3½ tbsp/50 g butter
salt and freshly ground pepper

Like everyone else, the fish-loving Portuguese consider Dover sole to be a prime-quality food. Here Maria Santos Gomes suggests a simple and delicious preparation that will delight both you and your dinner guests.

Dover-sole fillet has quite a supple texture, making it suitable for certain treatments that other more fragile fish would not withstand. According to Santos Gomes, sea bass falls into the same category. Once you have rolled up each fillet around its shrimp filling and secured it with a toothpick, you have excellent *paupiettes* that will stand up successfully to cooking without losing taste or texture.

The proper cohesion between these *paupiettes* and their accompanying sauce is achieved by the little gray shrimp. The sauce should be left to simmer for quite a while, because its success hinges on the various flavors melding properly. So take your time, and only add the *crème fraîche* at the last moment.

Purists might insist that Dover sole deserves to be paired with finer shellfish than the ones suggested here. Lobster and langoustines would be fine in this dish, provided that the sauce is not so highly seasoned as to mask their flavor.

1. First, prepare the sauce: Finely cut up the onion and sauté until golden. Add the quartered tomatoes, followed by the gray shrimp. Cover and sweat for 15 minutes.

2. Wash the clams in 3–4 changes of water. Place in a pot with water to cover, bring to a boil, and cook over high heat until they open. Strain the cooking water into the pan with the shrimp sauce. Bring the sauce to a boil, then purée in a blender and strain.

with shellfish sauce

3. Shell the pink shrimp. Fillet the soles and season. Top the fillets with the shrimp and roll up, fastening with a toothpick.

4. Place the paupiettes in a braising pan. Add the sauce, the crème fraîche and the clams, and simmer over low heat for 10 minutes. Arrange the fish rolls and clams on plates and pour over the sauce. Serve with rice separately.

Greek-style sea-

Preparation time: 30 minutes
Cooking time: 20 minutes
Difficulty: ★★

Serves 4

4 sea bream
14 oz/400 g celery
4 small tomatoes
3 medium carrots
3 onions

1 lemon
2 egg yolks
6½ tbsp/100 ml olive oil
6½ tbsp/100 ml white wine
1 pinch of cornstarch
¾ cup/200 ml *crème fraîche*
1 bunch of parsley
cilantro
saffron threads
salt and freshly ground pepper
butter

This dish is the perfect opportunity to become acquainted with one of the great classics of Greek cuisine, *avgolemono* sauce. Lamb in particular is often prepared with this egg and lemon sauce, giving body to the most delicate flavor combinations. To ensure success, you will need egg yolks that are absolutely fresh and the essential pinch of cornstarch to bind the sauce at the last moment.

Nikolaos Sarantos gives the starring role in this production to sea bream, although purists would never dream of using this famous sauce in anything but a lamb fricassee. In mitigation, let it be said that the sauce has been modified

slightly with the addition of saffron, that costly spice that has been prized since ancient times. In Roman mythology Jupiter even bedded down on saffron. Nikolaos Sarantos , uses it sparingly, to impart just the right golden tone to the sauce. Like him, you should avoid powdered saffron.

Olive oil has no competition in Greece. From an early age, Greek children are given bread dunked in olive oil and sprinkled with salt. The memory of this delicacy haunts them so that when they grow up and become chefs, they never fail to incorporate the aromatic oil in their favorite dishes.

1. Fillet the sea bream; reserve the bones. Place the parsley and the sliced carrots and onions in a saucepan and gently sweat in a little butter. Add the fish bones, moisten with white wine and simmer until the vegetables are soft. Press through a fine strainer.

2. Reduce the sauce and add the crème fraîche. Wash the celery and cut into thin strips; blanch and refresh under cold water. Glaze the tomatoes under the broiler. Season the fish fillets and set aside.

bream fricassee

3. Finish the sauce by binding it with the egg yolks and a pinch of cornstarch, and seasoning with the saffron and lemon juice. Deep-fry the celery strips.

4. Steam the sea bream fillets for 4–5 minutes. Pour the sauce onto the plates, top with the fish fillets and arrange the celery strips, broiled tomatoes and a few cilantro leaves all around. Garnish the edges of the plate with a few saffron threads.

Grouper with Naoussa

Preparation time: 1 hour
Cooking time: 15 minutes
Difficulty: ✷✷

Serves 4

4 medium eggplants
2¼ lb/1 kg grouper
5 oz/150 g each zucchini and potatoes
3 oz/80 g carrots
3 oz/80 g red bell pepper
4 tomatoes

2 cloves garlic
a little olive oil
oil for deep-frying
salt and freshly ground pepper
dill tips for garnishing

For the sauce:
¾ cup/200 ml *Naoussa boutari* (Greek red wine)
¾ cup/200 ml fish stock
a little butter

If you are not yet familiar with Naoussa wine, then it is time that you got to know this red nectar. The powerful flavor of this wine, particularly if it has been allowed to age, makes it ideal for this recipe, in which the fish is prepared *matelote* style (stewed in wine with onions). Note the Franco-Greek character of this dish, with the typically Greek stuffed eggplants on the one hand, and a very Gallic red-wine sauce on the other.

The grouper is known for abundant flesh that makes excellent eating. Grouper yields good fillets, and the bouquet of the red wine makes up for any imperfections, succeeding in conjunction with the eggplant in harmoniously melding all of the individual flavors.

To keep the eggplant "boats" nice and firm, the hollowed-out eggplant halves should be strewn with coarse salt and left to degorge overnight, then deep-fried. The boats will be filled with a mixture of finely diced vegetables and new potatoes.

The grouper can quite happily be replaced by a sea bass— or even milk-fed lamb, so highly prized by Greek gourmets.

1. Hollow out the eggplants, leaving a ⅛ in/½ cm thickness of flesh for the "boat." Deep-fry in plenty of olive oil and place on a grill upside down to drain.

2. Wash, scale and fillet the grouper, then remove all remaining bones. Cut the fillets into large cubes and sauté briefly in olive oil. Season.

wine in eggplant boats

3. Deglaze the pan with some red wine and cook for about 10 minutes. For the sauce, reduce the wine and fish stock by one third, strain and whisk in some butter. Cut all of the vegetables into coarse cubes and blanch separately.

4. Sauté the vegetables in butter. Fill the eggplants alternately with fish and vegetables, pour the sauce over and garnish with vegetable cubes and dill sprigs.

Monkfish in a shellfish

Preparation time: 2 hours
Cooking time: 30 minutes
Difficulty: ★★★

Serves 4

One 3¼ lb/1½ kg monkfish tail
1¾ oz/50 g pikeperch fillet
14 oz/400 g cultivated mussels
14 oz/400 g littleneck clams
½ egg white
4 tsp/20 ml heavy cream
1 cup/250 g butter
1 loaf white bread (unsliced)
¼ cup/60 ml olive oil
2 cloves garlic
1 large bunch of tarragon

1 bunch of flat-leaf parsley
1 sprig of thyme and rosemary
salt, freshly ground pepper, lemon

For the *mirepoix*:
2 shallots, garlic, ¼ leek
½ fennel bulb, 2 ribs celery
zest of 1 orange; 1 tomato
6½ tbsp/100 ml white wine,
2 tsp/10 ml pastis

For the carrot sauce:
generous 1 lb/500 g carrots
a little sugar
6½ tbsp/100 ml cream
6½ tbsp/100 ml chicken stock
cilantro, tarragon
8 tsp/40 g butter
orange zest

For the tarragon *coulis*:
2 tbsp/30 g butter
3½ tbsp/50 ml shellfish stock

Fritz Schilling admits to a weakness for the Mediterranean, where light and *joie de vivre* are so eloquently reflected in the colors, aromas and flavors of the cuisine. In this dish with Mediterranean overtones, the sweet carrot, the crisp crust and the tender monkfish flesh are placed on a bed of flavorful sauce that discreetly enhances the fish.

The monkfish crust is made from unsliced white bread with its crusts removed. Slightly stale (2-day-old) bread is best, as it is easier to cut into thin slices that do not fall apart. The size of these slices will obviously determine the cut of the monkfish fillet, which must usually be squeezed into shape before it can be rolled up like a cigarette. (The monkfish is supple enough to permit this treatment.) Mollusks are used for the stuffing; they are more varied-tasting, chewier and less expensive than crustaceans.

The carrot sauce should have the purity and uniformity of the light in the Mediterranean. The lightly caramelized carrots develop a subtle complexity of flavor. Puréed, they yield a bright, vivid liquid with a denser, sweeter taste. Once the sauce has been seasoned with cilantro, tarragon and orange zest, then carefully strained, this dish hands you sunshine on a plate.

1. To prepare the sauce, slice one carrot into fine julienne and deep-fry. Cook the remaining carrots in a covered pot over low heat with butter, salt, sugar and chicken stock. Add the cilantro, tarragon and orange zest. Set aside 4 carrots in a little of their cooking liquid. Add the cream to the remaining carrots, then purée the mixture and strain.

2. For the tarragon coulis, purée ⅓ of the parsley and ⅔ of the tarragon in a little water. Strain into a pot and bring to a boil. Cook the shellfish with the diced vegetables until they open. Drain, reserving the cooking liquor. Thicken the liquor with a beurre manié. Add to the coulis, whisk in 4 tsp/20 g butter and season.

crust with carrot sauce

3. Make a classic mousse with the pikeperch fillet. Set aside a few shellfish for the garnish, then shell and coarsely chop the rest and mix with the pikeperch mousse. Trim the crusts from the bread, then cut into 1/8 in/3 mm thick slices and lay on top of some plastic wrap.

4. Spread the slices of bread with the mousse, top with the monkfish fillets, season, and roll up tightly using the plastic wrap. Remove the wrap, then brown the fillets in oil with a little butter, garlic and thyme for 8–10 minutes. Spoon some sauce slightly off-center on the plates and decorate with a spiral of tarragon coulis. Place the monkfish fillets on top and garnish with the shellfish and the carrots.

Pikeperch with mayonnaise

Preparation time: 1 hour 30 minutes
Cooking time: 30 minutes
Difficulty: ✫✫

Serves 4

One 4½ lb/2 kg pikeperch
4 cloves garlic
1⅔ cup/400 ml Hermitage wine
cornstarch
1 sprig of wild fennel
2 basil leaves
1 sprig each of thyme and rosemary

For the ratatouille:
1 red and 1 yellow bell pepper

1 small eggplant
1 zucchini
4 small onions

For the mayonnaise:
2 egg yolks
4 tsp/20 ml fish stock
¼ cup/60 ml olive oil
salt, freshly ground pepper, lemon

For the tempura batter:
2 tbsp/30 g all-purpose flour
2 tbsp/30 g cornstarch
1 tsp/5 ml oil
water and white wine

Highly prized in Central Europe, whre it probably originated, the pikeperch is used here to demonstrate Fritz Schilling's skill with fish. This freshwater predator is at home in lakes, rivers and ponds. As a food, it is highly, and must be used within 48 hours of being caught. If it isn't slightly stiff and absolutely fresh, avoid it.

If pikeperch is not available, you may substitute another type of fish with similar qualities, even a sea fish such as turbot or sea bass. The recommended cooking method, pan-frying with herbs, is ideal for these fillets, which are served with mayonnaise.

For the "ratatouille" you'll need medium-sized vegetables, which should be cooked separately according to variety. The vegetables should still be crisp-tender before frying, so that they will retain an attractive texture and color when served. Fritz Schilling uses red and yellow bell peppers here in an allusion to two of the three colors of the German flag.

Before they are deep-fried, the vegetables are dipped in tempura batter; spearing the vegetable bits on toothpicks makes things easier and helps them keep their shape when fried.

1. Reduce the wine to ⅓ cup plus 1½ tbsp/100 ml. Bind with the cornstarch and add the basil and fennel. Simmer for 5 minutes and strain. Clean and fillet the pikeperch.

2. Make a mayonnaise with the egg yolks, olive oil, fish stock, salt, pepper and a little lemon juice. Blister the bell peppers under the broiler and remove their skins. Cut the vegetables into large chunks.

and ratatouille tempura

3. Combine all of the tempura batter ingredients. Lightly sauté the vegetable chunks. Pan-fry the pikeperch fillets with a clove of garlic and a sprig of rosemary and thyme. Dust all of the sautéed vegetables with flour, then dip in the tempura batter and deep-fry in olive oil.

4. Spoon a dollop of mayonnaise onto each plate, pipe with the red-wine sauce and use a toothpick to create an attractive pattern. Place a piece of pikeperch to the side and scatter the fried vegetables attractively all around.

Red mullet fillet with

Preparation time: 45 minutes
Cooking time: 20 minutes
Difficulty: ★★

Serves 4

4 red mullet fillets
7 oz/200 g bone marrow
1 sprig of thyme
¾ oz/20 g cumin seed
6½ tbsp/100 ml olive oil
sea salt
salt and freshly ground pepper

For the sauce:
1 shallot
3½ tbsp/50 g butter
1¼ cups/300 ml red wine (Pinot noir)
6½ tbsp/100 ml fish stock
¾ cup/200 ml veal demiglace

An essential ingredient of many versions of bouillabaisse, red mullet boasts a number of advantages: it is not only very lean, but is also rich in protein, iodine and phosphorus. Moreover, it is the tastiest member of the *Mullidae* or goatfish family, which gets its name from the beardlike chin barbels sported by its 50 or so different species. Try to buy the fish whole, because its liver is a great delicacy. If red mullet is unavailable, this recipe can also be made with pieces of sea bass.

You will also need a good marrow bone, from which you may remove the contents in advance if this is more convenient. The marrow should be soaked in ice water, wrapped in aluminum foil and refrigerated. The marrow is only very lightly cooked, but simply heated for a few seconds after being cut into rounds using a very sharp pastry cutter, which should be warmed slightly in hot water.

To give this dish the desired Mediterranean touch, it should be sprinkled with thyme flowers, a very useful, pretty and subtle-tasting herb available in the spring and summer. Deep-fry the thyme flowers (or fresh thyme) in very hot oil for a few seconds only: any longer could spoil their lovely color. These steps should be carried out at the very last moment, just before serving the red mullet piping hot.

1. Scale and fillet the mullets and remove any remaining bones. Trim the fillets and pan-fry in olive oil for 1 minute on the skin side and only 30 seconds on the flesh side.

2. Cut the marrow into rounds. Lay the mullet fillets on a platter, place the raw slices of marrow on the fillets and heat briefly in the oven.

bone-marrow crust

3. Toast the cumin seed in a dry skillet. Deep-fry the fresh thyme briefly in olive oil. Top the slices of marrow with the cumin and thyme and sprinkle with a little sea salt.

4. Lightly sauté the finely sliced shallot. Deglaze the pan with red wine and reduce by a third. Add the fish stock and the veal demiglace, reducing to a good consistency. Whisk in the butter and adjust the seasoning.

Dover sole shamrock

Preparation time: *45 minutes*
Cooking time: *10 minutes*
Difficulty: ✻

Serves 4

4 Dover soles
7 oz/200 g spinach
1 medium carrot
2 leeks
1 celery root
3 ribs celery
4 cups/1 l fish stock
salt and freshly ground pepper

For the salmon mousse:
7 oz/200 g fresh salmon

1 egg white
1 cup/250 ml cream
salt and freshly ground pepper

For the cod mousse:
3½ oz/100 g fresh cod
½ egg white
2 cups/500 ml cream
salt and freshly ground pepper

For the dressing:
3 tbsp syrupy reduced lobster stock
6½ tbsp/100 ml tarragon vinegar
¾ cup/200 ml olive oil
1 tbsp chopped chives
1 tbsp chopped chervil

Dover sole is becoming increasingly rare, and you may have to fall back on a fish with a less illustrious pedigree for this recipe. The explanation for this is simple: the soles are caught by trawlers in the North Sea and the English Channel using deep-sea dragnets, and overfishing is threatening the species' very survival. If you do not wish to be an accessory to the decline of the Dover sole, you could used turbot, sea bass, cod or halibut fillets.

This dish was created when the *Queen Elizabeth 2* put in at Cork, on the occasion of the Irish Prime Minister's lunch aboard the luxury liner. It contains a strongly symbolic component, consisting of green spinach, white fillet of Dover sole and orange salmon, in honor of the Irish flag: a harmonious composition arranged in the shape of a shamrock, that quintessentially Irish emblem.

The two different mousses may be prepared in advance, though the dish must be cooked just before serving. Let the fish rest for a few minutes, which makes slicing a good deal easier. If you'd like to chance your luck, there's nothing to stop you from adding a fourth leaf to the clover.

1. Fillet the soles. Flatten the fillets slightly with the blade of a knife, place them on a work surface covered with plastic wrap and season. Prepare the salmon mousse and spread this on the fillets, applying the mixture somewhat more thickly in the center. Wilt the spinach in oil and purée it with a pat of butter.

2. Prepare the cod mousse, blend with the spinach purée and spread on the fillets over the salmon mousse. Roll up the fillets lengthwise using the plastic wrap. Poach the fish roll for 10–12 minutes in fish stock, or steam for 8 minutes.

with crunchy vegetables

3. Cut the vegetables into fine julienne and sweat in a little butter. Season. Make the dressing by whisking together all the ingredients.

4. Cut the fish on the diagonal into 12 slices. Arrange on the plates with the vegetable garnish and pour the dressing all around.

Fillet of brill with bay

Preparation time: 1 hour
Cooking time: 1 hour
Difficulty: ✧

Serves 4

1 brill
8 bay leaves
14 oz/400 g lentils (preferably French lentils from Le Puy)
2¾ oz/80 g smoked bacon, finely diced
1 cup/250 ml cream
2 cups/500 ml milk

For the lentil stock:
1 medium carrot
1 onion, studded with cloves
2 cups/500 ml chicken stock
1 bouquet garni
salt and freshly ground pepper

Brill has a fine, smooth skin, and when fresh has red gills and is firm to the touch. Choose a large brill for this dish, so the fillets will hold their shape well when cooking. The white, very fine flesh of this flatfish requires close monitoring during the cooking process. The fillets are scored at intervals to insert dried bay leaves that lend their strong flavor to the fish.

Roger Souvereyns deserves accolades for his delicate lentil-cream sauce, which may be prepared several days in advance if this is more convenient. The only lentils that will do are the small green lentils from Puy-en-Velay, the only ones in France to carry a quality seal based on origin. The product of a favorable microclimate, these legumes grow in volcanic soil. These tiny lentils have a flavor as fine as their skin. Fortunately, it is no longer necessary to sort through the lentils for tiny pebbles, but spare a thought for the generations of cooks who had to do this as a matter of course.

This recipe would also work well with other white fish, such as turbot or John Dory, to name just two. Asparagus, shallots, peas or salsify could replace the lentils in the sauce.

1. Fillet the brill, cut into 4½ oz/125 g pieces and wash. Carefully score each piece 3 times at regular intervals and insert a bay leaf in each cut. Season the fish.

2. Rinse the lentils and blanch in boiling water. Cook in the chicken stock with the onion, carrot and bouquet garni. Remove and reserve 2¾ oz/80 g lentils when done, about 20 minutes, and continue cooking the remainder for a total of 1 hour. Drain, removing the vegetables, blend or process with the milk and the boiling hot cream. Pass through a strainer. Season and keep warm.

leaves and lentil-cream sauce

3. Steam the brill fillets for about 5 minutes. Fry the diced bacon over high heat for a few seconds and drain on paper towels. Reheat the whole lentils by steaming them.

4. Place a brill fillet on each warmed plate and spoon on some lentil-cream sauce. Surround with the whole cooked lentils and the diced bacon.

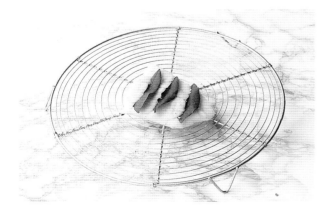

Pineapple tart with

Preparation time: 1 hour
Cooking time: 20 minutes
Difficulty: ★★

Serves 4

12 oz/350 g fresh pineapple
9 oz/250 g live crayfish
¾ oz/20 g yarrow, chopped
⅓ cup/80 g butter

1¾ oz/50 g puff pastry
2 cups/500 ml French sauternes
6½ tbsp/100 ml Swiss pine liqueur
a little olive oil
salt and freshly ground pepper

Pine liqueur, much prized in Switzerland and served after dinner, is virtually unknown outside that country. In this dish it lends an unexpected, slightly bitter touch that contrasts nicely with the sweet flavor of the pineapple.

This recipe will delight sweet-and-sour enthusiasts, particularly with its combination of pineapple and crayfish. For the record, let it be mentioned that Roger Souvereyns originally prepared this dish with foie gras in place of the crustaceans.

It is not always easy to buy live crayfish. Try to buy red-clawed crayfish, as they are more flavorful. The only trick in preparing them is removing the intestine, which may be done by twisting and pulling the center fin of the tail.

The pineapple should be fragrant and heavy for its size. The outer flesh of the fruit should then be finely diced (the core is generally too woody). The "eyes" and skin should be carefully removed before simmering the pineapple cubes for a couple of hours in a good sauternes and pine liqueur to preserve them. While not the most inexpensive of wines, sauternes' viscosity and sweet richness make it the perfect foil for the slightly tart fruit.

This dish might well be your first introduction to yarrow, an edible plant prized for its bitter aftertaste that has been almost forgotten in the kitchen. Its highly indented leaves have earned its most common species the name "milfoil" ("thousand leaves").

1. Peel the pineapple and remove the "eyes." Cut the flesh into small even dice.

2. Preserve the pineapple cubes by simmering for about 2 hours in sauternes and pine liqueur. Roll out the puff pastry on a baking sheet to a thickness of scant ⅛ in/2 mm and bake at 350 °F/180 °C until golden brown.

crayfish and pine liqueur

3. Toss the live crayfish for 2 minutes in hot olive oil in a covered pan. Remove from the pan, cool and shell.

4. Using a pastry cutter, cut circles out of the baked pastry. Place 1 on each plate and top with the preserved pineapple. Heat the chopped yarrow in the butter, add the crayfish tails, season, and carefully turn in the butter. Place the crayfish next to the pineapple tart and pour over a little butter.

Angulas

Preparation time: 10 minutes
Cooking time: insignificant
Difficulty: ✫

Serves 4

1¼ lb/600 g precooked elvers (young eels)
4 small *guindillas* (dried red seedless chiles)
4 cloves garlic, sliced thinly
olive oil

Angula is the Spanish term for the elver or glass eel, known in the French Basque country as *pibale* and elsewhere in France as *civelle*. Among the Spanish Basques, this creature is as highly prized as caviar. The tiny, transparent elvers are served piping hot in the earthenware dish in which they are cooked. In order to avoid damaging the eels, we recommend that you use a wooden fork when pan-frying them and when eating them.

Pedro Subijana, an eminent member of the *angula* fraternity in Hendaye (whose emblem is the *farol* or lantern used by eelers at night) recommends buying precooked elvers. You will thus be spared the necessary but tedious advance preparations in which the elvers are suffocated with tobacco smoke, freed of their slime, washed, blanched and dried. This time-consuming and painstaking process justifies the high price. By leaving it to the experts, you will also avoid the risk of failure when preparing this choice, not to mention extremely rare, dish.

Always white when caught, the *angulas* deserve a highly seasoned acompaniment, preferably one incorporating *girindella*, the region's red-hot chile pepper.

Take care to add just the right amount of olive oil, which the eels should absorbed almost in its entirety as they cook. Too much oil could spoil this dish with its carefully balanced flavors.

1. Untangle the prepared elvers in a bowl of water, then rinse in several changes of water.

2. Heat the olive oil and garlic in a pan, preferably earthenware. If you like your elvers spicy-hot, toss in the chiles at the beginning of cooking; otherwise add them only at the end.

(baby eels)

3. As soon as the garlic is golden, add the elvers, turning them quickly in the oil.

4. Keep the elvers on the move with a wooden fork so that they do not color. They should be served piping hot and glistening with oil, preferably in an earthenware dish and eaten with a wooden fork.

Grouper with

Prepartion time: 25 minutes
Cooking time: 20 minutes
Difficulty: ✲

Serves 4

1¼ lb/600 g thick grouper fillet
generous 5 oz/150 g small fresh cèpes or porcini
1¾ oz/50 g leaf spinach
1 onion, chopped

7 oz/200 g carrots, julienned
chervil
2 tsp/10 ml cognac
3½ tbsp/50 ml white wine
6½ tbsp/100 ml olive oil
salt and freshly ground pepper

Fortunate in having an almost year-round supply of various members of the cèpe family, Pedro Subijana freely admits to being crazy about these wild mushrooms— understandable considering their fine flavors. In this recipe the mushrooms are flambéed in cognac, which might shock some purists. But far from masking the flavor of these mushrooms, alcohol actually enhances it. In France, in particular, the cèpe (*Boletus edulis*), with its thick stalk and brown cap is highly appreciated for its dense, tasty flesh.

Spinach has been grown in Spain at least since the 6th century. Choose small, delicate leaves, and sauté them quickly. Their fresh taste will lighten the dish.

Grouper is a great classic of Spanish cuisine, especially the Basque variety from the *Cernidae* family, found in both the Atlantic and the Mediterranean. Grouper can grow to over 3 ft/1 m in length, and is particular sought after by fisherman.Once its considerable resistance has been overcome, it offers copious, firm flesh that can be broiled or grilled.

For this recipe, Pedro Subijana recommends cooking the fish on one side only. You will therefore need a very fresh fillet that has not been skinned. The skin should be scored lattice-fashion before the fish is cooked, so that the heat can penetrate the fillet more effectively.

1. Clean the mushrooms and separate the stalks from the caps. Reserve a few nice caps for later use. Heat some olive oil in a pan and gently sauté half of the chopped onion and the cèpes until they color slightly. Flambé with cognac, deglaze with white wine and add water to cover. Simmer over low heat for 15 minutes.

2. Purée the mixture in a food processor or blender, then press through a sieve. Add a little olive oil to lift the flavor and keep warm in a double boiler.

spinach and cèpes

3. Sauté the spinach in some olive oil and remove from the pan. Thinly slice the reserved cèpe caps and sauté in the same oil. Finely chop the remaining ½ onion and sweat in another pan without allowing it to color; spoon this mixture over the mushroom slices. Deep-fry the julienned carrot.

4. Clean and fillet the grouper, but do not skin. Season with salt and pepper and pan-fry over high heat, skin-side down, for about 4 minutes. Do not turn the fish. Just before serving, finish by crisping the skin under the broiler. Serve on a bed of spinach and cèpes, garnished with the sauce and some chervil.

Brill and langoustines

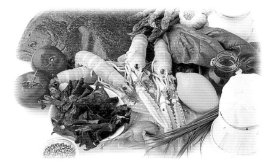

Preparation time: 45 minutes
Cooking time: 15 minutes
Difficulty: ☆

Serves 4

4 brill fillets (generous 5 oz/150 g each)
1 dozen 2¾ oz/80 g langoustines
generous 1 lb/500 g spinach
1 dozen asparagus tips
1 clove garlic
6½ tbsp/100 g butter

For the chive-cream sauce:
⅔ cup/150 ml *crème fraîche*
½ lemon
½ bunch of chives
salt and freshly ground pepper

For the dressing:
3½ tbsp/50 ml olive oil
juice of 1 lemon
2 oz/60 g shallots, chopped
1 tbsp chopped chives
3½ oz/100 g tomatoes, diced
1¾ oz/50 g black trumpet mushrooms
crushed coriander seed
salt and freshly ground pepper

On hot days in the summertime, light dishes with little or no sauce are generally preferred. Brill, with its exquisite, very firm, snow-white flesh is ideal choice for an entrée. It can tolerate only gentle and quick cooking, such as steaming or baking *en papillote* (in a foil or waxed-paper parcel).

For this recipe, you will need fillets from a brill weighing 6½–8¾ lb/3–4 kg to combine to best effect with the langoustines and spinach. The langoustines should also be fairly large; they will be pan-fried in olive oil before being combined with the bright-green spinach. The flavors of the crustacean and the vegetable complement each other beautifully. The medium-size spinach leaves should be stripped off their stalks before they are used.

As for the asparagus, the spears should be stiff and "snappy," since their flavor is dependent chiefly on their freshness. The grayish mushrooms with their earthy aroma will lend this dish a woodsy flavor.

The chive-cream sauce, a light, moderately lemony confection, should be prepared only at the very last minute and the chives added just before serving. Its consistency must be thick enough to coat the fish fillets without running all over the plate.

1. Strip the spinach leaves from their stalks, wash in several changes of water and sauté with a clove of garlic. Gently sauté the mushrooms in butter. Shell the langoustines and pan-fry the tails in butter. Snap off the woody ends of the asparagus, peel if necessary, then wash them and cook until crisp-tender in boiling salted water. Drain.

2. Bring some water to a boil in a steamer. Place the brill fillets on a piece of aluminum foil in the upper part of the steamer. Cover and steam for 2–3 minutes.

with chives

3. Reduce the crème fraîche in a saucepan. Season with salt and pepper, then add the juice of ½ lemon and ½ bunch of finely chopped chives. Prepare the dressing by combining the ingredients in a bowl.

4. Arrange a mound of spinach and 3 asparagus spears on each plate. Top with a brill fillet, coated in chive-cream sauce. Place the langoustines and mushrooms between the asparagus spears and spoon over some dressing.

Marinated eel

Preparation time: 40 minutes
Cooking time: 15 minutes
Difficulty: ✴✴

Serves 4

2 small eels
8 medium zucchini
⅓ cup/80 g butter
baking soda
garlic, marjoram, rosemary, sage
thyme
olive oil
salt

The lesser eel inhabits unpolluted waters such as the rice fields of the Po plain in Italy. Able to breathe outside of water, it can be found in damp meadows as well as in streams. It is an extremely slippery customer, managing to wrigle out of the grasp of many a fisherman. Gourments are particularly fond of elvers, young eels, sold in the French Basque country as *civelles* or *pibales*.

A fresh eel is by definition a live eel. If, unlike the protagonist of Boris Vian's postwar novel, *Froth on the Daydream*, you do not have the good fortune to spy one coming out of your water pipe, you'll have to transport it to the kitchen yourself, and slaughter it using a club or similar blunt instrument, then skin it. This is most easily

done by hanging it from a hook, snipping the skin at the top, and pulling it off with a sharp tug. Your fishmonger will be willing to handle this task for you.

Romano Tamani prefers the lesser eel to the plumper silver eel. In any case, some advance preparation is necessary for this dish, since the eel fillets must first of all be stuffed with herbs and then marinated in oil for 24 hours.

The zucchini purée is a pleasant accompaniment for the fish, because the sweet, melting quality of the vegetable harmonizes superbly with the flavor of the eel fillets, which are in turn set off to best advantage by the herb stuffing with its Provençal touch.

1. Carefully wash and clean the eels. Skin them and fillet them (2 fillets per eel). Chop the rosemary, sage, marjoram and thyme together with 2 cloves of garlic. Sprinkle the fillets with the herb mixture, a little oil and some salt.

2. Place the 4 fillets in a glass or similar container, cover with olive oil and marinate for 24 hours in the refrigerator.

in zucchini sauce

3. Roll up the fillets and secure them with a toothpick. Pan-fry them in a little oil.

4. Wash the zucchini and cut into pieces. Sauté with a little butter and baking soda. Add water to cover and boil for 10 minutes. Drain, transfer to a food processor and blend to a purée. Serve the eel fillets on a bed of zucchini purée.

Brandade of cod

Preparation time: 1 hour
Cooking time: 1 hour
Difficulty: ★★

Serves 4

One 5½ lb/2½ kg fresh cod
2¼ lb/1 kg potatoes
3 cloves garlic
1 bunch of flat-leaf parsley

4 slices of good white bread
1⅔ cups/400 ml veal stock
¾ cup/200 ml olive oil
¾ cup/200 ml cream
6½ tbsp/100 g butter
coarse salt
salt and freshly ground pepper

Brandade de morue is a Provençal dish whose name comes from *brandad*, "something stirred." Originally a very simple dish of salt cod, potatoes and oil, it has "stirred" the imaginations of numerous cooks, who have enriched it with new ingredients. Today it consists of cod emulsified in olive oil and milk, with garlic often added to intensify the flavor.

In this recipe, the brandade is bound with meat juices and is served alongside a pan-fried fillet of fresh cod. You will need a piece of fresh (as opposed to salt) cod that feels good and firm to the touch, sporting a shiny silver skin with mother-of-pearl glints.

The fish is "marinated" in coarse sea salt. Follow the natural shape of the fillets when salting them, and adjust the length of marinating time according to the thickness of the fish. It is then rinsed and marinated in oil to keep it tender. These tasks, which may seem tedious, can be done in advance.

Olives, chives and chopped parsley are appropriate garnishes for this economical and delicious dish, not only underscoring the individual flavors, but adding a vivid touch of Mediterranean color.

1. Fillet the cod. Liberally strew both sides of the fillets with coarse salt and let stand for 20 minutes. Rinse off the salt, pat the fish dry and cut four 4½ oz/120 g portions. Rub with olive oil and set aside. Reserve the remaining cod for the brandade.

2. Peel the garlic and preserve by simmering very gently for 1 hour in olive oil. Wash the potatoes and bake them in their skins. Trim the crusts from the bread, then cut the bread into cubes and deep-fry. Reduce the veal stock to 4 tbsp and whisk in the butter.

with garlic oil

3. Coarsely cube the remaining cod and poach in water until just cooked. Drain, removing skin and bones. Pound or blend to a purée in a mortar or food processor. Peel the potatoes and add while still hot to the fish purée. Gradually add the lukewarm olive oil and the cream, stirring constantly. Correct the seasoning.

4. Pan-fry the cod fillets in some olive oil for 4 minutes on each side. Place a dollop of brandade on each plate, arranging a piece of cod next to it and garnishing with a few croûtons and the preserved garlic cloves. Add a spoonful of meat juices and decorate with a few parsley leaves. Serve piping hot.

John Dory with

Preparation time: 1 hour
Cooking time: 15 minutes
Difficulty: ★★

Serves 4

One 3¼ lb/1½ kg John Dory
7 oz/200 g peas
7 oz/200 g snow peas
4 scallions

1 small fresh galangal root (or ginger root)
¾ oz/20 g sesame seeds
6½ tbsp/100 ml peanut oil
6½ tbsp/100 ml sesame oil
6½ tbsp/100 ml soy sauce
salt and freshly ground pepper

Asia abounds in exciting ingredients just waiting to be discovered by Western cooks. Take galangal, the fleshy underground stem of *Alpinia galanga* of the sedge family. Available in the West in dried sliced or powdered form, and less frequently, fresh, this rhizome bears a marked resemblance to its cousin, ginger, but is finer and sweeter, imparting a more intense flavor to the dishes it seasons. A lovely reddish brown in color, galangal is rich in eucalyptol, with a powerful aroma and flavor, and should therefore be used with care.

Lemongrass is common in Southeast Asia, and is used in both meat and fish dishes. It has a pungent citrus aroma and flavor that enhances rather than masks the taste of the other ingredients.

The John Dory is a flat, spiny fish with a huge mouth. Legend has it that the two black spots, one on either side of its body, are the fingerprints of Saint Peter. The John Dory is a fish whose tender but slightly bland flesh requires a well-seasoned accompaniment. This can be prepared in advance, like the snow peas, which must be refreshed after poaching.

1. Fillet the John Dory, remove the skin and cut into 4 equal pieces. Season with salt and pepper. Peel the galangal; reserve the skin and cut the flesh into fine shreds. Steam the fish.

2. Shell the garden peas and trim the snow peas. Blanch until crisp-tender, then drain, refresh and reserve. Pour the peanut and sesame oils into a skillet and heat until very hot. In another pan, sauté the peas and the sesame seeds in a tsp of the mixed oils.

galangal oil

3. Arrange a portion of fish on each of 4 plates and spoon the peas to the side. Top the fish with the julienne of galangal and the finely sliced scallions. Drizzle with a few drops of soy sauce.

4. Pour a tbsp of boiling oil over the fish. Serve at once.

Sea bream with potato "scales"

Preparation time: 1 hour
Cooking time: 40 minutes
Difficulty: ★★

Serves 4

Two 1¾ lb/800 g gilt-head sea breams
10 crayfish heads
2 chicken carcasses
1 generous lb/500 g potatoes
28 pearl onions

¾ oz/20 g shallots
2 tsp/10 g tomato paste
2 tsp/10 g tarragon
3½ tbsp/50 ml olive oil
¾ cup/200 ml fish stock
2 cups/500 ml peanut oil (for deep-frying)
2 tbsp/30 g butter
3½ tbsp/50 g sugar

12 chervil leaves
salt and freshly ground pepper

Originally from the Orient, where its skin was used to dye silk, the onion was introduced into Europe in ancient times. It has always been eaten by people of all social classes, and was recognized early on for its digestive properties. In this recipe, we used the pearl onion, whose size and flavor make it the ideal accompaniment.

The gilt-head sea bream is without doubt the tastiest of the sea breams. It is recognizable by the golden sickle between its eyes, which is reminiscent of a crown, hence another name by which it is occasionally known.

The potato "scales" can be made from any variety of potatoes that won't brown too quickly when blanched in oil: Yukon golds would be ideal, because they stay firm and hold their shape well. Cut the potatoes into very regular rounds, and the dish will be a delight to look at as well as to eat. This edible cloak naturally makes the fillets trickier to handle as they are cooking.

Gilt-head sea bream can be accompanied by any Mediterranean herb: basil, rosemary, bay leaf or thyme, for example. If the pearl onions are not your cup of tea, chanterelles may be substituted in this recipe, and the fish may easily be replaced by porgy, sea bass, pikeperch or turbot.

1. Fillet the fish. Peel the potatoes and cut into thin slices. Using a pastry cutter, stamp out ¾ in/2 cm disks from these. Wash and drain the potato disks, then blanch in 2 cups/500 ml peanut oil at 265 °F/130 °C for 1 minute. Peel the pearl onions and glaze them in water, sugar and salt, cooking until brown.

2. Drain the blanched potatoes and let cool. Cover the fish fillets with potato slices, overlapped to resemble scales. Meanwhile, brown the chopped, crushed chicken carcasses with the crushed crayfish heads and the chopped shallots.

in a chicken-and-crayfish *jus*

3. Meanwhile, gently brown the chopped chicken carcasses with the crushed crayfish heads and the chopped shallot. Sweat the mixture for 5 minutes and deglaze with the fish stock. Add the tomato paste and the chopped tarragon. Cook for 30 minutes over low heat. Strain the stock and reduce by two thirds. Correct the seasoning and whisk in 2 tbsp/30 g butter.

4. Season the sea bream fillets and pan-fry in olive oil, potato-side down. Place a fillet in the center of each plate and surround with the onions and the chicken-crayfish jus. Decorate with a few chervil leaves before serving.

Monkfish "tournedos" threaded

Preparation time: 1 hour
Cooking time: 30 minutes
Difficulty: ★★

Serves 4

2¼ lb/1 kg monkfish tail
4 small fresh sardines
4 anchovy fillets in oil

2 shallots
3 large leeks
2 cloves garlic
¾ cup/200 ml red wine
¾ cup/200 ml red-wine vinegar
4 tbsp/50 g tomato paste
1 bouquet garni
a little white wine
a little stock
6½ tbsp/100 g butter
salt and freshly ground pepper

The monkfish boasts lean, exceptionally fine flesh that is completely free from bones (bar the central one), and can be prepared in 1,001 different ways. For this recipe, 4 "tournedos" should be cut from the head end of the fillet.

To thread the "tournedos" with the anchovy fillets, you can make things easier for yourself by cutting the anchovies on the diagonal and freezing them. A larding needle will also be a help.

Sardines are slender silver-blue fish with semi-fatty flesh. They should be bought absolutely fresh and preferably ungutted. According to Dominique Toulousy, the small, very tasty Mediterranean sardines are the best. They are caught at night by the light if the *lamparo*, a large lantern that lights up schools of fish. It is tempting to assume that sardines originally came from the similar sounding Sardinia, but this is not the case: the main exporters of sardines are the Portuguese as well as the Italians.

The vinegar should be measured sparingly and reduced carefully. Its strong flavor is meant to enhance rather than mask the flavors of the other ingredients. Used too liberally, its acidity could spoil the dish beyond redemption. If you feel that the leek accompaniment is not enough on its own, our chef suggests an orange-flavored onion compote, which would harmonize superbly with the monkfish.

1. Cut 4 medallions from the monkfish tail. Wash the leeks carefully. Cut the white part into ⅜ in/1 cm thick rings. Place the anchovy fillets in the freezer to firm them up.

2. Using a larding needle, thread the monkfish with the anchovies. Proceed exactly as if you were larding meat.

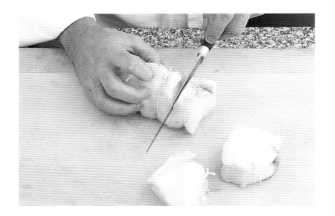

with anchovies in verjuice

3. Grind or finely chop the sardines, including their heads and bones. Sweat in a saucepan with the chopped shallots, the bouquet garni and the chopped garlic. Add the tomato paste and the vinegar. Reduce until all of the liquid has evaporated. Add the red wine and reduce by half. Strain and correct the seasoning.

4. Gently sweat the leek rings in a covered saucepan in some butter. Add a little white wine and stock and cook over low heat until soft. Pan-fry the monkfish "tournedos" until golden brown. Place one in the center of each plate, pour some sauce all around and garnish with the leek rings.

Whiting with watercress-

Preparation time: 35 minutes
Cooking time: 20 minutes
Difficulty: ★

Serves 4

4 large whitings
14 oz/400 g waxy potatoes
1 bunch of sorrel

1 bunch of watercress
10 tbsp/150 g butter
1¼ cups/300 ml mussel liquor
¾ cup/200 ml jellied white veal stock
a little lemon juice
a little olive oil
salt and freshly ground pepper

Gilles Tournadre has decided to center this dish around the whiting, that serviceable fish from the cod family. Our first priority here is to restore a certain thickness to the fish by placing one fillet on top of another and wrapping them both in a piece of plastic wrap. The protein in the fish flesh will cause the two fillets to stick to one another. Once this has happened, we need only remove the wrap and pan-fry the fish in clarified butter or olive oil, taking care to handle

it gently so it does not come apart as you cook it.

Sorrel and watercress both have distinctive flavors, so they simultaneously vie for attention and complement one another. Even if you are skeptical of the results, do try this surprising combination. The veal stock lightens things up a bit, softening the taste slightly and preventing the oxidation of the chlorophyll in the greens.

1. Place the watercress and sorrel leaves in a blender with the jellied veal stock and blend to a coarse purée.

2. Boil the potatoes in their skins. Peel, then crush with a fork while adding the butter.

buttered potatoes

3. Fillet and skin the whitings and remove remaining bones. Sandwich the fishes back together by placing one fillet on top of another. Dust the fillets with flour and brown them in clarified butter or olive oil in a nonstick pan.

4. Add the watercress-sorrel mixture to the potatoes and correct the seasoning. Heat the mussel liquor and add a few drops of lemon juice and olive oil. Arrange the whiting and the watercress-buttered potatoes on the plates and spoon over a little mussel liquor.

Gilt-head sea bream in a

Preparation time: 45 minutes
Cooking time: 35 minutes
Difficulty: ☆

Serves 4

Two 1¾ lb/800 g gilt-head sea breams
1 bulb of fennel
7 oz/200 g chanterelles
1 red bell pepper
4 roasted tomatoes
1 bunch of dill

1 bunch of cilantro
3½ tbsp/50 g butter
2 orange leaves
1 sprig of lemon balm
3½ tbsp/50 ml olive oil

2 cups/500 ml langoustine stock
a little honey
1 piece fresh ginger root
3½ tbsp/50 g butter
salt and freshly ground pepper

Spices have been traded in the port city of Rouen for centuries. Add to this Gilles Tournadre's innate curiosity, coupled with the chance to sample an impressive array of dishes cooked for him by a Chinese colleague, and you can see how this herb *jus* came into being. In it, sweet and sour tastes combine to season the highly esteemed gilt-head sea bream, recognizable by the golden crescent between its eyes. Low in fat, this fish is at its peak in spring.

Our chef, however, is fairly easygoing and would happily use other sea breams, provided they were absolutely fresh.

In fact you could even use porgy or red mullet, or fall back on John Dory in a pinch.

Whatever fish you decide on, Tournadre recommends that you braise it gently so that it will absorb the sauce well. Make sure to use the herbs and spices in balance, so that their strength doesn't mask the flavor of the fish, and their interplay does not leave unpleasant aftertastes.

Gilles Tournadre had his dinner guests' health in mind when he created this dish containing ginger, lemon balm and ornage blossom, all known for their medicinal virtues.

1. Prepare the vegetables, herbs and spices. Clean, scale and fillet the sea bream, reserving the bones and trimmings.

2. Combine the langoustine stock in a saucepan with all of the herbs, spices and honey. Simmer gently for 15 minutes. Bring the mixture to a boil and reduce by a third. Blend, strain and whisk in the butter.

herb *jus* with chanterelles

3. Cut the sea-bream fillets into large pieces and cook quickly in olive oil.

4. Finely slice the fennel and red bell pepper and sauté all of the vegetables and the chanterelles in butter. Spoon the vegetables into the center of 4 deep plates and sprinkle with chopped dill. Place the fish fillets all around. Pour over the jus and sprinkle with cilantro.

Dover-sole-stuffed cucumber with

Preparation time:	45 minutes
Cooking time:	15 minutes
Difficulty:	⋆

Serves 4

2 large cucumbers
6½ tbsp/100 g butter
2 tbsp/30 g whipped herb butter

For the filling:
Two 14 oz/400 g Dover soles

2 egg whites
¾ cup/200 ml heavy cream
fish stock
¾ oz/20 g shelled and skinned pistachios
salt, cayenne pepper, paprika

For the harlequin vegetable garnish:
1 yellow bell pepper
1 tomato
1 medium carrot

This recipe may also be prepared with a langoustine stuffing. The colors of the vegetables in the harlequin garnish harmonize beautifully with the striped cucumber, making the dish a delight to look at as well as to eat.

The cucumbers should be firm and regular in shape. First, sprinkle coarse salt over them and let stand for about 10 minutes. This rids them of excess liquid and any bitterness. Raw cucumbers are easy to work with, so it is not at all difficult to make the little tubs that will be filled with the fish mousse mixture. Although baking is a treatment more commonly reserved for zucchini and other vegetables, the flavor of the oven-braised cucumber brilliantly partners José Tourneur's Dover sole mousse.

When very fresh, the flesh of the Dover sole is very white and firm, and they are somewhat difficult to skin. To accomplish this last task, carefully nick the skin with a knife directly above the tail and pull the skin upward with a sharp tug.

The accompaniments must be of top quality. Above all, pick through the pistachios carefully. If even one of them is rancid, the stuffing, and hence the entire dish, will suffer.

1. Wipe the cucumber with a damp cloth. Using a fluting knife, remove strips of skin at even intervals to create a striped effect. Cut into 1¼ in/3 cm long sections and hollow these out, leaving the bottom intact. Blanch in boiling salted water and refresh in ice water. Drain upside down on a cloth.

2. Poach the sole in fish stock, then quickly fillet it. Let cool. Finely chop the fillets and add the egg whites and then the salt, paprika and a pinch of cayenne pepper. Once the stuffing firms up, work in the cream. You should have a glossy, well-bound paste. Add the chopped pistachios and correct the seasoning.

a harlequin vegetable garnish

3. Place the cucumbers in a buttered casserole, just touching. Season with salt and pepper and pipe in the stuffing. Cover with a piece of buttered paper and bake for 15 minutes at 350 °F/180 °C. Remove the paper halfway through cooking and brush the cucumbers with a little melted butter, then return to the oven until they brown slightly.

4. Cut small balls from the vegetables using a melon baller and cook in boiling water until tender. Arrange in a circle on each plate. Place a few stuffed cucumbers in the center and pour over some melted herb butter.

Preparation time: 1 hour 30 minutes
Cooking time: 20 minutes
Difficulty: ★★

Serves 4

4 small arctic char
8 spinach hearts
1 handful of spinach leaves
1 onion, 1 medium carrot
1 rib celery
1 tbsp capers, chopped
3½ oz/100 g tuna in oil
⅓ cup plus 1½ tbsp/100 ml *crème fraîche*
olive oil
dry vermouth

vegetable stock, to taste
salt, pepper, paprika

For the oil sauce (prepare the day before):
salmon caviar
black olive paste
1 bay leaf
1 tsp chopped chervil
1 basil leaf
pink peppercorns
extra-virgin olive oil (to taste)
salt and freshly ground pepper

To garnish:
chervil
basil leaves

Salmerino di fontanta (brook trout) and *salmerino alpino* (arctic char or salmon trout) are both highly esteemed fish, though very different in size. While the brook trout is nearly 40 in/1 m long and tips the scales at about 17½ lb/ 8 kg, the arctic char is just half that size and seldom exceeds 6½ lb/3 kg in weight. Both species live in the cold waters of alpine lakes, home also to the freshwater herring, one of the substitutes suggested by Luisa Valazza. Related to the salmon, brook trout and arctic char are very firm-fleshed fish and thus well-suited to rolling up around a filling.

Luisa Valazza recommends a modest-sized arctic char, between 14–16 in/35–40 cm in length, which will not be too fatty. If you can find no char, you may substitute trout, perch, or other freshwater fish.

The tuna filling is the dominant element in this dish, the oil sauce serving merely to set it off to good advantage. This recipe draws its inspiration from the Piedmontese *vitello tonnato*, thinly sliced poached veal served cold with a tuna and mayonnaise sauce. The stuffing prepared here by Luisa Valazza is considerably lighter than the traditional tuna sauce.

The oil sauce is very subtly seasoned, mainly thanks to the pink peppercorns with their surprising aroma. The black olive paste is what is left of the olives after pressing.

1. Prepare the oil sauce a day in advance: mix all the ingredients together in a bowl and refrigerate overnight.

2. Fillet the fish and remove remaining bones. Prepare a mousse by blending the surplus flesh with salt, pepper, the crème fraîche, a handful of lightly blanched spinach leaves and a shot of dry vermouth.

Arctic char

3. To prepare the vegetable and tuna fish sauce, lightly sauté the vegetables in olive oil, then add the tuna and capers. Braise lightly and moisten with the vegetable stock. Simmer briefly, then whip vigorously and keep warm. Blanch the spinach hearts.

4. Spread the fillets with the stuffing. Roll up the fillets and secure with a toothpick. Poach in vegetable stock for 8 minutes. Place 2 spinach hearts on each plate, and two spoonfuls of vegetable-tuna fish sauce to the side. Top with the fish roulades, and pour over a little oil sauce. Garnish with the chervil and basil leaves.

Cod with parsley, mustard

Preparation time: 30 minutes
Cooking time: 40 minutes
Difficulty: *

Serves 4

Four scant 9 oz/250 g portions skinned,
boned cod fillet
2 large Spanish onions
1 cup/250 g butter
1 cup/250 ml Hoegaarden weissbier (Belgian
top-fermentation beer)

1 tbsp Ghent or Dijon mustard
pinch of nutmeg
pinch of sugar
fine salt and freshly ground black pepper

For the crumb coating:
3½ oz/100 g fresh white bread crumbs
a few parsley leaves
2 small shallots

For our European cousins, the cod goes by more aliases than a confidence trickster. In France, for example, *cabillaud* is one name for fresh cod, while *morue* refers to the dried, salted fish. Germans call the fully grown North Sea variety *Kabeljau*, while the term *Dorsch* takes in the Baltic and juvenile North Sea forms of the fish. And in English of course, cod is cod, except when its scrod. Whatever name it goes by, however, it is important to choose an absolutely fresh fillet. This is a fish with fine, firm flesh, which, when carefully prepared, can be a true delicacy.

Parsley was apparently discovered by the Romans. We distinguish the flat-leaf variety from curly parsley, which has slightly less scent and flavor. This umbellifer is harvested the whole year round. Always look for brightly colored green stalks that are rigid and brittle and have very firm leaves.

Belgians are fond of cooking with beer. Hoegaarden weissbier, a light, fizzy ale made with top-fermentation yeast whose brewing process dates back to 1445, is ideal for this recipe. It has an almost imperceptible cloudiness and a refined flavor that lends an elegant bitter note to the cod and beautifully partners the onion coulis. To take the edge off its acridity, Guy Van Cauteren adds a tiny pinch of sugar.

1. Clean and trim the cod and cut into nine 3 oz/80 g portions.

2. Season the cod with salt and pepper and brush with mustard. Make a crumb coating out of bread crumbs and finely chopped parsley and shallots, and use to coat the mustard-covered fish. Pan-fry for 10 minutes in oil. Place under the broiler to finish cooking.

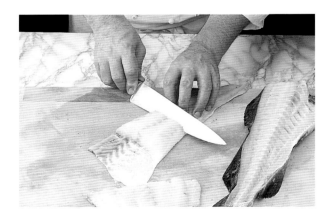

and onion purée

3. Peel and finely slice 2 large onions and cook gently in butter until reduced in volume. Moisten with the beer. Add salt, pepper and a pinch each of nutmeg and sugar. Start off braising on the stove, then transfer to a 400 °F/200 °C oven for 20 minutes. Remove from the oven and purée the onions in a food processor.

4. Whisk the butter into the onion purée. Pour this into the center of the heated plates and top with a piece of cod.

Sautéed lobster with

Preparation time: 1 hour
Cooking time: 2 hours
Difficulty: ★★★

Serves 4

Two female lobsters (1¼ lb/500 g each)
3½ oz/100 g bell-pepper *cassonade* (bought ready-made)
2 red bell peppers
4½ lb/2 kg fava beans (unshelled weight)
mirepoix: 3 medium carrots, 2 onions, diced

13 tbsp/200 g butter
6½ tbsp/100 ml heavy cream
olive oil
1 bunch of cilantro
parsley, garlic, thyme, bay leaf
fine and coarse salt and freshly ground black pepper

For the buckwheat crêpe batter:
8¾ oz/250 g buckwheat flour
6½ tbsp/100 ml whole milk
2 eggs

May the great Prosper Montagné forgive us, but we can't suppport him in his campaign to prepare lobster *à l'armoricaine* instead of *à l'amèicaine*.. The recipe for this dish was created by a certain Pierre Fraisse, a French chef who had just returned to his native land from the United States and who ran the Café Amèricain on the Boulevards.. French national pride, therefore, is saved: *sauce amèicaine* is actually a French invention. Basically, it is a recipe for chefs who can work quickly the live lobster must be cut up in a flash, flambéed with cognac and speedily cooked on a bed of garlic, shallots and tomatoes moistened with white wine before being served with a flourish.

Live lobsters have a disquieting tendency to scuttle around your kitchen, but live is the only way to buy them, as only then will they be absolutely fresh. Buy female lobsters, for their coral.

When preparing the vegetable accompaniment, take care to cook the favas only until crisp-tender. The bell-pepper *cassonade* can be purchased ready-made, but there is nothing to stop you from inventing your own method of preparing this condiment. You may also substitute sweet Hungarian paprika. As for the buckwheat flour, it is used to make delicious little crêpes (about 3 per person), which can be reheated just before serving.

1. Crack the claws and legs of the lobsters and halve their bodies. Reserve the creamy substance (tomalley) and the coral. Peel and dice the red bell peppers. Shell and skin the fava beans. Make the buckwheat crêpe batter.

2. Mix the coral with the crêpe batter. Make small crêpes in a nonstick pan. Add the herbs and spices to the diced carrots and onions.

bell-pepper cassonade

3. Sprinkle the lobster halves with the cassonade or paprika and flash-fry them in oil. Add the vegetables. Shell the lobsters, reserving their meat. Crush the heads and shells and return to the pot. Moisten with water and cook for 20 minutes. Put through a fine strainer.

4. Mix the tomalley with the butter and thicken the braising liquid with this mixture. Add the diced red bell pepper. Reheat the lobster and the crêpes in the oven. Cook the beans in the cream. Alternately layer the beans and the lobster inside circular molds and unmold on top of the crêpes. Arrange on heated plates.

Baked brill with

Preparation time: 20 minutes
Cooking time: 25 minutes
Difficulty: ★★★

Serves 4

One 3¼ lb/1½ kg brill
2 small zucchini
3½ oz/100 g spinach
1¾ oz/50 g potatoes
7 oz/200 g celery root

6½ tbsp/100 ml fish stock
3½ tbsp/50 ml dry white wine
⅓ cup/80 g butter
2 black olives
salt and freshly ground pepper

For the fish filling:
7 oz/200 g whiting
1 egg white
¾ cup/200 ml cream
salt and freshly ground pepper

The inspiration for this marvelous baked brill came to Freddy Van Decasserie from a trip to Japan. Brill is similar to turbot, but is more economical.

The composition of fillings must be geared to the variety of fish they are to stuff. Whiting or other lean fish goes well with brill. The fish should be seasoned with salt and pepper before the cream is worked in, since salt absorbs moisture and helps to thicken the stuffing. Either black pepper or a little cayenne pepper may be used here.

The zucchini "scales" require some explanation. Freddy Van Decasserie recommends small zucchini, which should

be cut into thin, even slices and placed overlapping on the fillet. Begin at the tip of the fish and work your way down to the bottom, laying the scales always from left to right, row by row.

For the remaining accompaniment choose firm celery root, which should feel heavy for its size. Peel it thickly and sprinkle the flesh with lemon juice, so that it doesn't discolor. Here, the potato helps bind the celery root purée.

Finally, the fillet is placed on the sauce, which you have emulsified just beforehand for a creamier consistency. The plates should be decorated with olives, capers and whelks.

1. Prepare the fish stuffing: Finely dice the well-chilled whiting and place in a food processor together with the egg white. With the motor running, add the salt and pepper. As soon as the mixture is smooth, add ¾ cup/200 ml ice-cold cream. Process for a total of 1 minute and push the mixture through a fine sieve.

2. Fillet the brill, season lightly and spread the fillets with the fish stuffing. Slice the zucchini thinly or shave on a mandoline. Sauté briefly in oil and place in overlapping rows on the fish fillets to resemble scales. Moisten with white wine and fish stock. Bake for 10 minutes at 350 °F/180 °C. Season with salt and pepper.

zucchini "scales"

3. Poach 7 oz/200 g celery root with 1¾ oz/50 g potatoes over high heat for 15–20 minutes. Purée everything and season with salt and pepper. Fill a piping bag with the puréed celery root and pipe onto the plates in the shape of the brill.

4. Strip the spinach leaves from their stalks. Blanch the leaves, refresh in cold water and press through a sieve. Reduce the liquid in which the fish fillets were cooked to the proper consistency. Remove from the heat and whisk in the butter. Whisk until the mixture is completely cool. Add 1 tbsp spinach purée and allow to dissolve over low heat before emulsifying with a hand-held blender. Strain the mixture and pour inside the piped celery root purée. Place a fillet of brill in the center and serve.

Scallops on a bed of

Preparation time: 20 minutes
Cooking time: 10 minutes
Difficulty: ★★

Serves 4

16 sea scallops
generous 1 lb/500 g Belgian endive
2 green apples
1 onion

1 beet
scant ½ oz/10 g curry powder
4 tsp/20 ml heavy cream
10 tbsp/150 g butter
3½ tbsp/50 ml green-apple juice
2 cups/500 ml peanut oil
2½ tbsp/40 ml olive oil
salt and freshly ground pepper

Geert Van Hecke, who hails from Bruges, is naturally crazy about *witloof*, the Flemish name for Belgian endive, which literally translates as "white leaf." This vegetable is none other than the shoot of the chicory plant, blanched by forcing in the dark. It made its first appearance in Belgium in 1850, having being grown inadvertently in the Botanical Gardens of Brussels. Since then, its season has been substantially extended by the development of early and late varieties. This vegetable is 95% water and therefore virtually calorie-free.

Look for white, firm specimens when buying. Discard any withered leaves, and rinse in plenty of water before cutting the vegetable into julienne (thin strips).

The pilgrimage routes of Saint James also lead through Belgium, and numerous pilgrims from this area have set off towards Santiago de Compostela with their famous scallop shells, which originally served as water ladles and later became their badge of identification. Paradoxically, you should if possible choose live scallops that haven't traveled far. Failing live scallops, you should buy dry packed scallops. The meat of this bivalve mollusk is extremely fragile and should therefore be cooked quickly, for no more than about 10 seconds on each side.

Go easy with the curry powder, as too much of its assertive taste could ruin this dish, which should be very subtly flavored. Serve the scallops piping hot.

1. Wash the scallops under running water, dry and refrigerate until needed. Peel the beet and cut into julienne. Deep-fry for several minutes in hot peanut oil.

2. Cook down the chopped onions and add 1 tsp curry powder. Moisten with 3½ tbsp/50 ml green-apple juice. Reduce by half and stir in the cream. Cook for 5 minutes over medium-high heat. Strain and whisk in the butter.

Belgian endive and apple

3. Clean and trim the Belgian endive, cut into julienne and gently sauté in butter for 2–3 minutes. Season with salt and pepper. Shave the unpeeled green apples into thin slices on a vegetable mandoline or with a knife, and set aside.

4. Season the scallops with salt and pepper, then sauté quickly in hot olive oil. Arrange the Belgian endive on a bed of green-apple slices. Top with a circle of overlapping scallops. Spoon the sauce all around and crown the scallops with the fried beet julienne.

Turbot cooked on the bone

Preparation time: *45 minutes*
Cooking time: *30 minutes*
Difficulty: ✶✶

Serves 4

1 turbot
1¾ lb/800 g young fava beans (unshelled weight)
30 small pearl onions
15 cloves garlic
1 shallot
7 oz/200 g smoked bacon

6½ tbsp/100 g butter
¾ cup/200 ml roast-meat juices
salt and freshly ground pepper

For the *beurre blanc*:
2 tbsp white wine
3½ tbsp/50 ml white-wine vinegar
1 shallot
6½ tbsp/100 g butter
6½ tbsp/100 ml cream
tarragon
1 pinch of crushed pepper
salt and freshly ground pepper

The turbot, a cold-water dweller, has fine, light flesh flesh which holds its shape well when cooked. The only drawback with turbot, apart from its cost, is the high degree of waste associated with its preparation. You will therefore need to choose a large fish if you want it to yield decent-sized pieces.

Gérard Vié recommends cutting up the turbot the day before you cook it, as it is his view that this fish actually improves if filleted in advance. The turbot should be cut into nice wide, thick pieces, drizzled with a little olive oil and refrigerated overnight.

The fava bean accompaniment is made tastier with the addition of the diced bacon, whose impact varies in inverse proportion to its size: in other words, the more finely it is diced, the more intense its flavor. As a great advocate of the increased consumption of legumes, Gérard Vié recommends navy beans, lentils or garden peas if fava beans are not your cup of tea.

Beurre blanc was created by a certain Madame Clèmence of Nantes, a cook by trade. Its preparation is made easier by using butter that consists of 82% fat, and a more acid reduction.

1. Cut the turbot down the middle, starting at the tail and stopping just short of the head. Blanch the shelled fava beans for 2 minutes in boiling water, slip them out of their skins and refrigerate.

2. Divide the fish into 7 oz/200 g portions. Season with salt and pepper. Bake in a 350 °F/180 °C oven in a mixture of oil and butter for about 12 minutes, basting frequently.

with a bean-and-bacon ragout

3. Lightly sauté the very finely diced bacon, the finely minced shallot and the fava beans in a little butter. Season, moisten with the meat juices and reduce by half, by which time the fava beans should be very tender. Brown 2 garlic cloves in their skins and the pearl onions over low heat in a little butter until done.

4. Prepare the beurre blanc: Place the chopped shallot, wine, crushed pepper and vinegar in a pan, bring to a boil and reduce to a syrup. Add the cream, then the butter a bit at a time, whisking constantly. Add the chopped tarragon and season with salt and pepper. Place a piece of turbot in the center of each plate. Arrange a spoonful of beans on one side of the fish and alternate the onions and the garlic cloves in an arc on the other side. Pour the beurre blanc all around.

Slightly salted cod

Preparation time: 1 hour 30 minutes
Cooking time: 20 minutes
Difficulty: ★★

Serves 4

One 2¼ lb/1 kg piece of fresh cod
1 generous lb/500 g coarse salt
8 tsp/40 g butter
salt and freshly ground pepper

For the brandade:
2 cups/500 ml milk
1 tbsp cream
1 clove garlic

3½ oz/100 g potatoes
1 sprig of thyme
1 bay leaf
olive oil

For the olive oil sauce:
2 shallots
½ green chile
½ green bell pepper
⅛ red bell pepper
roast-meat juices
a little olive oil

For the garnish:
a few basil leaves

Cod, a fish with fine, very delicate flesh, can be a bit bland, and has enjoyed varying fortunes over the last few decades. In bygone days, this fish found high favor with gourmets, and it is now very popular once more.

Choose a really fresh piece of fish, as thick as possible. It should be firm at the time of purchase, or it will fall apart during cooking. In this recipe, it is "marinated" briefly in salt, which firms up its texture and enhances its natural flavor, provided that the prescribed quantity of salt and the period of marination are not exceeded.

Following Jean-Pierre Vigato's instructions to the letter will yield a fish whose texture is similar to that of fresh cod, but with the some of the suppleness of the traditional brandade of cod from the south of France.

The olive oil sauce enlivened with both chile and bell pepper that accompanies both the cod and the *brandade* is also very southern European in style. A word or two should be said about the chile, which should be used in strictly measured doses. Whether you opt for the long *serrano*, the small, wavy *habanero* or the bird's eye chile, these chiles all contain fairly large amounts of capsaicin, whose heat can have a drastic effect on the uninitiated. Always discard the ribs and seeds of chiles, which are the hottest parts, and add a little chile at a time, tasting after each addition.

1. Fillet the cod and remove its skin and remaining bones. Reserve the trimmings. "Marinate" the fillets in coarse salt for 30 minutes. Soak in fresh water for 1 hour to remove excess salt. Cut into thick 6 oz/180 g fillets, season with salt and pepper and steam in butter.

2. To make the brandade, cook 100 g/3½ oz peeled potatoes in the milk with the clove of garlic, bay leaf and sprig of thyme. Lift out the solid ingredients and push the potatoes and garlic clove through a sieve. Cook the cod trimmings for the brandade in the same milk. Lift these out and drain.

with a spicy brandade

3. Transfer the cod trimmings to a bowl and stir in the olive oil and cream. Add the potatoes at the last moment. Keep warm in a double boiler over hot water.

4. Chop the shallots and sweat in a little butter. Add the meat juices and reduce by half. Add a mixture of green chile and green bell pepper that has been put through a juice extractor. Whisk in the olive oil. Blanch the green and red bell peppers. Peel, dice and stew in butter. Add to the sauce. Garnish with a deep-fried basil leaf.

Scottish salmon cooked

Preparation time: 1 hour 30 minutes
Cooking time: 25 minutes
Difficulty: ★★★

Serves 4

2 salmon fillets, cut into 12 oz/350 g squares
2 pigs' bladders (soaked in water for 48 hours)
¼ cup/60 g butter
2 large mushrooms

1 medium zucchini
1 medium carrot
1 generous lb/500 g seaweed
½ bunch of chervil
½ bunch of chives
4 tsp/20 ml fish stock
⅓ cup/80 ml extra-virgin olive oil
sea salt
salt and freshly ground pepper

Lyons is an important gastronomic capital, serving as a point of contact between neighboring regions and their specialties: Bresse with its poultry, the Charolais with its beef, and the alpine lakes with their wealth of fish. This has resulted in an authentic and inventive cuisine, of which the classic *poularde en vessie* (chicken cooked in a pig's bladder) is a good example, inspiring Jean-Pierre Vigato to create this recipe using fish in place of poultry.

Pigs' bladders have always been known for their watertightness. Medieval pilgrims used them as waterskins, pork butchers as shop signs. In the kitchen they are valued for their ability to seal food hermetically, concentrating flavors like the (much-later) pressure cooker. Pigs' bladders are usually available dried. They should be soaked in several changes of cold water for 48 hours. From past experience, Vigato recommends that you then fill the bladders with water to verify that they are free from leaks. You must then have patience, because sealing the bladders is no easy task. Once they have cooked and inflated, they become unstable and must be wedged in place. Vigato uses seaweed for this, but a deep plate of the right size would also do the trick.

In Vigato's opinion, Scottish salmon is the best. The cold waters of Scotland are known to be rigorously monitored, guaranteeing the quality of the environment of the fish, whether wild or farmed. The pieces of salmon should be cut from the fleshiest part of the fillet, along the backbone toward the head.

1. Soak the pigs' bladders in several changes of ice-cold water for 48 hours. Rinse well inside and out, and test for leaks by filling with water. Wash the vegetables, peeling the carrot, and slice them finely. Blanch the carrot and zucchini. Sweat the mushrooms in a little butter. Drain the vegetables and cut up the herbs. Divide the vegetables and herbs evenly between the two bladders.

2. Remove the skin and remaining bones from the 2 salmon fillets and place the fillets in their respective bladders with the vegetables. Add the butter and fish stock.

in a pig's bladder

3. Lightly inflate the bladder and tie shut with some string 1½–2 in/4–5 cm from the top. Fold over the top and again tie shut tightly to prevent any leakage during cooking.

4. Cook for 25 minutes in gently simmering water. Arrange the blanched seaweed on two platters and place an inflated bladder on each. Serve with two sauce boats, one containing olive oil, the other sea salt. The contents of each bladder serves 2.

Arctic char with

Preparation time: 15 minutes
Cooking time: 30 minutes
Difficulty: ✶✶

Serves 4

1¼ lb/600 g arctic-char fillets
¾ oz/20 g black truffles
generous 1 lb/500 g spinach
10½ oz/300 g cauliflower
1 tomato

3 cloves garlic
6½ tbsp/100 ml fish stock
1 small piece chile
1¾ oz/50 g Parmesan cheese
olive oil
salt and freshly ground white pepper

For the capellini dough:
2½ cups/300 g all-purpose flour
10 egg yolks
salt

In this recipe, the arctic char is served on a bed of freshly made capellini, also know as angel-hair pasta. Once again we have cause to admire the formidable creativity of theItalians, who are forever inventing new varieties of pasta, and annualy consume about 55 lb/25 kg per capita of it.

The egg-rich capellini are served with tiny cauliflower florets, whose flavor and crunchiness add an extra dimension to the dish. The cauliflower should be a firm specimen with very white, tightly packed florets. Note the clever structure of this easy-to-prepare brassica,

whose edible portion is well protected against frost and other damage by its large green leaves. According to Mark Twain, cauliflower is "nothing but a cabbage with a college education." Killjoys accuse this vegetable of bitterness, but this can be remedied by steaming it or changing the water between cooking stages.

The arctic char, *salmerino* in Italian, was once found chiefly in alpine lakes. It is fairly abundant in Lake Annecy in Haute-Savoie, but it is now farmed extensively. Its delicacy is best preserved by cooking over low heat, or braising.

1. Cook and purée the spinach, squeezing out all excess moisture. Mix the flour and the egg yolks, working in the spinach purée. Refrigerate the dough for 1 hour, then roll out thinly and cut into very fine capellini. Cook the cauliflower florets in boiling salted water; drain. Sauté in some olive oil with the salt, pepper and chile.

2. Cut the arctic char into pieces and braise over low heat in a little olive oil with a whole clove of garlic. Remove the fish. Add a small ladleful of fish stock to the cooking juices, as well as the pulp of 1 tomato and 1 tsp chopped truffles. Reduce for 2 minutes, then blend or process and press through a fine strainer.

black truffles

3. Cook the capellini in boiling water, then drain and mix gently with the cauliflower florets and the freshly grated Parmesan. In a small skillet, warm the whole garlic clove and the thinly sliced truffles in the olive oil.

4. Arrange a mound of capellini and some cauliflower in the center of each plate, pour some sauce all around and top with the fish pieces. Garnish with truffle slices.

Pandora with an oyster-

Preparation time: 15 minutes
Cooking time: 1 hour 30 minutes
Difficulty: ★★

Serves 4

10½ oz/300 g pandora fillets
3½ oz/100 g fresh morels
7 oz/200 g oyster mushrooms or chanterelles, according to season
1 clove garlic
1¾ oz/50 g shallots
1 piece of pork rind

2 eggs
¾ oz/20 g fresh ginger root
1 tbsp diced carrot, onion and celery
1 sprig of thyme
7 oz/200 g chervil
1 bay leaf
6½ tbsp/100 ml *crème fraîche*
¾ cup/200 ml olive oil
salt and freshly ground white pepper

For garnish:
peeled, diced tomato
parsley

This recipe delicately brings together the fruits of the earth and sea while respecting their contrasts and individual flavors. First, we have that highly prized wild woodland mushroom, the morel. Gianfranco Vissani believes that France has the best morels, expecially the conical variety, to whose delicacy and flavor he sings his praises. He combines them here with shallots to provide his dinner guests, and yours, with a gustatory jolt and to keep their taste buds on the alert. He is also full of praise for the cultivated mushroom, and reminds us that it it is the Tuscans to whom we owe the principles of growing mushrooms in layers.

Oyster mushrooms are used in the savory molded custard or *timbale* that accompanies the pandora, a typically Mediterranean fish that is similar to sea bream. Its somewhat lackluster flavor can be perked up with the addition of some fresh ginger. Be sure not to overdo it with this piquant rhizome, because its flavor can be overpowering. The ginger and the shallot, the two strongest-tasting ingredients in this dish, should be measured very carefully.

Care should be taken not to overcook the pandora, or its fragile, delicate flesh could wind up tasting insipid and mushy.

1. Skin the fillets and cut into 2½ oz/75 g pieces. Sauté the oyster mushrooms in olive oil with the thyme and the whole garlic clove.

2. Purée the oyster mushrooms in a blender with the eggs, the chopped chervil, half of the crème fraîche, and salt and pepper. Butter the dariole molds and fill with the custard mixture. Bake in a water bath for 40 minutes at 325 °F/160 °C.

mushroom *timbale* and morels

3. Heat some olive oil in a sauté pan and sweat the chopped shallots, the finely diced pork rind, a tablespoonful of finely diced carrot, onion and celery, the bay leaf and thyme. Add a quarter of the morels, the finely sliced ginger, and the cabbage, blanched and cut into thin strips. Moisten with fish stock and add the remaining crème fraîche. Reduce, blend to a purée and press through a fine-mesh strainer.

4. Sauté the remaining morels and the rest of the coarsely chopped, blanched cabbage leaves in butter. Pan-fry the fish fillets. Pour the sauce onto the plates and unmold the mushroom timbale in the center. Arrange the pandora fillets around it, alternating with the morels and cabbage leaves. Garnish with the peeled, diced tomato and sprigs of parsley.

Monkfish medallions with

Preparation time: 15 minutes
Cooking time: 15 minutes
Difficulty: ✶

Serves 4

14 oz/400 g monkfish fillet
salt and freshly ground pepper

For the basil-vinaigrette dressing:
¾ cup/200 ml extra-virgin olive oil
3½ tbsp/50 ml very fruity olive oil
juice of ½ lemon

a few basil leaves
salt and freshly ground pepper

For the vegetable garnish:
1¾ oz/50 g carrots
1¾ oz/50 g leeks
1¾ oz/50 g celery
salt

For garnish:
chervil leaves
small basil leaves

This original, simple and colorful dish is certain to appeal to devotees of a fresh, light style of cooking. The combination of hot monkfish medallions with the cold vinaigrette yields a lukewarm dish served with a cornucopia of finely sliced vegetables, with the scent and flavor of basil as the keynote.

Set aside any reservations you have concerning monkfish; its truly hideous appearance when whole should not deter you from enjoying the quality of its flesh. Just be sure that all the impurities, membranes and fibers have been removed from the tail, leaving only very supple, elegant white flesh. Cut the flesh into medallions, which should be broiled until just done before being served with the vegetable accompaniment,

The vinaigrette dressing plays a key role in the balance of this dish, its basil flavor helping to forge a link between the monkfish and the vegetables. To pull this off successfully, you should choose small basil leaves for preference, as their lemony flavor is not as aggressive as that of larger leaves. The vegetables are kept simple, prepared as a classic julienne. Another vegetable chosen at the market on account of its freshness could also be included in the mixture. In any case, pay attention to the respective cooking times of the vegetables, and cook separately those varieties requiring different treatment.

This summer dish can easily be made substituting different kinds of fish, for example turbot or salmon, for the monkfish.

1. Fillet the monkfish. Remove all membranes and slice into 16 medallions of the same size. Season.

2. Prepare the seasoned monkfish medallions for broiling by spacing them out at even intervals on a buttered baking dish or sheet.

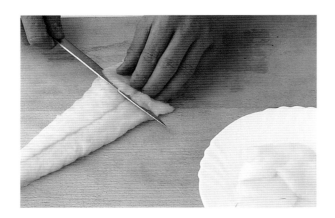

vegetables in a vinaigrette dressing

3. Prepare the basil vinaigrette: Combine the 2 olive oils together with the juice of ½ lemon, the salt and a generous grinding of pepper. Add the chopped basil and whisk everything together.

4. Clean the vegetables and cut them into strips. Blanch separately in boiling salted water and drain. Dry them and toss with the basil vinaigrette while still warm. Broil the monkfish medallions until just done, and season. Transfer to serving plates, garnish with the marinated vegetables and pour over the remaining dressing. Decorate with basil and chervil.

Salmon in a spinach

Preparation time: 20 minutes
Cooking time: 20 minutes
Difficulty: ★★

Serves 4

1 salmon (or 14 oz/400 g fillet)
3½ oz/100 g pike fillet
¾ oz/20 g caviar
32 large spinach leaves
1 shallot

1 egg
13 tbsp/200 g butter
6½ tbsp/100 ml heavy cream
6½ tbsp/100 ml whipped cream
2 cups/500 ml white wine
2 cups/500 ml fish stock
3½ tbsp/50 ml Noilly Prat (French dry vermouth)
freshly ground nutmeg
salt, freshly ground pepper

People should stop thinking of salmon as an "anywhere, anytime" food: it is suffering from overexposure and consumers are tiring of it. And that is hardly fair, for this choice fish merits the most sophisticated of preparations. In Scotland and Norway, salmon is farmed on a large scale. Of course there is also wild salmon, which offers delicious, fine flesh.

Scottish salmon has been awarded the French *label rouge* seal of quality, which is not given lightly. Therefore, if it is available, be sure to give it the starring role in this dish.

Whatever salmon you use, it should be absolutely fresh of course. It should be cut carefully into equal-sized portions

of 3½ oz/100 g. Larger pieces might lead to an imbalance with the other ingredients of this dish, according to Heinz Winkler.

Note that the cooking method employed in this recipe preserves the delicate color of the salmon, which contrasts beautifully with its cloak of bright green.

The spinach cloak is lined with a contrasting white fish mousse. Stem and blanch the spinach leaves and dry them in a cloth before spreading with the mousse, topping with the fish and making into little parcels. These should be wrapped tightly, in order to prevent the pike stuffing from leaking out.

1. Cut the well-chilled pike fillet into chunks. Season with salt and chop in the food processor. Add the egg, and gradually incorporate the heavy cream. Season with pepper and freshly ground nutmeg and push through a sieve. Lastly, gently fold in the whipped cream.

2. Fillet the salmon and cut into four cutlets about ⅜ in/1 cm thick and 3½ oz/100 g in weight. Blanch the spinach leaves, spread out over a cloth into 8 small rectangles and dry.

cloak with caviar cream

3. Spread each spinach rectangle with a ⅜ in/1 cm layer of fish mousse. Top with a well-seasoned salmon cutlet and envelop with the spinach. Place the salmon parcel in a gratin dish with a little fish stock and cook for 6 minutes in a preheated 400 °F/200 °C oven. Remove and drain on paper towels.

4. To prepare the sauce, bring the white wine, Noilly Prat and chopped shallots to a boil in a saucepan. Add the fish stock. Reduce by two thirds, whisk in the butter and simmer for 6 minutes. Blend and correct the seasoning. Add the caviar at the last minute, taking care not to boil any further. Serve the salmon on heated plates, garnished with the sauce and a few sprigs of chervil.

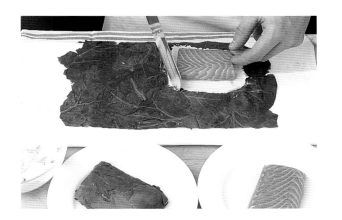

Chartreuse of scallops

Preparation time: 1 hour
Cooking time: 20 minutes
Difficulty: ★★

Serves 4

16 large sea scallops
12 cultivated mussels, 12 clams
1½ oz/40 g caviar, 8 cabbage leaves
2 tbsp/30 g butter

For the mussels:
¾ oz/20g each shallot, leek and celery
1 clove garlic, 3 peppercorns
1⅔ cup/400 ml water, ½ cup/125 ml white wine
4 tsp/20 ml olive oil
2 saffron threads
1 pinch of coarse sea salt

For the *nage*:
½ cup/125 ml stock from the mussels and scallop beards ("frills") or trimmings
2 oz/60 g carrots

2 oz/60 g snow peas
2 oz/60 g leek
1 shallot
1 bunch of cilantro
½ cup/125 ml dry wine
4 tbsp/20 ml Noilly Prat (French dry vermouth)
¼ cup/60 g butter
cayenne pepper

For the filling:
3½ oz/100 g langoustines
½ egg white
6½ tbsp/100 ml cream
1 tbsp whipped cream
salt and freshly ground pepper, cayenne pepper

Although cilantro looks something like flat-leaf parsley, its flavor is a good deal more pungent. It should therefore be used in moderation, lest it spoil the dish it is intended to enhance.

A *nage* (French for "swimming") is a court-bouillon in which the shellfish take their last dip. This is transformed into a sauce by reducing it and adding fine flavors. The latter are provided by the cilantro and the scallop beards —which are removed from the white meat when the shells are opened—as well as by the distinctively flavored cultivated mussels.

Incidentally, French cultivated mussels are known as *moules de bouchot*, *bouchot* signifying the stakes and wickerwork to which the mollusks attach themselves via a sticky substance that they secrete. This has led in the west of the country to the term *boucholeur* or *bouchoteur* for the mussel grower, rather than the *myticulteur* (*Mytilidae* is the marine mussel family) prevalent in other parts of France.

Harald Wohlfahrt recommends scallops from Scotland or Ireland, but those from Brittany (especially Baie de Saint-Brieuc) are also good.

1. Lightly sauté the diced vegetables and season with salt and pepper. Add the mussels and clams and sauté lightly. Add the white wine and water. Cook the mollusks until they open, then shell them and set aside. Clean the scallops, pull off and reserve their beards and shell them. Dry the white meat on paper towels. Cook the beards in the shellfish cooking liquor for 15–20 minutes, then strain.

2. Salt and pepper the cooked, chilled langoustine tails. Purée finely, then add the egg white, followed by the cream, which should be incorporated bit by bit. Press the mixture through a sieve and fold in the whipped cream. Correct the seasoning. Blanch and refresh the cabbage leaves and drain on paper towels. Butter 4 ramekins, line with the cabbage leaves and refrigerate.

in a vegetable *nage*

3. Using a piping bag, fill the ramekins with the langoustine stuffing. Quarter the scallops, season with salt and pepper and place on top of the stuffing. Tuck in the cabbage-leaf overhang to seal and steam for 6 minutes at 400 °F/200 °C. Cut the vegetables for the nage into fine julienne. Blanch each type separately and refresh in ice water.

4. Reduce the shellfish cooking liquid to a coating consistency. Add the wine and Noilly Prat and whisk in the cold diced butter. Add the vegetables, mussels and clams, and reheat gently. Arrange the cabbage-shellfish molds in the center of each plate. Surround with the vegetables, mussels and clams and pour over the nage. Top each chartreuse with a small mound of caviar and garnish with a few cilantro leaves.

Arctic char fillet with

Preparation time: 45 minutes
Cooking time: 8 minutes
Cooling time: 3 hours
Difficulty: *

Serves 4:

4 arctic char (12–14 oz/350–400 g)
1 tbsp oil
sea salt
freshly ground pepper

For the horseradish crust:
1¾ oz/50 g freshly grated horseradish
¼ cup/60 g butter
3 egg yolks

2 oz/60 g white bread
salt, freshly ground pepper, cayenne pepper

For the sauce:
¾ oz/20 g shallots, chopped
1 cup/250 ml fish stock
1 cup/250 ml dry riesling
2½ tbsp/40 ml Noilly Prat (French dry vermouth)
½ cup/120 g butter
2 tbsp whipped cream
a few drops lemon juice
1 bunch of shallots
salt and freshly ground pepper

For the garnish:
1¾ oz/50 g potatoes
1¾ oz/50 g beets
1 bunch of watercress

The state of Baden-Wurttemberg in southwestern Germany abounds in lakes, rivers and streams, and hence in freshwater fish. Harald Wohlfahrt confesses to a weakness for arctic char, whose slightly sweet flavor sets it apart within the salmon family. It must also be said that the exceptional geographical situation of our chef means that he can order fresh fish and have it delivered within the hour by a fisherman who knows where to find adequate supplies of this fish that is increasingly rare in the wild.

This light-eyed fish, which must be cooked at a uniform temperature, has a lot of bones, whjich you will have to spend somw time removing. The odd bone will still turn up even after you have executed this tedious procedure.

In terms of quantity, you will need about 12–14 oz/350–400 g arctic char per person. There is a lot of waste with large specimens, so that the smaller ones are relatively more economical. The flavor of arctic char is complemented superbly by the sharp horseradish, especially if the latter is grated just before use.

You will be delighted by the exquisite taste of the crisp fish skin, which not only serves to decorate the plate, but lends an element of contrast, inviting you to crunch into an otherwise soft and delicate dish.

If you are unable to get hold of arctic char, a fine sea trout will fit the bill quite nicely.

1. For the horseradish crust, cream the butter in a bowl. Add the egg yolks a little at a time, whisking constantly. Mix in the horseradish and the fine white bread crumbs. Season with salt and pepper and chill the mixture for 2–3 hours.

2. Scale, gut and fillet the fishes. Remove remaining bones and pan-fry quickly on the skin side in a little olive oil. Next, remove the skin and fry it in the hot pan until crisp.

horseradish and shallot butter

3. Place the fish fillets on a buttered baking sheet and cover with a thin slice of horseradish butter. Place under the broiler for a couple of minutes until the topping turns golden brown. Mix the riesling and Noilly Prat with the chopped shallot in a saucepan and reduce by two thirds. Add the fish stock and cream. Reduce by half and add the chilled diced butter. Correct the seasoning and add a few drops of lemon juice.

4. Blanch separately the cubed potato and beet, then sauté in separate pans in hot butter. Place the broiled fish fillets on heated plates and add the shallot butter. Decorate with the crisp skin and the watercress. Arrange the diced vegetables around the fish.

Grouper with a

Preparation time: 30 minutes
Cooking time: 15 minutes
Difficulty: ☆

Serves 4

1 small grouper (or four 5 oz/150 g fillets)
generous 1 lb/500 g zucchini, eggplant,
onions and red bell peppers, total weight, very
finely diced

2 cloves garlic
1⅔ cup/400 ml olive oil
thyme
chives
salt and freshly ground pepper

Grouper is especially popular in Italy. This large Atlantic fish might not be in the same size league as the giant Mediterranean grouper, which can reach a weight of 660 lbs/300 kg, but it does offer dense white flesh that doesn't fall apart during cooking.

Armando Zanetti is exceptionally proud of his miniature version of ratatouille, ascribing to it an importance inversely proportional to the size of its components. The quality and freshness of the vegetables and their proper cooking are crucial factors here. This is especially true for the red bell pepper, whose slightly indigestible skin must be removed. Dip the bell pepper in boiling water for several seconds, as you would do with a tomato; this should loosen the skin enough to allow its removal. In other cases—but under no circumstances in this recipe—our chef roasts halved or quartered peppers in the oven and then wraps them immediately in newspaper. The steam trapped in the newspaper condenses, helping to remove the skin of the peppers.

The mini-ratatouille should be on the *al dente* side. Carrots, peas and finely cut-up artichokes offer unexpected flavors, so long as the mixture is bound with high-quality olive oil.

1. Peel the onions and the red bell pepper. Finely dice the zucchini, eggplant, onions and bell pepper, placing them in separate bowls.

2. Sauté the finely diced vegetables in olive oil and garlic, adding them to the pan in the following sequence: onions, eggplant, zucchini and red bell pepper. Correct the seasoning and add the thyme.

"mini-ratatouille"

3. Fillet the grouper, but do not skin. Brown the fillets in a nonstick pan, starting with the skin side.

4. Place a metal ring in the center of the plate and fill with the mini-ratatouille. Top with the grouper and drizzle with a little extra-virgin olive oil. Decorate with a criss-cross pattern of chives.

Arctic char *in carpione*

Preparation time: 20 minutes
Cooking time: 35 minutes
Difficulty: ★★

Serves 4

2 arctic chars
1 head escarole, 2 heads radicchio
1 bunch arugula
2 cups/500 ml chicken broth
1⅔ cups/400 ml peanut oil
6½ tbsp/100 ml extra-virgin olive oil
3½ tbsp/50 ml balsamic vinegar
¾ cup/200 ml white-wine vinegar
¾ cup/200 ml *moscato* (Italian muscat wine)
pinch of sugar

1 tomato
1½ oz/40 g flour
3½ tbsp/50 g butter

4 leaves gelatin or 4 tsp powdered gelatin
scant ½ oz/10 g chives
2 tsp/10 g salt and freshly ground pepper

For the *carpione* mixture (prepare the day before):
2 cloves garlic
7 oz/200 g onions
2 bay leaves
1¾ oz/50 g sage
1 oz/30 g raisins
7 oz/200 g pine nuts

The arctic char inhabits cold, well-oxygenated waters and boasts colorful, firm yet tender flesh. One of the few disadvantages of this fish is its rarity in the wild. However, Piedmont in the northwest of Italy is a geographically blessed region, abounding in alpine lakes, and hence in wild arctic char. Armando Zanetti has an admirable way of increasing the keeping qualities of this fish, by preparing it *in carpione*, that is preserving it in a marinade originally intended for the Lake Garda fish, the carpione, based on a noble wine, for example the Italian *moscato*. In the Middle Ages, this was the method most commonly used in this region to preserve meat, fish and vegetables, usually with vinegar or white wine in large earthenware jars.

Make the *carpione* mixture at least a day in advance and remember that your aim is to obtain a gelatinous preparation, either naturally (which actually takes a good week) or with the aid of gelatine leaves, which are neutral in taste.

The fish does not take long to cook, since it is virtually cooking for the second time when you immerse it in the hot marinade. Its flesh should then be porous enough to absorb all the flavors of the latter. Before thjs, however, be sure to remove all the bones and the stubbornly adherent skin.

1. Prepare the carpione mixture: Heat the butter until it browns slightly, then add the sage, 2 cloves garlic, bay leaf and sliced onions. Sauté the mixture until golden brown. Add the pine nuts and raisins.

2. Deglaze with the vinegar and moscato. Bring to a boil, add the broth and a pinch of sugar and simmer for about 30 minutes.

with muscat wine

3. Fillet the arctic char and remove the remaining bones and the skin. Dredge in flour and pan-fry briefly in plenty of hot oil. Drain on paper towels. Soften the gelatin leaves in water. Strain the carpione cooking water and add the gelatin. Cover the char fillets with this hot liquid and refrigerate for 24 hours.

4. Wash the salad greens and slice into paper-thin shreds. Season to taste. Arrange a char fillet in the center of each plate, surround with little mounds of salad greens, a few cubed tomatoes, some pine nuts, onions and raisins, and garnish with some snipped chives.

Bacalao a

Preparation time: 1 hour
Cooking time: 20 minutes
Difficulty: ★★

Serves 4

Four 9 oz/250 g pieces of salt cod (soaked for 48 hours to remove excess salt)
1¾ lbs/800 g red onions
6 cloves garlic

6 dried red bell peppers
1 ham bone
olive oil
salt and freshly ground pepper

Salt cod is not only esteemed in Portugal, but also right along the eastern coastline of the Atlantic and the coast of the English Channel up to the North Sea, where the Norwegians are particulary fond of it. It is hardly surprising, therefore, that this Biscayan-style salt-cod recipe from the Spanish Basque country, the promised land of fish and crustaceans, is extremely common in those regions. Morevover, the Spanish claim that the process for salting the cod catch to preserve it traveled from their country to Norway..

The sauce *a la vizcaína* is a Basque recipe from the province of Vizcaya, and is made with the red or pink onions well known in most Mediterranean countries. These onions contain little sugar, giving the sauce a robust taste. If you want to give the sauce more body and creaminess, you can enrich the mixture with a piece of thick, fatty pork rind or, as here, a ham bone simmered with garlic and onion.

The advantage of a sauce like this is that it can be made all year round, and can also be enriched according to taste with the most varied vegetables, especially potatoes.

1. Desalt the cod 48 hours in advance. In a high-sided frying pan, gently brown the very finely sliced onions, the ham bone and half of the garlic. Cook slowly. Remove the bone.

2. Blanch the red bell peppers 3 times. Peel and seed them and add the flesh to the onions, sautéing gently for 3–4 minutes. Purée the mixture in a blender or food processor, then add the remaining garlic and correct the seasoning. (If the cod is still too salty, bring the water to a boil and blanch it twice).

la vizcaína

3. Pour some olive oil into a nonstick skillet and pan-fry the pieces of cod over a high heat for 7 minutes. Turn and cook for a further 5 minutes.

4. Cover the bottom of an earthenware casserole with the sauce and arrange the pieces of cod on top. Simmer for a few minutes over low heat. Serve piping hot.

Hake fillet with

Preparation time: 20 minutes
Cooking time: 10 minutes
Difficulty: ✳

Serves 4

1 large hake
20 large *kokotxas* (lower-jaw muscle of the hake)
2 cloves garlic
1 cup/250 ml olive oil
flat-leaf parsley
salt and freshly ground pepper

Nowadays, nearly everyone in Spain is familiar with the *kokotxa*, discovered by a female chef from San Sebastián. This is the V-shaped muscle used by the hake to move its lower jaw. Soft and gelatinous in texture, the *kokotxa* has become the hake-accompaniment supreme in the Basque country, with most restaurants including it on the menu.

Look for a good-sized hake weighing 6½–8¾ lb/3–4 kg, which should yield fine, very white fillets of an agreeable texture. As for the *kokotxas*, with all the will in the world, each fish has just one such muscle, so you may have to substitute the whole fish head, taking care to cook it very gently so as not to burn its precious gelatin.

It is this gelatin, by the way, that the *pil-pil* of the recipe stands for, as this is the name given to the thickening substance with which it surrounds the fish.

If no hake is available, you may substitute any fish whose head yields a lot of gelatin when cooked—or even cod—in this recipe.

1. Cut the hake fillets into portion-sized pieces. Skin and season the fillets. Heat the oil in an earthenware casserole and sauté the 2 finely sliced garlic cloves.

2. Remove the garlic when golden brown, reduce the heat and cook the fish fillets for 2 minutes on each side.

kokotxas al pil-pil

3. Add the kokotxas and season with the chopped parsley. Cook for a further minute, then remove from the heat.

4. Carefully shake the casserole with a gentle circular motion to thoroughly mix the oil and the fish juices. Serve immediately.

Basic recipes

Sauce américaine

Recipe: Spiny lobster with olives,
by Jacques Chibois

Ingredients:
2 lobsters (generous 1 lb/500 g each), 1 carrot, 1 onion, ⅓ cup plus
1½ tbsp/100 ml dry white wine, 2 tbsp cognac, 3½ tbsp/50 ml oil,
2 cups/500 ml veal or fish stock, 4 tomatoes, 1 tbsp tomato paste,
1 bouquet garni (parsley, thyme, bay leaf, chervil, tarragon), salt,
cayenne pepper, 10 tbsp/150 g butter.

Preparation:
*Sever the lobster heads from the tails. Halve the heads lengthwise,
and remove and discard the dark intestine running down the body, as
well as the stomach that is located at the top of the head. Place the
coral in a bowl and mix with 3½ tbsp/50 g butter. Finely dice the onion
and carrot. Heat the oil in a braising pan to very hot, then put in the
lobster pieces and sauté until the shell turns bright red. Add the
cognac, the white wine, the tomatoes, peeled, cored and chopped, the
bouquet garni, the tomato paste and 2 cups/500 ml veal or fish stock.
Cover the pan and cook for about 20 minutes. Remove the lobster and
bind the sauce with the coral butter. Bring to a boil and season with salt
and cayenne pepper. Pass through a fine sieve and whisk in 6½
tbsp/100 g butter to finish.*

Beer batter

Recipe: Perch fillets with *confit* tomatoes,
by Horst Petermann

Ingredients:
5¼ oz/150 g all-purpose flour, 2 eggs, 3 egg whites, ¾ oz/20 g sugar,
pinch of salt, 3½ tbsp/50 ml beer.

Preparation:
*Mix together the flour, 2 whole eggs, salt and sugar in a bowl.
Gradually add the beer to yield a smooth, supple batter. "Rest" the
batter in the refrigerator. Before using, beat the 3 egg whites to stiff
peaks and gently fold in.*

Brioche dough

Recipe: Russian salmon koulibiac,
by Michel Bourdin

Ingredients:
2 lbs 10 oz/1.2 kg all-purpose flour, 1½ oz/40 g sugar, 1 oz/24 g salt,
10 eggs, 1½ oz/40 g fresh yeast, ⅓ cup plus 1½ tbsp/100 ml milk,
2½ cups/600 g butter (at room temperature).

Preparation:
*Dissolve the yeast in the cold milk. Place the flour, salt, sugar and milk
in a mixing bowl, together with the yeast and eggs. Using a dough hook
attachment, knead for 10 minutes at medium speed. As soon as the
dough is supple and smooth, quickly mix in egg-sized pieces of the
softened butter. Knead thoroughly. Turn the dough out into a bowl in
which it has room to rise. Cover with a cloth, and allow to rest at room
temperature for about 1½ hours. Punch down the dough and
refrigerate overnight.*

Crêpe batter

Recipe: Russian salmon koulibiac,
by Michel Bourdin

Ingredients:
3½ oz/100 g all-purpose flour, 2 eggs, 1 cup/250 ml milk, pinch of
salt, 3½ tbsp/50 g butter, small bunch of chives.

Preparation:
*Sieve the flour into a bowl with the pinch of salt. Beat in the whole eggs
with a whisk, followed by the milk, a little at a time, until you have a
smooth batter. Melt the butter in a crêpe pan and remove from the heat
as soon as it turns nut brown in color. Pour the butter into the batter,
whisking constantly. Strain. Let stand for 20 minutes before making the
crêpes.*

Fritter batter

Recipe: *Fritto misto* of Dover sole,
by Philippe Dorange

Ingredients:
2¾ oz/80 g all-purpose flour, ¼ cup/60 ml water, 1 tsp/5 g salt, scant
teaspoon/4 g baking powder.

Preparation:
*Whisk the flour, baking powder, salt and water together in a bowl. Let
stand for ½ hour before making the fritters.*

Introducing the chefs

Fernando Adría

born May 14, 1962

Restaurant: **El Bulli**
Address: 30, Apartado de Correos Cala
Montjoi
17480 Rosas, Spain
Tel. (9)72 15 04 57; Fax (9)72-15 07 17

As a talented 21-year-old back in 1983, Fernando Adría received two Michelin stars for his culinary achievements in **El Bulli**, his restaurant on the Costa Brava whose kitchens had previously been run by his friend Jean-Louis Neichel. Awarded 19 points and four red chef's hats by Gault-Millau, Adría has also fared well with the Spanish restaurant guides: four stars in Campsa and 9.5/10 in Gourmetour. A winner of the Spanish National Gastronomy Award, Fernando Adría also received the European Culinary Grand Prix in 1994. When his work leaves him time, this chef is a great supporter of the Barcelona soccer team.

Hilario Arbelaitz

born May 27, 1951

Restaurant: **Zuberoa**
Address: Barrio Iturrioz, 8
20180 Oyarzun, Spain
Tel. (9)43 49 12 28; Fax (9)43 49 26 79

Born in the heart of the Spanish Basque Country, whose gourmet traditions form the emphasis of his cooking, Hilario Arbelaitz began his career in 1970 at **Zuberoa**, where he became chef in 1982. Since then, he has received numerous French and Spanish awards: two Michelin stars, three red chef's hats, and 17 points in Gault-Millau, as well as four Campsa stars. In 1993 he was named Best Chef in Euzkadi (the Basque Country), after being named Best Chef in Spain in 1991. He brings equal measures of enthusiasm to the Basque game of *pelota* and family life, and is very interested in the history and future of his profession.

Firmin Arrambide

born September 16, 1946

Restaurant: **Les Pyrénées**
Address: 19, place du Général de Gaulle
64220 Saint-Jean-Pied-de-Port, France
Tel. (0)5 59 37 01 01; Fax (0)5 59 37 18 97

Firmin Arrambide has been at the helm of this restaurant, not far from his place of birth, since 1986, garnering two Michelin stars, three red chef's hats, and 18 points in Gault-Millau for **Les Pyrénées**. His regionally inspired cuisine won him second place in the 1978 *Taittinger* awards and carried him to the finals of the *Meilleur Ouvrier de France* competition in 1982. True to his Basque origins, Arrambide hunts woodpigeon and woodsnipe in the fall, and also loves mountain climbing; occasionally, though, he enjoys simply soaking up the sun by the pool.

Jean Bardet

born September 27, 1941

Restaurant: **Jean Bardet**
Address: 57, rue Groison
37000 Tours, France
Tel. (0)3 47 41 41 11; Fax (0)3 47 51 68 72

Before opening a restaurant in Tours under his own name in 1987, Jean Bardet traveled throughout Europe, working mainly as a sauce chef at the **Savoy** in London. A member of *Relais et Châteaux*, *Relais Gourmands*, and the Auguste Escoffier Foundation, he was awarded four red chef's hats in Gault-Millau (19.5) and two Michelin stars. In 1982 he had the honor of preparing dinner for the heads of state at the Versailles Summit. Jean Bardet is an enthusiastic cigar smoker (American Express awarded him the title of Greatest Smoker in the World in 1984) and in the fall indulges his passion for hunting, together with friends.

Giuseppina Beglia

born May 16, 1938

Restaurant: **Balzi Rossi**
Address: 2, Via Balzi Rossi
18039 Ventimiglia, Italy
Tel. (0)18 43 81 32; Fax (0)18 43 85 32

Since 1983 her restaurant has towered over this famous vantage point and the caves of the **Balzi Rossi** ("red cliffs"), but Giuseppina Beglia herself is just as well known in Italy for the television cookery programs broadcast under her direction between 1985-90. A member of *Le Soste*, the prestigious Italian restaurant chain, she holds two Michelin stars, three red chef's hats in Gault-Millau (18) and 82/100 in the Italian Gambero Rosso guide. In 1992 she won the first ¡Golden Key of Gastronî, which was donated by Gault-Millau to chefs out of France. Guiseppina Beglia has a great interest in floral decorations and loves to go skiing in the nearby Alps.

Michel Blanchet

born June 16, 1949

Restaurant: **Le Tastevin**
Address: 9, avenue Eglé
78600 Maisons-Laffitte, France
Tel. (0)139 62 11 67; Fax (0)1 39 62 73 09

After a topnotch training in 1967–71 at **Maxim's**, **Lutétia**, and **Ledoyen**, Michel Blanchet took over the reins at **Tastevin** in 1972; today, the restaurant boasts two Michelin stars. Blanchet's talents have more than once carried him through to the final rounds of prestigious competitions: the *Prosper Montagné* prize (1970 and 1972); the *Taittinger* prize (1974), and the *Meilleur Ouvrier de France* competition in 1979. Michel Blanchet is a *Maître Cuisinier de France* and a member of the Culinary Academy of France. A great nature-lover, he enjoys rambling through the woods— sometimes collecting mushrooms—as well as cycling and hiking.

Michel Bourdin

born June 6, 1942

Restaurant: **The Connaught**
Address: Carlos Place, Mayfair
London W1Y 6AL, England
Tel. (0)171 491-0668; Fax (0)171 495-3262

One of the old and distinguished line of French chefs in Great Britain, Michel Bourdin has been delighting London diners at the **Connaught** since 1975. The recipient of numerous prizes (*Prosper Montagné, Taittinger*) since training at **Ledoyen** and under Alex Humbert at **Maxim's**, he has been Chairman of the British branch of the Culinary Academy of France since 1980. In addition, he is a member of the 100 Club, and, like Paul Haeberlin, is also an honorary member of the *Chefs des Chefs* association. His pastry-chef colleagues, the twins Carolyn and Deborah Power, have made the Connaught famous for its desserts.

Christian Bouvarel

born April 26, 1954

Restaurant: **Paul Bocuse**
Address: 69660 Collonges-au-Mont-d'Or,
France
Tel. (0)4 72 42 90 90; Fax (0)4 72 27 85 87

The youngest chef at **Paul Bocuse** had famous teachers, training under Raymond Thuillier at **Ousteau de Baumanière** in Baux-de-Provence in 1971 and Paul Haeberlin at the **Auberge de l'Ill** in Illhaeusern in 1972, before coming to work at this celebrated restaurant in Collonges in 1975. Christian Bouvarel has played his part in the success story of this restaurant, with its three Michelin stars, four red chef's hats in Gault-Millau (19), and four stars in the Bottin Gourmand guide, and was named *Meilleur Ouvrier de France* in 1993. A native of Lyons, he is an enthusiastic nature-lover and spends his scarce leisure hours mountain climbing whenever possible.

Carlo Brovelli

born May 23, 1938

Restaurant: **Il Sole di Ranco**
Address: 5, Piazza Venezia
21020 Ranco, Italy
Tel. (0)3 31 97 65 07; Fax (0)3 31 97 66 20

One sun—it was only fitting that the Italian restaurant guide Veronelli should pay tribute to this restaurant with the sun in its name by awarding it this distinction. Looking back on a 120-year-old family tradition, **Il Sole di Ranco** is run in a masterly fashion by Carlo Brovelli, who took over the reins in 1968 after training at the College of Hotel Management in La Stresa. A member of the *Le Soste, Relais et Châteaux* and *Relais Gourmands* chains, the restaurant has received many accolades: two Michelin stars, three chef's hats in Gault-Millau, (18), 84/100 in the Italian Gambero Rosso. Carlo Brovelli loves cycling and soccer.

Jean-Pierre Bruneau

born September 18, 1943

Restaurant **Bruneau**
Address: 73-75, avenue Broustin
1080 Brussels, Belgium
Tel. (0)24 27 69 78; Fax (0)24 25 97 26

For over 20 years, Jean-Pierre Bruneau has run the restaurant bearing his name which stands in the shadow of the imposing Koekelberg Basilica in the center of Brussels. The sophisticated creations of this Belgian *Maître Cuisinier*" have won him many distinctions: three Michelin stars, four red chef's hats in Gault-Millau, three stars in Bottin Gourmand, and 94/100 in the Belgian restaurant guide Henri Lemaire. He is also a member of *Traditions et Qualité*. Outside of the kitchen, he enjoys hunting and motor racing (first hand), and also collects old automobiles.

Michel Bruneau

born February 11, 1949

Restaurant **La Bourride**
Address: 15-17, rue du Vaugueux
14000 Caen, France
Tel. (0)2 31 93 50 76; Fax (0)2 31 93 29 63

"Normandy is proud of herself"—this is the motto of Michel Bruneau, who never tires of enumerating the sumptuous produce of the Calvados region on his extensive, tempting menu. Starting off his career in the midst of the plantations in Ecrécy, on the banks of the Guigne (1972-82), he then moved to **La Bourride** in Caen, where he has been since 1982. There he continues to delight gourmets with his inventive cooking, steeped in regional traditions, which has also impressed the critics: two Michelin stars and three red chef's hats in Gault-Millau (18). In his spare time, Michel Bruneau enjoys cooking for friends. He plays soccer and sometimes accompanies his son to the skating rink.

Alain Burnel

born January 26, 1949

Restaurant **Oustau de Baumanière**
Address: Val d'Enfer
13520 Les Baux-de-Provence, France
Tel. (0)4 90 54 33 07; Fax (0)4 90 54 40 46

Alain Burnel served his apprenticeship in Beaulieu at **La Réserve de Beaulieu** (1969–73), in Nantes at the **Frantel** under Roger Jaloux, in Marseilles at **Sofitel**, and in Saint-Romain de Lerps at the **Château du Besset**, where he served as chef in 1978–82 before taking over the reins from the famous Raymond Thuillier in Baux, whose restaurant is now owned by the Charial family. Alain Burnel has earned two Michelin stars and three white chef's hats in Gault-Millau (18), and is a member of *Traditions et Qualité, Relais et Châteaux*, and *Relais Gourmands*. In his free time this chef is a keen cyclist, and was even once a participant in the Tour de France.

Jan Buytaert

born October 16, 1946

Restaurant **De Bellefleur**
Address: 253 Chaussée d'Anvers
2950 Kapellen, Belgium
Tel. (0)3 664 6719; Fax (0)3 665 0201

Despite being a dyed-in-the-wool Belgian who has spent a large part of his career in his native country—first at the **Villa Lorraine** in Brussels from 1973–4—Jan Buytaert worked for two years in the kitchens of **Prés et Sources d'Eugénie** in Eugénie-les-Bains under Michel Guérard (1974–5). In 1975, after this French interlude, he opened his current restaurant, which has earned him two Michelin stars and is one of the best in the region.
This Belgian *Maître Cuisinier* loves gentle activities, such as hiking and horseback riding, and also enjoys gardening.

Jacques Cagna
born August 24, 1942

Restaurant **Jacques Cagna**
Address: 14, rue des Grands Augustins
75006 Paris, France
Tel. (0)1 43 26 49 39; Fax (0)1 43 54 54 48

This distinguished chef has worked in the most famous restaurants of the French capital—1960 at **Lucas Carton**, 1961 at **Maxim's**, and 1964 at **La Ficelle**—and was even Chef to the French National Assembly (1961–62) before opening a restaurant under his own name in 1975, for which he has received high honors: two Michelin stars, two red chef's hats in Gault-Millau (18), and three stars in Bottin Gourmand. Jacques Cagna is a Knight of the *Mérite Nationale des Arts et des Lettres*. He knows his way around Asia, speaks fluent Japanese, and is a fan of classical music, opera, and jazz.

Stewart Cameron

born September 16, 1945

Restaurant **Turnberry Hotel & Golf Courses**
Turnberry KA26 9LT, Scotland
Tel. (0)1655 331 000; Fax (0)1655 331 706

Since 1981, the kitchens of the Turnberry Hotel—one of only two 5-star Scottish restaurants—have had a real Scot at the helm: Stewart Cameron, who previously worked at **Malmaison**, the restaurant of the Central Hotel in Glasgow. This chef is also a member of the Taste of Scotland and of the British branch of the Culinary Academy of France. In 1986 and 1994 he was privileged to play host to the participants of the British Golf Open in his restaurant. When he gets the chance, Stewart Cameron goes hunting or fishing. A rugby fan, of course, he is one of the Scottish XV's most faithful supporters.

Marco Cavallucci

born May 20, 1959

Restaurant **La Frasca**
Address: 38, Via Matteoti
47011 Castrocaro Terme, Italy
Tel. (0)543 76 74 71; Fax (0)543 76 66 25

Two Michelin stars, four chef's hats in Gault-Millau (19), one sun in Veronelli, 89/100 in Gambero Rosso: what more could Mario Cavallucci want? Working in perfect harmony with the restaurant's proprietor and sommelier, Gianfranco Bolognesi, this young, energetic chef has already received many accolades. A member of the *Le Soste* restaurant chain since 1978, he has vigorously supported Italy's great culinary tradition.
This extraordinarily busy chef still manages to find a little spare time for fishing, reading, seeing the occasional movie, and playing cards, soccer, and billiards.

Francis Chauveau

Born: September 15, 1947

Restaurant: **La Belle Otéro**
Address: Hôtel Carlton (7th floor)
58, La Croisette
Cannes 06400, France
Tel. (0)4 93 69 39 39; Fax (0)4 93 39 09 06

Although born in Berry in the northwest of France, Francis Chauveau's encounter with Provençal cooking has led to outstanding results, which visitors to the legendary Palace-Hotel in Cannes—holder of two Michelin stars—have been enjoying since 1989. Francis Chauveau gained his first experience as a chef in the **Hôtel d'Espagne** in Valençay, continuing his career at the **Auberge de Noves** in 1965. Later, he worked in prestigious restaurants, such as the **Auberge du Père Bise**, the **Réserve de Beaulieu**, the **Terrasse** in the Hotel Juana in Juan-les Pins, and in the famous restaurant **L'Amandier** in Mougins in 1980–89.

Jacques Chibois

Born: July 22, 1952

Restaurant: **La Bastide St-Antoine**
Address: 45, avenue Henri Dunant
06130 Grasse, France
Tel. (0)4 92 42 04 42; Fax (0)4 92 42 03 42

During the course of a career involving many moves, Jacques Chibois has met numerous famous names in French gastronomy: Jean Delaveyne in Bougival, Louis Outhier in La Napoule, Roger Vergé in Mougins, and the famous pastry chef Gaston Lenôtre. Since 1980 he has often worked under Michel Guérard, and was awarded two Michelin stars during his time at **Gray d'Albion** in Cannes (1981–95). He opened **La Bastide Saint-Antoine** in Grasse in 1995. In his spare time, Jacques Chibois is an enthusiastic cyclist and nature-lover, as well as an avid hunter and angler.

Serge Courville

Born: December 9, 1935

Restaurant: **La Cote 108**
Address: Rue Colonel Vergezac
02190 Berry-au-Bac, France
Tel. (0)3 23 79 95 04; Fax (03) 23 79 83 50

Serge Courville mentions his three teachers—Roger Petit, Robert Morizot and Jean-Louis Lelaurain—with warmth. Although not much interested in accolades, he has nonetheless reached the finals of numerous culinary competitions (*Prosper Montagné* prize, 1971, *Trophée National de l'Académie Culinaire*, 1972, *Taitinger* prize, 1973). Since 1972, he and his wife have run *La Cote 108*, which in 1982 received one Michelin star.
When not working, Serge Courville enjoys cooking for friends. He is also a passionate reader and cyclist, and spends a lot of time in the wilds, fishing or gathering mushrooms.

Bernard Coussau

Born: September 15, 1917

Restaurant: **Relais de la Poste**
Address: 40140 Magescq, France
Tel. (0)5 58 47 70 25; Fax (0)5 58 47 76 17

Bernard Coussau's name is synonymous with the characteristic cuisine of the Landes region in southwest France. At the **Relais de la Poste**, opened in 1954 and the continuous holder of two Michelin stars since 1969, this Honorary Chairman of the *Maîtres Cuisiniers de France* offers diners fine regional cuisine in the surroundings of a superbly preserved old coaching inn. At the summit of an extraordinary career, this chef is an officer of the *Mérite Agricole*, a Knight of the Legion of Honor, and of the *Palmes Académiques*. An old rugby fan, he supports the Dax team, and is also an automobile enthusiast.

Jean Coussau

Born: May 6, 1949

Restaurant: **Relais de la Poste**
Address: 40140 Magescq, France
Tel. (0)5 58 47 70 25; Fax (0)5 58 47 76 17

A worthy heir to the mantel of his father Bernard, Jean Coussau is a *Maître Cuisinier de France*, and a member of the J.R.E. (Young Restauranteurs of Europe) and of the French *Haute Cuisine* association. Following an exemplary Franco-Spanish career at the **Café de Paris** in Biarritz, the **Plaza-Athénée** in Paris, and the **Ritz** in Madrid, since 1970 he has worked with his father in the kitchens of the **Relais de la Poste** in Magescq. In 1976 he reached the finals of the Best Sommelier in France competition. Jean Coussau shares his father's passion for hunting and is also an enthusiastic golfer.

Richard Coutanceau

Born: February 25, 1949

Restaurant: **Richard Coutanceau**
Address: Place de la Concurrence
17000 La Rochelle, France
Tel. (0)5 46 41 48 19; Fax (0)5 46 41 99 45

Richard Coutanceau, whose restaurant boasts a marvelous location in "green Venice" between Marais Poitevin and the Côte Sauvage, started his career in Paris at **L'Orée du Bois** in 1968. He then moved to La Rochelle and the **Hôtel de France et d'Angleterre**, where he worked in 1968–82. This native of Charentais has received many distinctions: two stars in Michelin, three red chef's hats and 17 points in Gault-Millau. His restaurant belongs to the *Relais Gourmands* chain, and he is also a member of the Young Restaurateurs of Europe. Richard Coutanceau is an enthusiastic tennis player and an avid fisherman, who has the good fortune to live on the coast.

Jean Crotet

Born: January 26, 1943

Restaurant: **Hostellerie de Levernois**
Address: Route de Combertault
21200 Levernois, France
Tel. (0)3 80 24 73 68; Fax (0)3 80 22 78 00

Amid a splendid park of Louisiana cedar, willow, and ash, through which a small river flows, Jean Crotet offers discerning diners a sophisticated cuisine which has been awarded two Michelin stars and three stars in Bottin Gourmand. He is a *Maître Cuisinier de France*, as well as a member of the *Relais et Châteaux* and *Relais Gourmands* chains. In 1988, after working for 15 years at the **Côte d'Or** in Nuits-Saint Georges, he settled down in Levernois, near Beaune. In his spare time Jean Crotet enjoys fishing, flying a helicopter, playing tennis, hunting, and gardening.

Claude Dupont

born: June 7, 1938

Restaurant: **Claude Dupont**
Address: 46, avenue Vital Riethuisen
1080 Brussels, Belgium
Tel (0)2 426 0000; Fax (0)2 426 6540

The Belgian and French gourmet restaurant guides have positively showered awards on Claude Dupont's cooking: two Michelin stars since 1976, three stars in Bottin Gourmand, three white chef's hats in Gault-Millau (17), and 92/100 points in the Belgian Henri Lemaire guide. In 1967 he was awarded the *Prosper Montagné* prize, and in 1973 the Oscar of Gastronomy. In addition, this chef ran the Belgian Pavillion at the 1970 World Fair in Osaka, before opening a restaurant under his own name in Brussels. In his leisure time Claude Dupont occupies himself by making things with his hands, gardening, playing tennis, and swimming.

Michel Del Burgo

Born: June 21, 1962

Restaurant: **La Barbacane**
Address: Place de l'Église
11000 Carcassonne-La Cité, France
Tel. (0)4 68 25 03 34; Fax (0)4 68 71 50 15

This young man from Picardy has worked in the kitchens of Alain Ducasse in Courchevel, Raymond Thuillier in Baux-de-Provence, and Michel Guérard in Eugénie-les-Bains. After a short stay in the Rhône valley and Avignon (1987–90), in 1991 Michel Del Burgo was appointed chef of **La Barbacane** in the center of Carcassonne by Jean-Michel Signoles. In 1995 he was awarded his second Michelin star, the Lily of the Restaurant Trade, and the Gault-Millau Golden Key, as well as three red chef's hats and 18 points in the Gault-Millau guide. Michel Del Burgo appreciates the cooking of his fellow chefs in the Land of the Cathars and is also fond of music, motor sport, and hiking.

Éric Dupont

born: April 16, 1966

Restaurant: **Claude Dupont**
Address: 46, avenue Vital Riethuisen
1080 Brussels, Belgium
Tel (0)2 426 0000; Fax (0)2 426 6540

Éric Dupont has had a truly star-studded training, serving successive apprenticeships with the Brussels Masterchef Freddy Van Decasserie (*Villa Lorraine*), Pierre Wynants (*Comme Chez Soi*), and Willy Vermeulen (*De Bijgaarden*). Nowadays he works with his father Claude Dupont in the family business. The apple never falls far from the tree, and it does not seem unreasonable to place high hopes on this young chef who founded the Brussels college of hotel management C.E.R.I.A.
Éric Dupont is an ardent traveler and loves sports, such as swimming, tennis, and horseback riding.

Joseph Delphin

Born: September 4, 1932

Restaurant: **La Châtaigneraie**
Address: 156, route de Carquefou
44240 Sucé-sur-Erdre, France
Tel. (0)2 40 77 90 95; Fax (0)2 40 77 90 08

A Maître Cuisinier de France and member of the Culinary Academy of France, Joseph Delphin delights gourmets from the Nantes area with his culinary skills. A Knight of the Mérite Agricole, this chef has also received the Vase de Sèvres award from the French President. His restaurant, La Châtaigneraie (one Michelin star), is located on the banks of the Erdre, and can be reached by road, river, or helicopter. You are sure to be won over by the warmth of the welcome from the Delphin family, as Jean-Louis, a member of the Young Restaurateurs of Europe, works here with his father. Joseph Delphin enjoys cycling and takes part in the Tour de France.

Lothar Eiermann

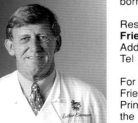

born: March 2, 1945

Restaurant: **Wald- & Schloßhotel
Friedrichsruhe**
Address: 74639 Friedrichsruhe, Germany
Tel (0)7941 60870; Fax (0)7941 61468

For over 20 years Lothar Eiermann has worked at Friedrichsruhe, the summer residence of the Prince von Hohenlohe-Öhringen which belongs to the *Relais et Châteaux* chain. Before this, he traveled throughout Europe, working as a chef in Switzerland in 1964–72 in the **Grappe d'Or** in Lausanne and in the **Hotel Victoria** in Glion. He then worked in the **Gleneagles Hotel** in Scotland, traveled south to England, and returned to Scotland, where he managed a hotel in 1972–3. This Bordeaux-wine enthusiast also has a degree in economics from the University of Heidelberg, and depending on the season, enjoys skiing, cycling, or playing tennis. He is also a fan of the American author Philip Roth.

Philippe Dorange

born: May 27, 1963

Restaurant: **Fouquet's**
Address: 99, avenue des Champs Élysées
75008 Paris, France
Tel (0)1 47 23 70 60; Fax (0)1 47 20 08 69

Is it actually necessary to introduce the legendary **Fouquet's** in these pages? Surely not, nor the prestigious restaurants in which Philippe Dorange has worked in the past: Roger Vergé's **Le Moulin de Mougins** (1977–81), Jacques Maximin's **Negresco** in Nice (1981–88), and **Ledoyen** in Paris, where he was chef in 1988–92. All in all, a fine career path for a young chef whose Mediterranean origins are reflected in his culinary preferences, a fact which is particularly esteemed by his Champs-Elysées clientele. When not in the kitchen, Philippe Dorange likes to box, drive sports cars, or play soccer.

Jean Fleury

born: April 22, 1948

Restaurant: **Paul Bocuse**
Address: 69660 Collonges-au-Mont-d'Or, France
Tel (0)4 72 42 90 90; Fax (0)4 72 27 85 87

After a highly promising début in his hometown of Bourg-en-Bresse—the chief town of Bresse, a region renowned for its outstanding produce—Jean Fleury achieved fame as a chef in the **Hotel Royal** in Évian (1968–9) and in the Brussels **Hilton** (1971–78). Winner of the *Prosper Montagné* prize in 1976, he was named Best Chef in Belgium in the same year, and won the *Meilleur Ouvrier de France* competition in 1979. In 1985 he left the kitchens of the **Arc-en-ciel** in Lyons, following Paul Bocuse to his famous restaurant in Collonges. Jean Fleury loves traveling and hiking and collects antique cookbooks, from which he enjoys drawing inspiration.

Constant Fonk

born: September 1, 1947

Restaurant: **De Oude Rosmolen**
Address: Duinsteeg 1
1621 Hoorn, the Netherlands
Tel (0)229 014752; Fax (0)229 014938

Thanks to Constant Fonk, the town of Hoorn in north Holland has had a two-Michelin-starred restaurant since 1990. After his first highly promising steps in the Amsterdam **Hilton** (1965–6), and the **Amstel Hotel** (1966–7), hef returned to his hometown, where in 1967 he began work in **De Oude Rosmolen**, finally taking over the reins of the kitchen in 1976.
A lover of fine cuisine and good wines, he especially enjoys partaking of both with like-minded people. As far as sport is concerned, golf is his favorite form of exercise, and makes a change from the kitchen.

Louis Grondard

born: September 20, 1948

Restaurant: **Drouant**
Address: 16-18, rue Gaillon
75002 Paris, France
Tel (0)1 42 65 15 16; Fax (0)1 49 24 02 15

It was no small job to have catered for the members of the jury of the prestigious *Goncourt* literary prize every year since 1990. Rather, it required someone with the skills of this chef, who was named *Meilleur Ouvrier de France* in 1979. Louis Grondard served his apprenticeship at **Taillevent** and at **Maxim's**, first in Orly, then in Roissy. He then achieved his first successes in the Eiffel Tower restaurant and in the famous **Jules Vernes**. To quote Michel Tournier, "The stars [two in Michelin] fall as his due from heaven." Louis Grondard has also been favored with three white chef's hats and 17 points in Gault-Millau. He loves literature, music and opera, and enjoys scuba diving when on vacation.

Philippe Groult

born: November 17, 1953

Restaurant: **Amphyclès**
Address: 78, avenue des Ternes
75017 Paris, France
Tel (0)1 40 68 01 01; Fax (0)1 40 68 91 88

A devoted pupil and colleague of Joël Robuchon at **Jamin** in 1974–85, this native Norman now runs his own restaurant, to the satisfaction of diners and critics alike. Named *Meilleur Ouvrier de France* in 1982, today Philippe Groult has two Michelin stars and three red chef's hats (18) in Gault-Millau. In 1988 he was a contender in the Culinary Olympics" in Tokyo, and one year later took over the reins in the kitchen at **Amphyclès**. He has been a member of *Devoirs Unis* since 1978. Philippe Groult is an ardent traveler, a connoisseur of the Far East, and an enthusiastic martial arts practitioner.

Marc Haeberlin

born: November 28, 1954

Restaurant: **Auberge de L'Ill**
Address: 2, rue de Collonges-au-Mont-d'Or
68970 Illhaeusern, France
Tel. (0)3 89 71 89 00; Fax (0)3 89 71 82 83

This worthy heir to the Haeberlin dynasty will certainly not disappoint the gourmets who, once lured by the success of his father Paul, return to this temple of Alsatian cuisine. Three Michelin stars, four red chef's hats (19.5) in Gault-Millau, and four stars in Bottin Gourmand are the impressive distinctions garnered by this former student at the College of Hotel Management in Illkirch. Completing his training with Paul Bocuse and the Troisgros brothers, he proved his skills in Paris at the *Lasserre* in 1976. When time allows, Mark Haeberlin occupies himself with painting and automobiles. In winter he skis on the slopes of the Vosges.

Michel Haquin

born: September 27, 1940

Restaurant: **Le Trèfle à 4**
Address: 87, avenue de Lac
1332 Genval, Belgium
Tel. (0)2 654 0798; Fax (0)2 653 3131

Not far from Brussels, on the shores of Lake Genval, Michel Haquin successfully pursues a culinary career which began in 1961 in the Belgian capital. There, in1977–85, he ran a restaurant under his own name. As a Belgian *Maître Cuisinier* and member of the Culinary Academy of France, this chef was admitted to the Order of the Thirty-three Masterchefs and was awarded the Oscar of Gastronomy. The guidebooks have showered him with honors: two Michelin stars, three red chef's hats in Bottin Gourmand, and 91/100 in the Belgian guide Henri Lemaire. In his leisure time, Michel Haquin enjoys reading and traveling.

Paul Heathcote

born: October 3, 1960

Restaurant: **Paul Heathcote's**
Address: 104 - 106 Higher Road,
Longridge PR3 3 SY, England
Tel. (0)1772 784969; Fax (0)1772 - 785713

This young British chef is very open to culinary influences from the other side of the English Channel. After working with Michel Bourdin at the **Connaught**, he spent two years with Raymond Blanc at the **Manoir au Quatr'Saisons** in Oxfordshire and worked at the **Broughton Park Hotel** in Preston, before finally opening his own restaurant (two Michelin stars) in 1990. In 1994, the Egon Ronay guidebook awarded him the enviable title of Best Chef of the Year. An enthusiastic sportsman, Paul Heathcote loves sports such as soccer, squash, and skiing.

Eyvind Hellstrøm

born: December 2, 1948

Restaurant: **Bagatelle**
Address: Bygdøy Allé 3
0257 Oslo, Norway
Tel. 22 44 63 97; Fax 22 43 64 20

No other chef in Scandinavia has received as many accolades as Eyvind Hellstrøm. He is strongly influenced by French gastronomy, with which he became familiar in the course of his training under famous chefs, such as Guy Savoy, Alain Senderens, Bernard Loiseau, and Fredy Girardet. A member of *Eurotoques* and *Traditions et Qualité*, Eyvind Hellstrøm was awarded two Michelin stars for his restaurant in 1982. A passionate wine connoisseur and a lover of Burgundies in particular, this chef often visits the wine cellars of Beaune and the surrounding area. He enjoys traveling and skiing, and is a fan of the Swedish skier Ingmar Stenmark.

Alfonso Iaccarino

born: January 9, 1947

Restaurant: **Don Alfonso 1890**
Address: Piazza Sant'Agata,
80064 Sant'Agata sui due Golfi, Italy
Tel. (0)81 878 0026; Fax (0)81 533 0226

In 1973, Alfonso Iaccarino named his restaurant, with its marvelous view of the Gulf of Naples and Salerno, after his grandfather. A member of the *Le Soste, Relais Gourmands*, and *Traditions et Qualité* chains, this chef has garnered numerous honors: two Michelin stars, four chef's hats in Espresso/Gault-Millau, one sun in Veronelli, and 92/100 in Gambero Rosso. In 1989 he was awarded the title Best Wine Cellar in Italy for his collection of superb Italian and French wines. In his private life, Alfonso Iaccarino is a true sportsman and particularly enjoys racing and cycling. He also loves nature, painting, and traveling.hter Sportsmann. Außerdem liebt er die Natur, Malerei und Reisen.

André Jaeger

born: February 12, 1947

Restaurant: **Rheinhotel Fischerzunft**
Address: Rheinquai 8,
8200 Schaffhausen, Switzerland
Tel. (0)52 625 3281; Fax (0)52 624 3285

André Jaeger can proudly claim to have successfully inspired Swiss and even European gastronomy with an eastern flavor. His restaurant, which he opened in 1975, boasts two Michelin stars and four red chef's hats in Gault-Millau (19). Named 1995 Chef of the Year by Gault-Millau, he was awarded the Golden Key of Gastronomy in 1988 and appointed Chairman of the *Grandes Tables* in Switzerland. He is also a member of *Relais et Châteaux* and *Relais Gourmands*. A connoisseur of wines from around the world, André Jaeger is also very interested in contemporary art and collects automobiles.

Roger Jaloux

born: May 20, 1942

Restaurant: **Paul Bocuse**
Address: 69660 Collonges-au-Mont-d'Or,
France
Tel. (0)4 72 42 90 90; Fax (0)4 72 27 85 87

As the loyalest among the loyal pupils of Paul Bocuse, Roger Jaloux joined his mentor in his restaurant in 1965, which incidentally received its third Michelin star in the same year. Everything there is to say about this celebrated restaurant in Collonges and the accolades it has received has already been said: it was here that Roger Jaloux prepared for the competition for the prestigious title of *Meilleur Ouvrier de France*, which he won in 1976. In his spare time, Roger Jaloux enjoys the arts, such as painting and singing, and numerous sports, including tennis, cycling, and skiing.

Patrick Jeffroy

born: January 25, 1952

Restaurant: **Patrick Jeffroy**
Address: 11, rue du Bon Voyage
22780 Plounérin, France
Tel. (0)2 96 38 61 80; Fax (0)2 96 38 66 29

A Breton with a penchant for solitude, Patrick Jeffroy settled down in a village in the Côtes-d'Armor *département*, where he serves innovative, delicious food in his restaurant, established in 1988 and now boasting one Michelin star and three red chef's hats in Gault-Millau (17). The earlier part of his career was spent in Abidjan in the Ivory Coast (1972) and the **Hôtel de l'Europe** in Morlaix back in France (1977-87). Patrick Jeffroy has had his Michelin star since 1984. He is also a *Maître Cuisinier de France*, and a recipient of the *Mandarine Impériale* first prize. Out of working hours, he enjoys going to the theater and the movies.

Émile Jung

born: April 2, 1941

Restaurant: **Le Crocodile**
Address: 10, rue de l'Outre
67000 Strasbourg, France
Tel. (0)3 88 32 13 02; Fax (0)3 88 75 72 01

Behind the sign of the crocodile—an allusion to Napoleon's Egyptian campaign—is Émile Jung's restaurant, highly rated by food lovers and a veritable temple of Alsatian cuisine, boasting no fewer than three Michelin stars, three white chef's hats in Gault-Millau (18), and three stars in Bottin Gourmand. The awards hardly come as a surprise, considering that this chef's career took him from **La Mère Guy** in Lyons to **Fouquet's** (1965) and **Ledoyen** (1966) in Paris. Émile Jung is a *Maître Cuisinier de France* and member of *Relais Gourmands* and *Traditions et Qualité*. A passionate oenologist, he is particularly well versed in Alsatian wines.

Dieter Kaufmann

born: June 28, 1937

Restaurant: **Zur Traube**
Address: Bahnstraße 47,
41515 Grevenbroich, Germany
Tel. (0)2181 68767; Fax (0)2181 61122

Dieter Kaufmann harbors a great love of France, and that country knows how to repay him: with two Michelin stars and four red chef's hats in Gault-Millau (19.5) he figures among the most highly esteemed non-French chefs, and was named Gault-Millau 1994 Chef of the Year. He is a member of the prestigious *Traditions et Qualité*, *Relais et Châteaux*, and *Relais Gourmands* chains. With over 30,000 bottles and some remarkable vintages, his restaurant, which he has run since 1962, boasts what is without a doubt the most important wine cellar in Germany. A bibliophile and polyglot, Dieter Kaufmann is also an enthusiastic traveler.

Örjan Klein

born: May 15, 1945

Restaurant: **K.B.**
Address: Smalandsgatan, 7
11146 Stockholm, Sweden
Tel. 86 79 60 32; Fax 86 11 82 83

At the pinnacle of a career based largely in the Swedish capital (**Berns** in 1966–7 and **Maxim's** of Stockholm in 1971–9), Örjan Klein joined forces with Ake Hakansson in 1980 to open **K.B.**, which boasts one Michelin star. Named Chef of the Year in 1993, Örjan Klein is also a *Nordfishing* Trondheim and Swedish Academy of Gastronomy gold-medallist (1976 and 1983, respectively). A nature-lover, he enjoys gardening and hiking. He also writes (cook)books and keeps fit by playing tennis and skiing.

Robert Kranenborg

born: October 12, 1950

Restaurant: **La Rive/Hotel Amstel Inter-Continental**
Address: Prof. Tulpplein, 1
1018 GX Amsterdam, the Netherlands
Tel. (0)20 622 6060; Fax (0)20 520 3277

No one becomes chef of **La Rive** (one Michelin star)—the restaurant of the Inter-Continental, the most prestigious hotel in Amsterdam—overnight. In fact, Robert Kranenborg had a string of successes as glowing references when he began work there in 1987: **Oustau de Baumanière** in Baux-de-Provence (1972–4), **Le Grand Véfour** in Paris (1975–7), and **La Cravache d'Or** in Brussels (1979–86). In 1994, Robert Kranenborg was named Chef of the Year. When he is able to escape from the kitchen, he enjoys playing the drums and sports—golf being his favorite.

Étienne Krebs

born: August 15, 1956

Restaurant: **L'Ermitage**
Address: 75, rue du Lac
1815 Clarens-Montreux, Switzerland
Tel (0)21 964 4411; Fax (0)21 964 7002

As chef-proprietor of a magnificent house on the shores of Lake Geneva, Étienne Krebs is a happy man: a member of the Young Restaurateurs of Europe and *Grandes Tables Suisses*, he boasts one Michelin star and three red chef's hats in Gault-Millau (18), as well as the title of Chef of the Year 1995 for French-speaking Switzerland. After training with the greatest Swiss chefs—Fredy Girardet in Crissier and Hans Stucki in Basel—he ran the **Auberge de la Couronne** in Cossonay in 1984–90, before finally opening **L'Ermitage** in Montreux. Étienne Krebs enjoys walking and cycling around the lake, as well as cooking for his family.

Jacques Lameloise

born: April 6, 1947

Restaurant: **Lameloise**
Address: 36, place d'Armes
71150 Chagny, France
Tel. (0)3 85 87 08 85; Fax (0)3 85 87 03 57

The third generation of his family to bear the name, Jacques Lameloise has, since 1971, also carried on the tradition of running the family restaurant. Cutting his professional teeth at Ogier's in Pontchartrain, in 1965–9 he worked at the Parisian temples of gastronomy **Lucas Carton**, **Fouquet's**, **Ledoyen**, and **Lasserre**, not forgetting the **Savoy** in London. The **Lameloise** can boast three stars in both Michelin and Bottin Gourmand, as well as three red chef's hats in Gault-Millau (18), and is a member of the *Relais et Châteaux*, *Relais Gourmands*, and *Traditions et Qualité* chains. Jacques Lameloise is especially interested in antiques and old automobiles, and enjoys golf and occasionally skiing.

Erwin Lauterbach

born March 21, 1949

Restaurant: **Saison**
Address: Strandvejen, 203
2900 Hellerup, Denmark
Tel. 39 62 48 42; Fax 39 62 56 57

In 1972–3, Erwin Lauterbach served the cuisine of his native Denmark at the **Maison du Danemark** in Paris—a time of which he has many fond memories. In 1977–81 he cooked in Malmö, Sweden at **Primeur**, after which he returned to Denmark. Opened in 1981, **Saison** boasts one Michelin star. Erwin Lauterbach is also member of the Danish Academy of Gastronomy, and a virtuoso proponent of Danish culinary traditions. An admirer of naive painting, he is an ardent visitor of museums and exhibitions. Of all the sports, he most enjoys playing soccer.

Dominique Le Stanc

born December 7, 1958

Restaurant: **Chanteclerc—Hôtel Negresco**
Address: 37, Promenade des Anglais
06000 Nice, France
Tel. (0)4 93 16 64 00; Fax (0)4 93 88 35 68

Some of the biggest names in the world of gastronomy have watched over the early stages of Dominique Le Stanc's career. After serving an apprenticeship with Paul Haeberlin, he worked with Gaston Lenôtre, Alain Senderens, and Alain Chapel, and became *chef de partie* under the latter before putting out his own shingle, first at the **Bristol** in Niederbronn-les-Bains (1982–84), then in Monaco and Eze. A member of the Italian chain *Le Soste*, he has been head chef of **Negresco** since 1989, earning this celebrated establishment two Michelin stars and three red chef's hats in Gault-Millau (18). An enthusiastic athlete, he takes part in triathlons and water-skis.

Michel Libotte

born May 1, 1949

Restaurant: **Au Gastronome**
Address: 2, rue de Bouillon
6850 Paliseul, Belgium
Tel. (0)61 53 30 64; Fax (0)61 53 38 91

Since 1978, Michel Libotte has presided over the kitchens of **Au Gastronome**, rated 94/100 in the Belgian restaurant guide Henri Lemaire. French critics have also been unstinting in their praise, awarding his establishment two Michelin stars and three stars in Bottin Gourmand. Michel Libotte has won the title of Best Cook in Belgium, and is a member of *Eurotoques* and the Culinary Academy of France. His restaurant, which lies close to the Franco-Belgian border, serves a highly individual, imaginative cuisine. Michel Libotte collects firearms as a hobby, and keeps fit by swimming and playing tennis regularly.

Léa Linster

born April 27, 1955

Restaurant: **Léa Linster**
Address: 17, route de Luxembourg
5752 Frisange, Luxembourg
Tel. 66 84 11; Fax 67 64 47

Léa Linster is the first, and to date the only, woman to receive the highest gastronomic accolade, the *Bocuse d'Or*, awarded to her in Lyons in 1989 by the master himself in well-earned recognition of her daily efforts to make the generous cuisine of Luxembourg better known to the dining public. Converting her parents' inn into an *haute cuisine* restaurant in 1982, this chef received her master craftsman's diploma in 1987. In addition to her obvious enthusiasm for fine cuisine, Léa Lister enjoys walks in the wild and stimulating conversations with diners in her restaurant.

Régis Marcon

born June 14, 1956

Restaurant: **Auberge et Clos des Cimes**
Address: 43290 Saint-Bonnet-le-Froid, France
Tel. (0)4 71 59 93 72; Fax (0)4 71 59 93 40

In 1995, at only 39 years of age, Régis Marcon was awarded the *Bocuse d'Or*, with his neighbor Michel Troisgros serving as godfather—just one more glowing distinction in a career already crowned with accolades: the *Taittinger* prize in 1989, the *Brillat-Savarin* prize in 1992, and several-time finalist in the *Meilleur Ouvrier de France* competition (1985, 1991, 1993). In 1979 he opened a restaurant in his village, which was designed to resemble "a cloister bathed in light." It has earned him three red chef's hats in Gault-Millau (17). The eye of a painter is apparent in the restaurant, and this is what Régis Marcon, a great sportsman and medal-winning skier, as well as a passionate lover of nature, once hoped to become.

Guy Martin

born February 3, 1957

Restaurant: **Le Grand Véfour**
Address: 17, rue de Beaujolais
75001 Paris, France
Tel. (0)1 42 96 56 27; Fax (0)1 42 86 80 71

It would be impossible to summarize Guy Martin's career in just a couple of sentences—two Michelin stars, three white chef's hats in Gault-Millau (18), three stars in the Bottin Gourmand, and 18.5/20 in Champérard. This young prodigy of gastronomy studied first with Troisgros, then in his native region, chiefly in Divonne. In 1991 he took over the reins of **Le Grand Véfour**, that jewel among Parisian restaurants at which the *litterati* of the French metropolis have rubbed shoulders for over 200 years, made famous by Raymond Oliver. Guy Martin remains true to the memory of his mother and to his native region of Savoy, of whose culinary history he is a fervent devotee. He also loves music, painting, and Gothic art.

Maria Ligia Medeiros

born August 9, 1946

Restaurant: **Casa de Comida**
Address: 1, Travessa das Amoreiras
1200 Lisbon, Portugal
Tel. (0)1 388 5376; Fax (0)1 387 5132

Since 1978, Maria Ligia Medeiros has run the kitchens of a cozy restaurant owned by Jorge Vales, a former actor of the *Casa de Comedia* theater—hence the pun of the restaurant's name (*comida* means food). There, in the heart of the historic Old Town of the capital, she serves traditional Portuguese dishes with skill and flair, for which she was awarded a Michelin star several years ago. In addition to *haute cuisine*, she loves classical music and spends a large part of her leisure hours reading.

Dieter Müller

born July 28, 1948

Restaurant: **Dieter Müller**
Address: Lerbacher Weg,
51469 Bergisch Gladbach, Germany
Tel. (0)2202 2040; Fax (0)2202 204940

Dieter Müller had already beaten a career path across several countries and continents by the time he settled down in his native Germany in 1992. From 1973 onward he served as head chef of various establishments in Switzerland, Australia (Sydney), Japan, and Hawaii, collecting numerous awards along the way, including the title of Chef of the Year in the Krug guidebook in 1982 and in Gault-Millau in 1988. Today, he boasts two Michelin stars and four red chef's hats (19.5), as well as a National Gastronomy prize. A member of *Relais et Châteaux* and *Relais Gourmands*, his hobbies are photography and collecting old recipes, as well as playing ice hockey and soccer.

Jean-Louis Neichel

born February 17, 1948

Restaurant: **Neichel**
Address: Beltran i Rózpide, 16 bis
08034 Barcelona, Spain
Tel. (9)3 203 8408; Fax (9)3 205 6369

Thanks to his training under such culinary celebrities as Gaston Lenôtre, Alain Chapel, and Georges Blanc, Jean-Louis Neichel is a European chef *par excellence*. For 10 years he brought his invaluable experience to bear while running **El Bulli** in Rosas, where Fernando Adría is now head chef, before opening his own restaurant in Barcelona in 1981, esteemed in particular for its collection of old Armagnacs and Cognacs. Awarded two Michelin stars and 9/10 in Gourmetour, Jean-Louis Neichel is also a member of *Relais Gourmands*. His leisure hours are devoted to oil painting (landscapes), his family, and sports (tennis, cycling, skiing).

Pierre Orsi

born July 12, 1939

Restaurant: **Pierre Orsi**
Address: 3, place Kléber
69006 Lyons, France
Tel. (0)4 78 89 57 68; Fax (0)4 72 44 93 34

Pierre Orsi's career reads like a dream. Named *Meilleur Ouvrier de France* in 1972, he has worked with the culinary greats of his generation: with Bocuse in 1955–8, then at **Lucas Carton**, with Alex Humbert at **Maxim's**, and at **Lapérouse** in Paris. There followed a stint in the United States from 1967–71, after which he returned to Lyons and put out his shingle at the edge of the *Tête d'Or* quarter. His superb restaurant, which boasts one Michelin star and three stars in Bottin Gourmand, is a mecca for gourmets. A member of *Relais Gourmands* and *Traditions et Qualité*, Pierre Orsi is also interested in table decoration and collects *objets d'art* and antiques.

Georges Paineau

born April 16, 1939

Restaurant: **Le Bretagne**
Address: 13, rue Saint-Michel
56230 Questembert, France
Tel. (0)2 97 26 11 12; Fax (0)2 97 26 12 37

Georges Paineau had the unusual good fortune to start off his career under Fernand Point at **La Pyramide** in 1960. Since then, he drew ever closer to Brittany, stopping off in La Baule (1962) and Nantes (1963), before settling at **Le Bretagne** in Questembert, close to the Gulf of Morbihan, where he now collects stars (two in Michelin and four in Bottin Gourmand) and Gault-Millau chef's hats (four red, 19 points). He works with his son-in-law, Claude Corlouer. His restaurant, an old coaching inn, is a member of *Relais Gourmands* and *Relais et Châteaux*. A gifted painter, Georges Paineau also loves literature and rugby.

Paul Pauvert

born July 25, 1950

Restaurant: **Les Jardins de la Forge**
Address: 1, place des Piliers
49270 Champtoceaux, France
Tel. (0)2 40 83 56 23; Fax (0)2 40 83 59 80

Professionally speaking, Paul Pauvert took his first steps at the **Café de la Paix** in Paris. In 1972–4 he served a stint in the kitchens of the Transatlantic Shipping Company's famous ocean liner *Grasse*, after which he worked at the hotel *Frantel* in Nantes at the invitation of Roger Jaloux. In 1980 he opened his own restaurant in his home town, at the site where his ancestors had once run a forge. The holder of one Michelin star, Paul Pauvert is also a member of the Culinary Academy of France and the Young Restaurateurs of Europe. The border area between Anjou and Nantes where he lives offers ample opportunity for the hunting, fishing, and horseback riding which he enjoys.

Horst Petermann

born May 18, 1944

Restaurant: **Petermann's Kunststuben**
Address: Seestraße 160,
8700 Küsnacht, Switzerland
Tel. (0)1 910 0715; Fax (0)1 910 0495

After serving his apprenticeship in Hamburg, Horst Petermann continued his career in Switzerland, in Saint Moritz, Lucerne and Geneva. He cooked in the kitchens of Émile Jung at **Le Crocodile** in Strasbourg, and at the Culinary Olympics in Tokyo in 1985, where he figured among the prizewinners. Further accolades received were the Golden Key of Gastronomy in 1987, Chef of the Year in 1991, four red chef's hats in Gault-Millau (19), and two Michelin stars. The success of his restaurant is also ensured by his master pastry chef, Rico Zandonella. As well as being a keen sportsman, Horst Petermann is passionate about his work and enjoys cultivating the friendships he has made through it.

Roland Pierroz

born August 26, 1942

Restaurant: **Hôtel Rosalp-Restaurant Pierroz**
Address: Route de Médran,
1936 Verbier, Switzerland
Tel. (0)27 771 6323; Fax (0)27 771 1059

Since 1962, Roland Pierroz has worked in this popular winter-sports resort in an equally popular restaurant. The holder of one Michelin star, four red chef's hats and 19 points in Gault-Millau, and three stars in Bottin Gourmand, he was awarded the Golden Key of Gastronomy in 1980 and named Chef of the Year in 1992. Roland Pierroz trained in Lausanne (Switzerland) and London, and is a member of *Relais et Châteaux* and *Relais Gourmands*, as well as Vice-chairman of the *Grandes Tables Suisses*. A native of the Valais, he enjoys hunting and playing golf.

Jacques & Laurent Pourcel

born September 13, 1964

Restaurant: **Le Jardin des Sens**
Address: 11, avenue Saint Lazare
34000 Montpellier, France
Tel. (0)4 67 79 63 38; Fax (0)4 67 72 13 05

Although specializing in different areas, these inseparable twins underwent the same training, serving apprenticeships with Alain Chapel, Marc Meneau, Pierre Gagnaire, Michel Bras, Michel Trama, and Marc Veyrat. Together with their business partner, Olivier Château, they opened the **Jardin des Sens** in a house made of glass and stone in 1988, and have since collected stars in various guides: two from Michelin and three red chef's hats in Gault-Millau (17). Both chefs are *Maîtres Cuisiniers de France* and members of *Relais Gourmands*.

Stéphane Raimbault

born May 17, 1956

Restaurant: **L'Oasis**
Address: rue Honoré Carle,
06210 La Napoule, France
Tel. (0)4 93 49 95 52; Fax (0)4 93 49 64 13

After working for several years in Paris under the watchful eye of Émile Tabourdiau at **La Grande Cascade**, followed by a stint with Gérard Pangaud, Stéphane Raimbault spent nine years in Japan, where he ran the **Rendez-vous** restaurant in the Hotel Plaza d'Osaka in Osaka. After returning to France in 1991, he took over **L'Oasis** in La Napoule, with his brother as pastry chef. The recipient of two Michelin stars and three red chef's hats in Gault-Millau (18), he was also a f nalist for the title of *Meuilleur Ouvrier de France*. In addition, he is a *Maître Cuisinier de France* and a member of *Traditions et Qualité*.

Paul Rankin

born October 1, 1959

Restaurant: **Roscoff**
Address: 7, Lesley House, Shaftesbury Square
Belfast BT2 7DB, Northern Ireland
Tel. (0)1232 331 532; Fax (0)1232 312 093

Paul Rankin has had an international career, working first in London with Albert Roux in **Le Gavroche**, then in California and Canada. It was not, however, in Canada, but on a cruise in Greece that he met his Canadian wife Jeanne, whose skills as a pastry chef have delighted diners at **Roscoff** since 1989. Named Best Restaurant in the United Kingdom by the Courvoisier guidebook in 1994–5, it is only a wonder that **Roscoff** has just one Michelin star. Paul Rankin also presents the BBC television program *Gourmet Ireland*. He loves traveling and wine, plays soccer and rugby, and practices yoga.

Jean-Claude Rigollet

born September 27, 1946

Restaurant: **Au Plaisir Gourmand**
Address: 2, rue Parmentier
37500 Chinon, France
Tel. (0)2 47 93 20 48; Fax (0)2 47 93 05 66

Jean-Claude Rigollet began his career at **Maxim's** under Alex Humbert, then arrived in the Loire valley, working first at **Domaine de la Tortinière** in Montbazon (1971–7), then at the famous **Auberge des Templiers** of the Bézards (1978–82), not far from Montargis. In 1983 he became chef at **Plaisir Gourmand** in Chinon in the Touraine, the home of Rabelais. He received one Michelin star in 1985. Although he comes from the Sologne, Jean-Claude Rigollet also cooks in the style of the Touraine, and his wine cellar is a testament to his extensive knowledge of regional wines.

Michel Rochedy

born July 15, 1936

Restaurant: **Le Chabichou**
Address: Quartier Les Chenus,
73120 Courchevel 1850, France
Tel. (0)2 47 93 20 48; Fax (0)2 47 93 05 66

Michel Rochedy received his earliest professional instruction from André Pic, the celebrated chef from Valence, in 1954–6. Originally from the Ardèche, Rochedy arrived in Savoy in 1963 and succumbed to the charms of the region. His restaurant **Chabichou**, which specializes in Savoy cuisine, has earned him two Michelin stars and three red chef's hats in Gault-Millau (17). A *Maître Cuisinier de France* and member of *Eurotoques*, he is also the chairman of the tourist information board of Courchevel. In his spare time, Michel Rochedy enjoys art and literature, fishes, and plays soccer and rugby.

Joël Roy

born November 28, 1951

Restaurant: **Le Prieuré**
Address: 3, rue du Prieuré,
54630 Flavigny-sur-Moselle, France
Tel. (0)3 79 26 70 45; Fax (0)3 86 26 75 51

In 1979, while still in the employ of Jacques Maximin at the **Hôtel Negresco** in Nice, Joël Roy won the *Meilleur Ouvrier de France* competition. Shortly afterwards, he became head chef at the **Frantel** in Nancy. In 1983 he opened **Le Prieuré**, which looks like a modern cloister with its arcades and garden. His one-Michelin-starred establishment is in the Lorraine, a region he loves for its traditions and natural beauty.
An expert on fish, he is especially fond of river angling, and also enjoys cycling in his spare time.

Santi Santamaria

born July 26, 1957

Restaurant: **El Racó de Can Fabes**
Address: Carrer Sant Joan, 6
08470 San Celoni, Spain
Tel. (9)3 867 2851; Fax (9)3 867 3861

Since 1981, Santi Santamaria has taken great pleasure in serving specialties from his native Catalonia to his discerning clientele. His restaurant, which is just a stone's throw away from Barcelona, at the foot of Montseny National Park, has been awarded three Michelin stars and 8/10 in Gourmetour. In addition, Santi Santamaria is a member of *Relais Gourmands* and *Traditions et Qualité*. He also organizes gastronomic seminars, on herbs in the spring and on mushrooms in the fall. These gourmet workshops are always a great success. In his free time, Santi Santamaria enjoys reading.

Ezio Santin

born May 17, 1937

Restaurant: **Antica Osteria del Ponte**
Address: 9, Piazza G. Negri
20080 Cassinetta di Lugagnano, Italy
Tel. (0)2 942 0034; Fax (0)2 942 0610

Ezio Santiní culinary talents have been common knowledge since 1974, when he became chef at the **Antica Osteria del Ponte**. Three Michelin stars, four red chefís hats in Gault-Millau (19.5), one sun in Veronelli, and 92/100 in Gambero Rosso: these honors justify the high regard in which he is held by his fellow Italian chefs, who have elected him Chairman of *Le Soste*, an association of the best restaurants in Italy. Ezio Santin enjoys reading in his spare time. He is an enthusiastic fan of Inter Milan soccer club and interested in modern dance.

Nadia Santini

born July 19, 1954

Restaurant: **Dal Pescatore**
Address: 46013 Runate Canneto sull'Oglio, Italy
Tel. (0)376 72 30 01; Fax (0)376 70304

Since 1974 Nadia Santini has presided over the kitchens of **Dal Pescatore**, which was opened in 1920 by her husband's grandfather. The outstanding reputation of this restaurant is impressively documented in both Italian and French restaurant guides: two Michelin stars, four red chef's hats in L'Espresso/Gault-Millau (19), one sun in Veronelli, and 94/100 in Gambero Rosso. A member of *Le Soste*, *Relais Gourmands*, and *Traditions et Qualité*, she was awarded the prize for the Best Wine Cellar of the Year by L'Espresso/Gault-Millau in 1993. Nadia Santini is interested in history, especially the history of the culinary arts, from which she draws inspiration.

Maria Santos Gomes

born August 10, 1962

Restaurant: **Conventual**
Address: Praça das Flores, 45
1200 Lisbon, Portugal
Tel. (0)1 60 91 96; Fax (0)1 387 5132

The **Conventual** is located in the historic Old Town of Lisbon, right by the Parliament. There, in 1982, Dina Marquez engaged the young chef Maria Santos Gomes—to the great delight of Lisbon politicians, who dine there regularly. Much of the restaurant's decor comes from the former cloister of Igreja (hence the restaurant's name). Maria Santos Gomes' inventive cuisine has already earned her one Michelin star. In 1993, she won first prize in the Portuguese Gastronomy Competition, which always takes place in Lisbon. In addition to cooking, she loves literature, going on walks, and traveling.

Jean-Yves Schillinger

born March 23, 1963

Succession in the Schillinger culinary dynasty is guaranteed thanks to this brilliant young chef, who has shown himself in all respects worthy of his predecessors. In 1988–95 he worked with his father in Colmar. Prior to this he had worked in prestigious restaurants, such as the **Crillon** in Paris, in **Jamin**, where he was Joël Robuchon's sous chef, and even at **La Côte Basque** in New York. He is also a member of the Young Restaurateurs of Europe, as well as of the *Prosper Montagné* and the French *Haute Cuisine* associations. Jean-Yves Schillinger is very active and especially enjoys golf, skiing, and motorcycling.

Nikolaos Sarantos

born December 5, 1945

Restaurant: **Hôtel Athenaeum Inter-Continental**
Address: 89-93, Syngrou Avenue
117 45 Athens, Greece
Tel. (0)1 902 3666; Fax (0)1 924 3000

From 1971-88, Nikolaos Sarantos traveled around the Mediterranean and the Middle East, honing his culinary skills in the various Hilton Hotels in Teheran, Athens, Corfu, Kuwait City, and Cairo before finally settling down at the **Athenaeum Inter-Continental** in 1988. Nikolaos Sarantos is a member of the jury at international cooking competitions in San Francisco, Copenhagen, and Bordeaux. Chairman of the Chef's Association of Greece, he is also a great sports fan, and an avid tennis, soccer, and basketball player.

Rudolf Sodamin

born April 6, 1958

Restaurant: **Passenger vessel** *Queen Elizabeth 2*
Home port: Southampton, England

The Austrian Rudolf Sodamin (pictured standing next to his colleague Jonathan Wicks) currently works for the Cunard Line shipping company, which owns several other magnificent liners besides the QE2. This *chef de cuisine*/pastry chef has attracted much favorable attention in numerous restaurants in Austria, France, Switzerland, and the United States. In New York, he worked in the kitchens of the famous **Waldorf-Astoria**. He is a member of the *Prosper Montagné* and *Chefs des Chefs* associations. Although Sodamin enjoys jogging, his favorite sport is still skiing in his home town of Kitzbühel.

Fritz Schilling

born June 8, 1951

Restaurant: **Schweizer Stuben**
Address: Geiselbrunnweg 11,
97877 Wertheim, Germany
Tel. (0)9342 30 70; Fax (0)9342 30 71 55

A chef since 1972, Fritz Schilling opened his restaurant in the Main valley near the romantic little town of Wertheim in 1990. His refined and versatile cuisine, which cultivates the best German gastronomic traditions, has already earned him two Michelin stars and four red chef's hats in Gault-Millau (19.5). A member of *Relais et Châteaux* and *Relais Gourmands*, his restaurant is one of the best in Germany. In his spare time, Fritz Schilling loves listening to pop music. He is a passionate driver, enjoys playing golf, and likes most beach sports.

Roger Souvereyns

born December 2, 1938

Restaurant: **Scholteshof**
Address: Kermstraat, 130
3512 Stevoort-Hasselt, Belgium
Tel. (0)11 25 02 02; Fax (0)11 25 43 28

Roger Souvereyns has presided over the **Scholteshof** since 1983. This eighteenth-century farmstead has a large vegetable garden, which used to be tended by his friend and gardener Clément, and which is the source of the wonderful fresh fruit and vegetables used in his cooking. Roger Souvereyns has two Michelin stars, four red chef's hats in Gault-Millau (19.5), and 95/100 in the Belgian restaurant guide Henri Lemaire. A member of *Relais et Châteaux*, *Relais Gourmands*, and *Traditions et Qualité*, he is a collector of antiques and old paintings. He also loves opera and enjoys swimming and cycling.

Jean Schillinger

born January 31, 1934
died December 27, 1995

This former Chairman of the *Maîtres Cuisiniers de France* was a symbol of Alsatian gastronomy: The well-known restaurant **Schillinger** in Colmar, France (1957-95) boasted two Michelin stars, three red stars in Gault-Millau (17), and three stars in Bottin Gourmand. Jean Schillinger, a Knight of the *Mérite* Order, was the third generation of a family which had been in the restaurant business since1893. For over 20 years he worked to heighten the profile of French cuisine throughout the world, from Japan to Brazil and Australia.

Pedro Subijana

born November 5, 1948

Restaurant **Akelaré**
Address: 56, Paseo del Padre Orcolaga
20008 San Sebastián, Spain
Tel. (9)43 21 20 52; Fax (9)43 21 92 68

Since 1981, Pedro Subijana has had his own restaurant overlooking the Bay of Biscay. Awarded two stars in Michelin and 9/10 in Gourmetour, he was named Best Cook in Spain in 1982. Subijana underwent a traditional training at the College of Hotel Management in Madrid and at Euromar College in Zarauz, and became a cooking teacher in 1970. In 1986 he became Commissioner General of the European Association of Chefs, whose headquarters is in Brussels. He presents food programs on Basque Television and on *Tele-Madrid*. Pedro Subijana loves music and the movies.

Émile Tabourdiau

born November 25, 1943

Restaurant **Le Bristol**
Address: 112, rue du Faubourg Saint-Honoré
75008 Paris, France
Tel. (0)1 53 43 43 00; Fax (0)1 53 43 43 01

Since 1964, Émile Tabourdiau has worked in only the most famous of restaurants: First at **Ledoyen**, then at **La Grande Cascade**, and finally, since 1980, at **Le Bristol**, located in the immediate vicinity of the Élysée Palace and boasting magnificent large gardens. A former pupil of Auguste Escoffier, Émile Tabourdiau is a member of the Culinary Academy of France, and was the winner of the *Prosper Montagné* prize in 1970, as well as *Meilleur Ouvrier de France* in 1976. His restaurant has one Michelin star. In his spare time he loves painting, and enjoys playing tennis and spending time in his garden.

Romano Tamani

born April 30, 1943

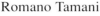

Restaurant: **Ambasciata**
Address: 33, Via Martiri di Belfiore
46026 Quistello, Italy
Tel. (0)376 61 90 03; Fax (0)376 61 82 55

Romano Tamani is the only one of our top chefs to hold the coveted title of *Commendatore della Repubblica Italiana*, a distinction conferred on him by his native Italy in 1992. This Lombardian, who learned his craft in London and Switzerland, is without doubt one of the most skillful representatives of Italian gastronomy to be found. Together, he and his brother Francesco have run the **Ambasciata** since 1978. Accolades received include two Michelin stars, three chef's hats in Espresso/Gault-Millau, one Veronelli sun, and 90/100 in Gambero Rosso, as well as membership of the prestigious Italian chain *Le Soste*. Cooking is Tamani's consuming passion, but he also loves the sea..

Laurent Tarridec

born May 26, 1956

Restaurant: **Le Restaurant du Bistrot des Lices**
Address: Place des Lices,
83990 Saint-Tropez, France
Tel. (0)4 94 97 29 00; Fax (0)4 94 97 76 39

That this Breton, a pupil of Michel Rochedy, could set himself up on the Côte d'Azur of all places, and after only one year (1995) walk off with one Michelin star and three red chef's hats in Gault-Millau (18), is testimony to his extraordinary adaptability. Before this, he honed his skills in Brittany at the **Lion d'Or**, in Paris, and in the Rhone valley at the **Beau Rivage**. Laurent Tarridec is interested in politics, as well as anything related to the sea. He also skis, rides a motorcycle, and, since living in Saint-Tropez, has discovered the game of *boules*.

Dominique Toulousy

born August 19, 1952

Restaurant: **Les Jardins de l'Opéra**
Address: 1, place du Capitole
31000 Toulouse, France
Tel. (0)5 61 23 07 76; Fax (0)5 61 23 63 00

Dominique Toulousy has lived in Toulouse only since 1984. Hanging out his shingle on the Place du Capitole, he reaped accolades by the dozen: Golden Key of Gastronomy (1986), three red chef's hats in Gault-Millau (18), and two Michelin stars, as well as the title of *Meilleur Ouvrier de France* (1993). Before this, he had his first successes in Gers, a region known for its generous cuisine. Dominique Toulousy is a member of the Young Restaurateurs of Europe, the *Prosper Montagné* association, *Eurotoques*, and *Traditions et Qualité*. He enjoys poring over old cookbooks and loves gardening, tennis, and swimming.

Gilles Tournadre

born June 29, 1955

Restaurant **Gill**
Address: 8 & 9, quai de la Bourse
76000 Rouen, France
Tel. (0)2 35 71 16 14; Fax (0)2 35 71 96 91

Even a Norman can occasionally be persuaded to leave his native region in order to learn his craft: Gilles Tournadre started out his career at **Lucas Carton**, followed by the **Auberge des Templiers** of the Bézards and **Taillevent**, before ending up—on his own two feet—in Bayeux, and in 1984, back in his hometown. His career successes have justified all these changes: the young gastronome can boast two Michelin stars and three red chef's hats (17 points) for his restaurant near Rouen cathedral. A member of the Young Restaurateurs of Europe, this enthusiastic sportsman loves judo, golf, and motor sports, and is also a passionate conservationist.

José Tourneur

born January 4, 1940

Restaurant: **Des 3 Couleurs**
Address: 453, avenue de Tervuren
1150 Brussels, Belgium
Tel. (0)2 770 3321; Fax (0)2 770 8045

The three colors which José Tourneur chose in 1979 as the logo and name of his restaurant are those of the Belgian national flag. The restaurant, which is wholly dedicated to Belgian cuisine, has one Michelin star and was awarded 88/100 in the Belgian restaurant guide Henri Lemaire. A self-taught cook, Tourneur gained further experience in Brussels and Nice, won the *Prosper Montagné* prize in 1969, and was *chef de cuisine* at the Brussels **Carlton** in 1969-79. He is also a member of the Order of the 33 Masterchefs of Belgium, the Culinary Academy of France, and the Vatel Club. His other interests all revolve around the sea: he loves ships, and enjoys fishing, and water-skiing.

Luisa Valazza

born December 20, 1950

Restaurant: **Al Sorriso**
Address: Via Roma, 18
28018 Soriso, Italy
Tel. (0)322 98 32 28; Fax (0)322 98 33 28

Taking their cue from the name of the restaurant which she and her husband Angelo have run since 1981 in their hometown in the Piedmont region, the food critics have all "smiled" on Luisa Valazza, awarding **Al Sorriso** two Michelin stars, four chef's hats in Espresso/Gault-Millau (19.2), one sun in Veronelli, and 90/100 in Gambero Rosso. Luisa Valazza, who is also a member of the Le Soste chain, remains modest in the midst of this avalanche of praise, carefully cooking the recipes she has amassed since 1971 in the **Europa** in Borgomanero. She is passionately interested in the arts, especially painting and literature. She frequently visits museums and is also an enthusiastic practitioner of winter sports.

Guy Van Cauteren

born May 8, 1950

Restaurant: **T'Laurierblad**
Address: Dorp, 4
9290 Berlare, Belgium
Tel. (0)52 42 48 01; Fax (0)52 42 59 97

Before opening his restaurant **T'Laurierblad** (The Bay Leaf) in 1979, Guy Van Cauteren was taught by some of France's most outstanding chefs: Alain Senderens at **Archestrate** in Paris, and the Allégriers at **Lucas Carton** (1972-4). He then spent several years cooking at the French Embassy in Brussels (1974-9). Since then, he has acquired two Michelin stars, three red chef's hats in Gault-Millau (17), and 89/100 in the Belgian restaurant guide Henri Lemaire. In addition, he was the fortunate recipient of the bronze **Bocuse** in 1993, and holds the title of *Maître Cuisinier de Belgique*. Guy Van Cauteren collects old books and enjoys traveling. In his spare time, he relaxes by cycling.

Freddy Van Decasserie

born October 10, 1943

Restaurant: **La Villa Lorraine**
Address: 75, avenue du Vivier d'Oie
1180 Brussels, Belgium
Tel. (0)2 374 3163; Fax (0)2 372 0195

Freddy Van Decasserie started off at **La Villa Lorraine** in 1963 as a kitchen boy and worked his way up the hierarchy until he became head chef and the recipient of numerous awards: two Michelin stars, three red chef's hats in Gault-Millau (18), three stars in Bottin Gourmand, and 92/100 in Henri Lemaire. He is a *Maître Cuisinier de Belgique* and a member of the Culinary Academy of France and *Traditions et Qualité*. In his spare time, he stays fit by being a training partner to the racing cyclist Eddy Merckx . He also swims and goes to the occasional soccer match.

Geert Van Hecke

born July 20, 1956

Restaurant: **De Karmeliet**
Address: Langestraat, 19
8000 Bruges, Belgium
Tel. (0)50 33 82 59; Fax (0)50 33 10 11

Geert Van Hecke was introduced to his craft by Freddy Van Decasserie at the **Villa Lorraine** in 1977, then served a stint with Alain Chapel at the famous **Cravache d'Or** in Brussels, finally opening his own restaurant in a renowned historic house in the heart of Bruges, the "Venice of the North." To date, his cooking has earned him two Michelin stars, three stars in the Bottin Gourmand, three red chef's hats in Gault-Millau (18), and 92/100 in Henri Lemaire. A winner of the Best Chef in Belgium award, he is also a member of **Traditions et Qualité**. He settled in Bruges, a well-preserved medieval town and popular tourist destination, as he is interested in art and enjoys visiting museums.

Gérad Vié

born April 11, 1943

Restaurant: **Les Trois Marches (Trianon Palace)**
Address: 1 boulevard de la Reine
78000 Versailles, France
Tel. (0)1 39 50 13 21; Fax (0)1 30 21 01 25

The chef of the **Trois Marches** (since 1970) started his career at the tender age of 13 at **Lapérouse**. There followed stints at **Lucas Carton**and the **Plaza-Athénée** in Paris and **Crillon Tower's** in London, as well as three years with the Compagnie des Wagons-Lits (1967–70). Today, Gérard Vié can boast two Michelin stars and three red chef's hats (18). Recipient of the Silver Table award from Gault-Millau in 1984, he was presented with the Golden Key of Gastronomy in 1993. A fan of the theater, opera, and movies, he collects paintings and is a *Chevalier des Arts et Lettres*. He also loves hiking and swimming.

Jean-Pierre Vigato

born March 20, 1952

Restaurant **Apicius**
Address: 122, avenue de Villiers
75017 Paris, France
Tel. (0)1 43 80 19 66; Fax (0)1 44 40 09 57

Jean Pierre Vigato started off as a sommelier and served an apprenticeship in various restaurants before his first major successes at **Grandgousier** in Paris in 1980–3. In 1984 he set up on his own, opening **Apicius** in his native Paris. The restaurant, named after a famous Roman epicure, was awarded its first Michelin star in 1985, and its second two years later. It also boasts three red chef's hats in Gault-Millau (18). A member of *Relais Gourmands*, Jean-Pierre Vigato was Gault-Millau Best Chef of the Year in 1988, and chef at the French Pavillion at the 1992 World's Fair in Seville, Spain.

Gianfranco Vissani

born November 22, 1951

Restaurant **Vissani**
Address: 05020 Civitella del Lago, Italy
Tel. (0)744 95 03 96; Fax (0)744 95 03 96

With a rating of 19.6 and four chef's hats, Gianfranco Vissani got a near-perfect report card from Espresso/Gault-Millau—the best in all Italy. Two Michelin stars, one Veronelli sun, and 87/100 in Gambero Rosso complete the guidebook honors showered on the restaurant run by Vissani since 1980 as a family concern with his wife, mother, and sister. One of the selling points of his establishment is his own-production olive oil, an indispensable flavor in his Mediterranean cooking. In his spare time, this gourmet collects clocks and relaxes by listening to classical music or reading. In addition, he is a fan of the AC Milan soccer club.

Jonathan F. Wicks

born June 14, 1962

Restaurant: **Passenger vessel *Queen Elizabeth 2***
Home port: Southampton, England

In 1980-7, Jonathan Wicks (pictured seated next to his colleague Rudolf Sodamin) worked at a number of prestigious London restaurants, including the **Mayfair Intercontinental**, the **Grosvenor House** in Park Lane, and the **Méridien** in Piccadilly, where he made his way up the ranks to sous chef. In 1987 he became chef aboard the luxury ocean liner QE2. The home port of the vessel is Southampton, but the constant change of scenery suits this travel-loving gourmet. Although rugby is the main sport in his hometown of Bath in England, Jonathan Wicks plays football and sails in his spare time. He also collects porcelain plates and loves having breakfast in bed.

Heinz Winkler

born July 17, 1949

Restaurant: **Residenz Heinz Winkler**
Address: Kirchplatz 1,
83229 Aschau im Chiemgau, Germany
Tel. (0)8052 17990; Fax (0)8052 179 966

At only 31 years of age, Heinz Winkler already boasted three Michelin stars—how on earth did he do it? Perhaps by training at the **Victoria** in Interlaken, under Paul Bocuse, and at **Tantris** in Munich, before opening the **Residenz Heinz Winkler** in 1991. To crown it all, this gastronome has three white chef's hats (18) and was Chef of the Year in 1979, as well as Restaurateur of the Year in 1994 in Gault-Millau. Heinz Winkler is a member of *Relais et Châteaux*, *Relais Gourmands*, *Traditions et Qualité*, and the Italian chain *Le Soste*. He enjoys poring over old cookbooks, playing golf, and skiing.

Harald Wohlfahrt

born November 7, 1955

Restaurant: **Schwarzwaldstube**
Address: Tonbachstrasse 237,
72270 Baiersbronn, Germany
Tel. (0)7442 49 26 65; Fax (0)7442 49 26 92

Harald Wohlfahrt started work at the **Schwarzwaldstube**, the restaurant of the Hotel Trauben-Tonbach in the heart of the Black Forest, in 1976, and has been chef there since 1980. He learned his trade at **Stahlbad** in Baden-Baden and **Tantris** in Munich. Voted Chef of the Year in 1991 by Gault-Millau, he currently boasts three Michelin stars and four red chef's hats (19.5). He is also a member of *Relais Gourmands* and *Traditions et Qualité*. While his main interests, unsurprisingly, are the traditions of eating and cooking, Harald Wohlfahrt is also an outstanding athlete, with swimming, soccer, and cycling being his favorite sports.

Armando Zanetti

born December 11, 1926

Restaurant: **Vecchia Lanterna**
Address: Corso Re Umberto, 21
10128 Turin, Italy
Tel. (0)11 53 70 47; Fax (0)11 53 03 91

A native Venetian, Armando Zanetti ran the **Rosa d'Oro** in Turin in 1955–69 before opening the evocatively named **Vecchia Lanterna** (Old Lantern) restaurant in the same city in 1970. Today, our chef, who devotes himself chiefly to the traditional cuisine of his native country, now proudly boasts two Michelin stars and four chef's hats in Espresso/Gault-Millau (19.2/20). In his spare time, Armando Zanetti tirelessly researches European cuisine of the past. He derives special pleasure from trying new dishes, both his own and those of his fellow chefs.

Alberto Zuluaga

born March 31, 1960

Restaurant: **Lopez de Haro y Club Nutico**
Address: Obispo Orueta, 2
48009 Bilbao, Spain
Tel. (9)4 423 5500; Fax (9)4 423 4500

As a Basque from the Spanish province of Vizcaya on the Bay of Biscay, Alberto Zuluaga is especially proud to be able to exercise his profession in the true capital of his native province. He has been chef of the five-star luxury restaurant **Club Nautico** in the banking district of Bilbao since 1991. Before this, in 1987–91, he cultivated his love of Basque cuisine and culinary traditions at the **Bermeo** in the same city, earning the title of Best Cook in *Euzkadi* (the Basque Country) in 1988. It goes without saying that he enjoys playing Basque *boules* in his spare time, but he also likes motor racing, and is an enthusiastic mushroom hunter when time allows.

Glossary

ADJUST THE SEASONING: To season a dish with salt and pepper, or with herbs and spices, toward the end of preparation, in order to round out the taste.

AÏOLI: A garlic mayonnaise from the Provence region in France (Fr. *ail* = garlic), which is served with steamed or boiled salt-water fish, hard-boiled eggs or vegetables.

AL DENTE (Ital. "to the tooth", i.e. "firm to the bite"): Term that describes the stage to which pasta and vegetables are to be cooked, i.e. crisp-tender rather than soft.

ASPIC: A transparent savory jelly of fish or meat stock, used as a garnish or to make a meat, fish or vegetable mold.

BASTE: To moisten roast meats such as roast beef, duck, suckling pig or similar with their hot juices, using a spoon or bulb baster, to prevent them from drying out and to give them an appetizing brown crust.

BÉCHAMEL SAUCE: Creamy sauce made from flour, butter and milk, served hot. Named after the Marquis de Béchamel, private chamberlain to Louis XIV.

BLANCH: To briefly cook foods, especially vegetables, in boiling water, in order to remove harsh tastes or smells, or to destroy germs or enzymes.

BLINI: A small Russian crêpe made from buckwheat flour, usually topped with sour cream, caviar or smoked salmon.

BOUQUET GARNI: A bunch of fresh herbs tied together and used to season soups, stews and braises. Usually consists of thyme, bay leaf and parsley, but may also contain rosemary, marjoram, lovage, fennel, leek or celery, according to the dish and region.

BRAISE: To cook foods by first searing them, then adding a little liquid (water, stock, meat juices, gravy or wine), covering tightly, and cooking slowly until done. The braised ingredients are thus cooked in the fat, liquid and steam.

BREAD: To dredge meat, poultry or fish in a mixture of flour, beaten egg and bread crumbs before shallow- or deep-frying.

BROIL: To cook food very quickly under a hot overhead element (broiler).

BROWN: To pan-fry or braise until brown, that is to cook a tender cut of meat on a piece of bacon in some butter or a little liquid over a moderate heat until an appetizing brown.

CARPACCIO: Raw meat, usually beef, sliced paper-thin and dressed with oil and lemon juice or an olive-oil vinaigrette, and served as an appetizer.

CHANTILLY, (À LA): Any dish, hot, cold, savory or sweet, accompanied by or prepared with whipped cream.

CHARLOTTE: Dessert made from puréed fruit or custard spooned into a dish lined with ladyfingers, wafers or buttered slices of bread.

CHARTREUSE: A soufflé made (for example) from finely chopped seafood or meat, vegetables and bacon, cooked in a water bath and served warm.

CLARIFY: 1. To remove cloudy substances from soups and sauces by stirring in lightly beaten egg white, heating carefully and then straining. 2. To heat butter and skim off the separated milk solids, leaving a cooking medium that can be heated to a higher temperature without burning.

COCKLES: A group of mollusks with two hinged, heart-shaped, ridged shells with brown stripes, common in the shallow coastal waters of the Atlantic and the Mediterranean, which are eaten raw drizzled with lemon juice, fried, or steamed.

CONSOMMÉ (Fr. "accomplished", "consummate" (adj.)): Bouillon made from meat or poultry, boiled down very slowly and then clarified, and eaten hot or cold.

CORAL: The roe of crustaceans, e.g. scallops or lobsters, held by connoisseurs to be a particular delicacy.

CRÈME ANGLAISE (Fr. "English cream"): Pouring custard or sauce for sweet dishes made from confectioner's sugar, egg yolk, milk and a bit of salt, rounded out with cream.

CROÛTONS: Slices or cubes of bread, toasted or fried until crisp and served with soups, braises or salads.

CRUDITÉS: (Fr. "raw food") Raw vegetables, usually sliced into strips or sticks, and served as an appetizer with dips and cold sauces.

DECORATE: To garnish a food, for example with sprigs of herbs or attractively cut slices of vegetables or fruit.

DEEP-FRY: To cook or brown foods in more than enough very hot fat or oil to cover, thereby forming a crust that seals in flavor and moisture.

DEFAT: To skim or pour off the fat that rises to the surface of sauces or soups.

DEGLAZE: To dissolve the rich sediment of cooking juices sticking to the bottom of a pot or pan by adding a liquid such as wine or meat stock and stirring over heat.

DIJONNAISE: French term for dishes prepared with light Dijon mustard—a special, creamy type of mustard made from mustard seeds steeped in the sour, fermented juice of unripe grapes. Dijonnaise also refers to a mayonnaise with mustard flavoring, served with cold cuts.

FARCE, FORCEMEAT (Fr. *farce* = "filling", "stuffing"): Finely chopped mixture of meat or fish with herbs and spices for filling turnovers or pies or stuffing poultry. Mushrooms, vegetables, rice, bread crumbs or egg are also mixed with meat or offal and used as a stuffing.

FLAMBÉ: (Fr. *flamber* = "to flame") To douse a dish in spirits and ignite, in order to enhance it with the flavor of the alcohol.

FOLD IN: To add ingredients to a uniform mixture, carefully and gently incorporating them using a figure-eight motion rather than stirring hard.

GALANTINE: A piquantly seasoned dish based on meat, fish or poultry that is boned, stuffed, poached and covered with aspic.

GARNISH: 1. (v) To arrange side dishes around a main ingredient, or to decorate a dish. 2. (n) The decorative side dish itself, for example dumplings or savory custard shapes in a soup, and snipped herbs in a sauce.

GAZPACHO: A cold vegetable soup of Spanish origin, made from ripe tomatoes, red bell peppers, cucumber, olive oil and bread crusts (sometimes rubbed with a cut clove of garlic).

GLAZE: To apply a shiny coating to food by brushing its surface with its own juices, jelly, aspic or sugar.

GRILL: 1. To fry or toast on an oventop grill. 2. To cook over hot coals; to barbecue.

GRATINÉE, GRATINATE, COOK AU GRATIN: To scatter bread crumbs, cheese and bits of butter over cooked foods and broil them briefly before serving, so that a brown crust is formed.

HOISIN SAUCE: A piquant, reddish-brown sauce made from fermented soybean paste, flour, salt, sugar and red rice. As a natural dye, it lends its color to many Chinese dishes.

JULIENNE: Finely sliced vegetables used as a soup garnish or as an accompaniment to a main course.

LARD: To thread through or wrap lean meat with strips of bacon (*lardons*), truffle slices or garlic cloves, in order to prevent the meat from drying out and to give it additional flavor.

LIAISE: To thicken or bind sauces and soups by stirring egg yolk and cream, milk or butter into the simmering liquid.

MARINATE: To steep meat, fish or poultry in a mixture of oil, vinegar or lemon juice, herbs and spices. This has the effect of reducing cooking time and flavoring the food.

MOUSSE (Fr. "froth, foam"): A rich, lightly sweetened or savory dish that owes its delicate, foamy consistency to stiffly whipped egg white and/or whipped cream.

PARFAIT: (Fr. "perfect") A cold dish made from a delicate *farce* or stuffing, thickened with gelatin or egg white, spooned into molds and chilled, and turned out when set. A sweet parfait is a chilled dessert made from custard, gelatin, ice cream and cream, served in a tall glass.

PERSILLADE: A mixture of finely chopped parsley and garlic, or cold slices of beef or ham with vinegar, oil and a great deal of parsley (Fr. *persil* = "parsley").

PHYLLO PASTRY: A pastry dough made from high-gluten (wheat) flour, water and oil (fat), rolled out paper-thin and then cut into sheets, brushed with oil or butter and layered. Frequently used in Middle Eastern, Turkish, Greek, Austrian and Hungarian dishes. Puff pastry may replace it in some recipes.

POACH: To cook ingredients in a small amount of simmering liquid.

PURÉE: To process or blend soft ingredients to a uniform mass.

REDUCE: To boil down a sauce or roasting juices so that the liquid evaporates, the sauce thickens and the flavor is intensified.

REFRESH: To immerse a hot food in cold water, or drain it and hold it under running cold water, in order to cool it quickly.

REMOULADE: A herb mayonnaise containing chopped tarragon, chervil, parsley, dill pickles and capers. Also available in stores, it is served with cold meat dishes, fish and shellfish.

ROAST: To brown or crisp foods by exposing them to dry heat; this gives nuts and seeds a fuller flavor.

ROUX: Flour sweated with an equal amount of butter, used to thicken soups or sauces.

SABAYON: A light, airy sauce made from egg yolk, sugar and white wine or champagne. Served warm with savory foods, or cold with sweet dishes.

SAFFRON: Spice obtained from the dried stigmas and style branches of the saffron crocus. Since the little threads must be hand-picked, genuine saffron is the most expensive spice in the world. Only small amounts, however, are needed to flavor and color different foods such as fish dishes, rice, curries, braises and desserts.

SAUCE AMÉRICAINE: (Fr. "American sauce".) Sauce made by searing diced root vegetables and crushed lobster shells, flambéeing with brandy, deglazing with white wine and whisking in butter. Served with fish and shellfish.

SAUTÉ (Fr. *sauter* = "to jump"): To fry foods in a small amount of hot butter or oil.

SCALD: To pour boiling water over fruit, vegetables or shelled nuts in order to facilitate peeling.

SCALLOPS: A mollusk with a characteristic fan-shaped shell. It moves about by opening and closing its shell with the help of its large adductor muscle. It is this muscle and the orange coral or roe that are eaten. Scallops are usually prepared and served in the shell.

SCORE: To make decorative cuts in fish or meat on both sides, so that the pieces do not burst, but rather curve evenly when cooked.

SEAR: To brown meat or other ingredients in a little hot fat.

SHALLOW-FRY: To cook in a pan in a depth of oil small enough so that the ingredient in question always stays in contact with the bottom of the pan (i.e. does not float).

SHRIMP: A small, pincerless crustacean with long antennae, slender legs and a long, plump body. Color varies according to species, but most turn reddish-orange when cooked. They are found in both cold and warm waters, as well as in fresh and salt water. Their firm, moist flesh forms the basis of a variety of dishes in many countries.

SIMMER: To cook foods in a liquid at just below boiling point. The liquid is simmering when bubbles rise to the surface.

SOUFFLÉ: (Fr. *souffler* = "to blow (up)") A light, airy sweet or savory dish based on eggs, and served hot or cold. A hot soufflé gets its airy texture from the stiffly beaten egg white that is folded into a warm sauce or a purée.

SPOON-MOLD: To form little dumplings or similar by scooping them out individually from a dough mixture and shaping them with a teaspoon or tablespoon prior to cooking them in boiling water or in broth.

STEAK TARTARE: Wafer-thin slices of raw beef or raw ground beef, dressed with chopped onions, pickled gherkins, capers or parsley, and seasoned with salt and pepper.

STEAM: To cook foods above boiling water in a dish with a perforated insert, a saucepan with a petal steamer, or in special stacking metal or bamboo pots.

STEW: To cook foods in their own juices or with a very small amount of additional liquid, usually also with a little added fat.

STRAIN: To pass or press a soup, sauce or other liquid through a strainer, sieve or cheesecloth.

STOCK : Liquid in which meat, fish, grains or vegetables have been cooked, which forms the basis of sauces. Also available canned.

STOCK: A seasoned bouillon for cooking fish or boiling meat.

SWEAT: To cook vegetables (especially onions) or flour over a low heat in fat without browning.

TERRINE: Dish made from finely chopped meat, poultry, game, fish or vegetables, cooked in a deep, straight-sided mold and served chilled.

TO CARVE: To cut meat, poultry or fish into slices, or to cut up for serving. A large, very sharp knife and a carving board are essential for this process.

TRUFFLE: A large edible fungus that grows wild, with a bulbous stem and a fleshy brown cap. Can be found in fall near oak and chestnut trees.

VELOUTÉ: (Fr. *velours* = "velvet") A white, creamy, basic sauce made from butter, flour, and veal or poultry stock, seasoned with salt and pepper.

VINAIGRETTE: Salad dressing based on vinegar (Fr. *vinaigre*) and oil, often also containing (Dijon) mustard.

WATER BATH: A gentle method of cooking whereby foods are cooked in a pot placed inside another larger pot containing boiling water, or in a special double-boiler pot; this prevents the food from scorching.

Index